A Flower for
Every Day

A FLOWER FOR
EVERY DAY

MARGERY FISH

CAPITAL BOOKS INC.

First published 1965
By Studio Vista Publishers, London
Reissued 1973
By David and Charles (Holdings) Limited
First published as a paperback 1981
By Faber and Faber Limited
Reissued 1991
By Faber and Faber Limited
Reissued in paperback 2000
By B.T. Batsford
9 Blenheim Court
Brewery Road
London N7 9NT

Printed and bound by
The Cromwell Press, Trowbridge, Wiltshire.

A catalogue record for this book is available from the British Library.

ISBN 0 7134 8555 8

ISBN 1-892123-25-8

Capital Books Inc.
22841 Quicksilver Drive
Sterling, Virginia 20166

Contents

Foreword

In the 21st century we take it for granted that our gardens will provide us with enjoyment all through the year; but this is a relative recent assumption. It's true that the great country houses ensured that flowers were available for arrangements whatever the season, but in more humble gardens, the winter months tended to provide a relatively bleak and colourless prospect.

Margery Fish changed all that. She believed that even in gardens of a relatively modest size and with limited resources, plants should, and could, be chosen to provide flowers and a fascinating garden prospect on every day of the year.

In this inspiring book she makes it clear how it's done. From hellebores, snowdrops and unusual periwinkles in January to heathers and fragrant winter honeysuckles in December, Mrs Fish chooses the best of the familiar, and the obscure, to give us daily delights.

In addition, and justifiably without qualms, she makes it clear that foliage can be as important as flowers in creating exciting plant pictures, in both winter and summer, and that the two together can brighten the dark days of winter as well as enhance the summer scene.

Margery Fish grew an extraordinary range of plants, her choice extending from familiar roses and perennials to bulbs and other plants that were rare in her time and are as uncommon today. But some of the plants which she recommended that were hard to find in her own time are now available in garden centres and from mail-order nurseries. Her own nursery at East Lambrook Manor in Somerset played a crucial role in distributing the plants she discovered and about which she enthused.

This book, together with *An All-the-Year-Round Garden* originally published seven years earlier, made a compelling argument for a change in the restrictive horticultural thinking of the time. Her books helped bring about our present assumption that we can indeed have flowers in our gardens on every day of the year.

Graham Rice
February 2000

3

~ 1 ~

January

No one would say that January is the best month for gardening, but when I think about it, it seems to me that I've had some of my best gardening days in that month.

We all expect the first month in the year to bring frost and snow, bitter winds and icy rain, but there are days when the ground is neither too hard nor too wet, when the sun shines and the air is warm, and then a walk round the garden will show that spring is very near. There are many days in a normal January when one can weed and plant, and if that is not possible one can always prowl and peer.

Many of January's flowers are small and would hardly be noticed in midsummer, but when the scene is bare each tiny flower receives the admiration it deserves. There is time to look into the flowers and study them, and to marvel at the exquisite workmanship.

The first snowdrops open in January and there are many interesting hours to be spent lifting up those dainty heads and comparing the formation of the flowers. The excitement begins when the flowers show just above the ground, each tiny white bud protected on each side by its green spathes as it pushes through the soil. It always interests me to see how the bigger snowdrops increase in size after they have been out for a few days. The flowers get perceptibly bigger and the stalks longer.

Interest in snowdrops grows, every year. And with the interest more and more varieties are available, for old gardens can still produce some treasures, and a certain amount of hybridising is going on. The snowdrops vary in size and shape, the markings are different and the colour and shape of the leaves.

This specialisation does not detract in any way from the joy we get in the ordinary snowdrop, *Galanthus nivalis*, which we can all have in large quantities, to naturalise in grass, to plant under trees and hedges and to grow in a nursery to be lifted and planted in bowls for the house. This little snowdrop increases fast and seeds itself generously, so once it has been introduced to a garden it will do the rest.

The double form of the common snowdrop increases far quicker in my garden than the single one. This is a pity for, though I like them both, to me the single form has more grace than the double. I have these snowdrops in grass and in my heavy clay soil they do not usually flower until February. Many of the named varieties, which are growing in beds of soil lightened with peat, flower in January, and I always think those under the trees have a hard time getting through the grass in such solid soil.

G. *elwesii* is the first to flower in my garden. It is usually recommended to plant this snowdrop in sun but I do not think it makes a great deal of difference. I grow it under a north hedge and it flowers well and increases fast. It has the most glaucous leaves of any; they are wide and clasp the stem of the flower. Another distinguishing feature is the extra green blotch at the top of the inner petals. Sometimes the two blotches run together so that the inner petals are almost all green.

The best named variety of G. *elwesii* is G. *whittalli*, a particularly fine plant with inner segments very heavily marked with green. With me it flowers after the ordinary G. *elwesii*, although that snowdrop continues in beauty for very many weeks.

G. *atkinsii** is another of the large early snowdrops that is said to like the sun but which also seems to do quite well in shade. It opens its long-petalled flowers in January and makes a most handsome clump, for the flower stems are often 12 in high. Purists complain that the individual flowers of this snowdrop are often imperfect, but the imperfections are not very noticeable and the general effect is good.

Another early snowdrop which has particularly big flowers is named G. 'John Grey'* after the raiser, a great gardener who lived in Saxmundham and who is also responsible for the double form of the green-eyed dianthus, Musgrave's Seedling. G. 'John Grey'* does not look very big when it first opens but gains in stature as the days go by and finishes up with flowers that are probably bigger than any.

A small snowdrop that opens early is G. *graecus**, easily distinguished by its narrow, twisted leaves. It also has double markings on its inner segments, but this is variable.

Years ago I was given a very attractive double snowdrop which had very neatly packed double petals which were quite green inside, so that the whole centre of the flower was green. Experts have been arguing about its name ever since I started to distribute it, and it was generally considered to be a form of G. *plicatus*, but it flowers much earlier than true G. *plicatus*. It has been named for me by Mrs Mathias of the Giant Snowdrop Company as G. 'Ophelia', a cross made by Mr H.A. Greatorex of Witton, Norwich, with the double form of the ordinary snowdrop. Mr Greatorex made several crosses and they are all lovely, but the only one I know intimately is G. 'Ophelia'. It increases quite well and, in addition to its very great double centre, has the engaging habit of lifting its outer petals when it has been out a little while, so that they look like wings.

The famous *nivalis* seedling, G. 'Samuel Arnott'*, does not open until February. It was developed by the late Walter Butt (who is also responsible for the lovely pale form of *Iris unguicularis*) and he planted it in his garden at Chalford in Gloucestershire. He left this garden some years before his death and lived first in West Porlock and then with a daughter. His garden in Chalford was bought by Brigadier and Mrs Mathias and they realised the value of the snowdrops that had by then multiplied, and they started the Giant Snowdrop Company and made available to the public the wonderful snowdrops growing in that fabulous hillside garden. In February it must be fairyland, with glades of snowdrops on those steep slopes. Brigadier and Mrs Mathias and their devoted gardener have done a great deal to encourage the interest in snowdrops. They seek out every old and rare variety and by degrees build up stocks so that all can share.

Before the Company was started there were enthusiasts collecting snowdrops, but I am sure there was nothing like the fever that has developed since. When there is a stand of these snowdrops it is surrounded all through the day, with the experts peering and comparing, for every time there are a few new varieties, some are seedlings raised by collectors, others found in old and forgotten gardens.

One does not usually connect scent with snowdrops but there is one that has perfume, *G. alleni*, which is considered to be a little more temperamental than most of them.

To see their real beauty I think snowdrops should be planted at eye level, or higher. I grow many of mine under the willows in my ditch garden. Large stones are used to support the bank and the angles made by the stones are ideal for little colonies or single clumps of all the different varieties. With several new varieties added to the collection each year I can see the time coming when I shall run out of niches. The small ones go in troughs or raised beds, because the ditch garden becomes rather like a jungle in high summer.

Most of the spring snowdrops like to grow in shady, moist places but need to be fairly dry in the summer, so between tree roots is a position that suits them, especially when the trees are growing on a hill. The autumn flowering types do best in a warm, sunny position.

Though the ordinary snowdrop, *G. nivalis*, sows itself with great liberality, it is not safe to leave entirely to nature the propagation of the rarer species. Germination of the seed is not always good and the late E. A. Bowles, who was an ardent collector, advocated waiting till the seed pods are beginning to turn yellow and sowing the whole pod without disturbing it.

The irises that flower in January, apart from the various forms of *I. unguicularis* and *I. histrio* and *I. histrioides*, are not easy. Most of them will flower the first year and after that are seen no more. Shown on the stands at Vincent Square they look so inviting and easy that one is tempted over and over again. 1 have tried several times to please *I. alata**, the scorpion iris from the Mediterranean region. It is pale lavender-blue, with a golden keel, and is said to be hardy, although it needs a fairly sheltered spot. Wintry rain and wind play havoc with its delicate flowers, and it is recommended to plant it in a light, limy soil in sun. But even with everything its heart could desire it may not succeed and is probably safer in an alpine house. I have no alpine house and the things I want to grow are those that will succeed out of doors, but some of the more temperamental plants don't fancy my heavy clay soil. (I believe that *I. alata** is one of the irises that break up into tiny bulbs after flowering.) *Iris vartani*, *alba*, is another that didn't, although it flowered the first year. It is worth a struggle and coming from Palestine is usually planted in a scree in full sun. Its flowers are white or white veined with blue and violet, with a golden crest. *Iris danfordiae* has the reputation of flowering the first year and never again; the reason given is that after flowering the bulbs split up into little grains too small to flower. Of course, in a well-conducted garden these little bulblets should grow up in time but they seldom do, and I suppose are either forked up or buried. I once asked a well known Dutch bulb grower how the trade was able to produce decent-sized bulbs of *Iris danfordiae* and was told that there was no difficulty in the rich soil of Holland! Regular feeding with bone-meal and potash is said to help them to flower, and they should be given a well-drained position.

This iris is a sturdy little plant, with greeny yellow flowers made greener by green markings. It is seldom more than 6 in, and to me is so much the embodiment of spring that now I take no chances and make sure I get my flowers indoors. It is surprisingly cheap and makes a very good bulb for growing in bowls in a mixture of peat, charcoal and crushed shell. I bury the bowls under a heap of peat and when the tips of the leaves are well through bring them indoors. It is amazing how soon they flower when they get into the house. All the bulbs go out into the garden after flowering and I usually get a flower or two outside but never a real show. The bronzed ferny leaves of *Corydalis cheilanthifolia* make a lovely background for this iris. *Iris histrioides* flowers well outside and if left alone will increase most satisfactorily and produce its dazzling blue flowers faithfully in January and February each year. It is not perturbed by ice or snow but its delicate petals are sometimes torn to shreds by strong winds. It was one of my January pleasures for many years until greed overcame discretion and I thought it was a pity to have only one clump in the garden. So after it had finished flowering I lifted the clump and divided it into several which I planted in different parts of the garden. It has taken several years to forgive me. If I had waited till late summer it wouldn't have known. It needs to be kept dry in the summer and some growers put a pane of glass flat on the ground after the leaves have died down and leave it till early autumn.

It is usually recommended to plant winter aconites—eranthis—at the base of deciduous trees, where they can naturalise to their heart's content. The ordinary type, E. hyemalis, increases almost too fast for some people, but those I planted at the foot of a willow many years ago made no attempt to colonise. Though they came up regularly they did not increase, and it was only when I dug them up and planted them in the grass under the variegated sycamore on the lawn that they began to do well. Now they come up in different parts of the garden and by degrees I am getting colonies in the grass in several shady places. The ones under the sycamore do the best and those are the ones I see from the house and whose company I enjoy every time I go into the garden. A few mild days in January and the little golden heads appear, each with its ruff of emerald-green. When the common one started to increase for me I had a little flutter in the less common types, which prolong the flowering season. E. cilicica* has deep yellow flowers and there is a suggestion of bronze in the toby frills. E. tubergenii* is a hybrid between the two, with large and showy flowers, which last for a long time. It has a more sturdy habit of growth. E. tubergenii 'Guinea Gold'* doesn't flower till March. It has deep golden flowers on bronze stems and is scented. I have heard of but never seen the rare white Japanese aconite, E. pinnatifida, with blue anthers and blue backing to its petals. It needs to be grown in shade, in light leafy soil, and must be protected from slugs.

The cyclamen that bloom in the winter have an added attraction for me because flowers and leaves come together and each corm makes a neat little clump with brilliant flowers above the dark green leaves. The autumn-flowering C. neapolitanum* looks best in a mass because the flowers come first and one needs a close planting to get a good effect. And then the handsome marbled leaves follow in great profusion and make a carpet to last throughout the winter.

The leaves of the winter-flowering types are smaller and never produced in such quantities. It has made it much easier now that they are all called C. orbiculatum*, and the only one that has individual status is C. o. coum*, which is recognisable because its round, dark leaves have no marblings. Before, even the experts found it difficult to distinguish between C. hiemale*, C. vernum*, C. atkinsii* and C. ibericum*, even before the varieties had lived together for a while and added to the population with unlawful children.

I like to grow my cyclamen in the shelter of the dwarf conifers that line the central path through the terrace garden; they seem to like the slight shade and I feel that they are safer from disturbance under the trees. *C. neapolitanum** grows in the upper part of the garden and the different colours of the winter ones on the lower terraces. It is exciting to come on those neat little clusters of flowers and leaves in the heart of the winter, flowers that can be any shade of pink to deep magenta, and white with shadings of pink. The ones we used to call *ibericum** and *atkinsii** make better clumps than *C. coum*. The flowers grow on erect stems among the leaves and one doesn't realise what is going to happen until the bright cerise or pink flowers shine out among the round, dark leaves. *C. coum* is much less neat: the buds on rather long stems lie about on the ground and take an unconscionable time to open, and the general effect is rather straggling. This is particularly noticeable in the case of the deep cerise form, for the flowers are rather small and there always seems to be too much stem. The white and pink forms of *C. coum* are much more compact; for one thing the flowers are bigger and chubbier. I have white *C. coum* growing in a small trough and it is a wonderful sight for over two months, as it is covered with bloom and, nestling among stones, looks neat and compact.

It is strange that the winter-flowering cyclamen seem to produce their seedlings at the same time as the autumn ones. In January one notices the many little seedlings growing round the parent corms, just as the seedlings of the pink and white *C. neapolitanum** appear in the winter.

I do not find the winter cyclamen colonise as well as the others but that may be from lack of room, as space under the little conifers is restricted. If one has bare soil under large trees where the cyclamen can seed freely there will soon be a carpet of winter flowers as thick as any autumn colonies. I know several gardens where winter cyclamen have done this under mulberry, ilex and beech trees, but here they have the scene to themselves. I do not think cyclamen do so well in grass, although I have seen *C. coum* holding its own in grass. This cyclamen in its spindly cerise form is particularly attractive in grass and makes more show than when grown in the open.

C. pseud-ibiricum, which sometimes flowers in January, does not seem to be included in the renaming operation yet, and it certainly cannot be included in the *orbiculatum** group for its leaves are oval and as jagged as those of *C. repandum*. This aristocrat is quite distinct and worth the trouble it takes to find it, and then to grow it when found. I have heard that it is not quite hardy, but mine survived the cruel winter of 1962–3 although they missed their flowering that disastrous year.

I have been buying *C. pseud-ibericum* for years and trying it in different places in the garden. It used to be easier to get than now. Each time, after a brief appearance, it disappeared. I had almost decided to give up trying when I saw a wonderful specimen flowering in Mr E. B. Anderson's garden when he lived in Porlock. It was growing in a steep bank, which Mr Anderson called the "cliff", and its corm was planted under a stone. After seeing that plant and admiring the large cerise flowers, which are deliciously scented, I hunted for three more corms and planted them under stones on high banks facing south in my ditch.

It is one of the excitements of the January prowl to look for flower buds on *C. pseud-ibiricum*. And they cannot be missed, for they are more than an inch long, in brilliant cerise, and rolled up like little umbrellas.

~ Part Two ~

Though January is not the month for most of them to flower, there are often odd blooms on the periwinkles, particularly *Vinca minor alba** and *Vinca major*. I can feel quite friendly towards *Vinca major* when it produces its clear blue flowers on a winter's day. Even its foliage is welcome then, for there is no thing more fresh and luxuriant and I have never seen it blemished by the most severe frost. Later on, of course, we curse it for the very qualities that charm us in mid-winter, but its habit of alighting on any available piece of soil and proceeding to raise a family becomes tedious after a bit. *V. acutiloba** can be nearly as tiresome, but again one is forgiving in the winter when there are beautiful flowers in deep slaty blue. It isn't quite as luxuriant as *V. major*, but it has a longer reach and penetrates more deeply into forbidden territory. I know people who consider this periwinkle a treasure and recommend it for clothing different places in the garden. Obviously it doesn't leave its appointed place in their gardens to appear in the middle of clumps of cherished treasures, which is the way it amuses itself in my garden.

There is one periwinkle which will flower all through the winter if it is given a good position and if the weather is kind. Sometimes *V. acutiloba** is sold for *V. difformis*, but the true plant, which comes from south-west Europe, has pale slaty blue flowers and neat, medium-sized leaves. It is not always reliably hardy and it grows differently from other periwinkles. Instead of growing down a bank or wall it likes to work up. Put it in an open bed and it will grow to about a foot and then proceed to flower. Under a tree it does much better because it fancies itself as a climber and will elbow its way through the branches of a tree to several feet. A bad frost will blacken its leaves, but they usually recover when the cold spell is over. In Italy it is used as a bedding plant and it makes quite a pleasant pot plant for a cool house. The late Canon Ellacombe grew it under a spreading pine in his garden at Bitton in Gloucestershire, and it flowered well all through the winter. In the average garden it would do very well under a shrub or tree growing at the foot of a south or west wall.

There are several hellebores to make the garden interesting in January. Some, of course, start to flower in December, or even November, and many more will open in February. One that never fails to make a good show about the middle of the month and continues for four or five weeks is *H. kochii**. It is not affected by heavy frost or snow, and being more compact than some is not damaged by wind. It is sometimes described as primrose but I would call it greenish white or very pale green, with the colour deepening at the centre and at the edges of the petals. The flowers are easy to recognise because they open so widely that they are almost flat, and the petals are waved, which makes them even flatter. This is really the only one of the "Lenten Roses" which is correct in calling itself *H. orientalis*. It has become usual to term all the "Lenten Roses" *H. orientalis* although they are hybrids of the various species. I was given another hellebore said to be another form of *H. kochii**, which is taller and later, and not nearly so distinct as the early one, with its neat flowers and buds and jaggedly toothed leaves. I grow my early *H. kochii** opposite the dining-room window, with a north wall behind it. This has many advantages: the wall gives protection, the paler hellebores show up best against the wall, and I can enjoy the flowers as I eat my breakfast.

If one is lucky enough to possess *H. lividus,* that will open in January too. It is very difficult to find the real thing, and many of the plants sold as *lividus* are a cross between *H. lividus* and *H. foetidus* with very little evidence of *lividus* blood, except the very distinctly netted, pointed leaves. The flowers of the real plant are quite distinct; little globes of pinkish green herald the flowers, which are green with a rosy tinge, and there is a crimson tinge to the undersides of the leaves. Sometimes this hellebore is grown in a cool house, and then one discovers that it has a delicate scent. It certainly needs a sheltered position for it will be 18 in when fully grown and its woody stems seem particularly brittle.

*H. corsicus**, which starts its long weeks of flowering in January, is a much tougher plant than *H. lividus*, but not a very long-lived one. It too has woody stems which can snap off in a gale if grown in an exposed position without any support. While most hellebores do best in shade, *H. lividus*, *H. corsicus** and *H. foetidus* need a well-drained soil and can stand a certain amount of sun. I give them all a little unobtrusive support when they need it, although I know that this shocks some gardeners. The flower trusses of *H. corsicus** in particular can be very heavy, and in their native home are either very dwarf or lie about on the ground. This is all right when growing on a rocky bank, but we would miss much of their beauty if we let it grow like that in an English garden. The flowers of *H. corsicus** last for months, and it is only when the seed is ripe and new growth comes up from the centre of the plant that the old stems can be removed.

There are at least three different forms of *H. foetidus*—our native plant, the

Italian form, which grows straighter and is rather taller, and one that Mr Bowles found in the Valley of the Roja. Buds start to open towards the end of January and during February and March, and sometimes later. When in full bloom the plants are among the most beautiful in the garden.

I noticed the slightly different form of *H. foetidus* the first time I visited the late Mr Bowles' garden at Enfield, long before I had read his books and learned that he had found a particularly fine form in his travels with Reginald Farrer. It seemed to have larger, darker flowers and more finely cut leaves, with shades of red at the stalk junctions. Mr Bowles liked to plant *H. foetidus* among bergenias and hostas to show up the beauty of the finely cut leaves by contrasting it with more solid foliage.

Even our native form can become a handsome, statuesque plant if grown where it has space to develop. In its native haunts it is often huddling under hedges and bushes and grows bent and crooked. *H. foetidus* has its own beauty of contrast, the whole top of the plant green at its palest and freshest, with maroon to edge the flowers, and below leaves so dark that they are nearly black.

All the hellebores are good planted among shrubs, and there are some lovely shrubs that flower in January. The witch hazels are not planted as often as they might be and yet they are excellent dual-purpose subjects. The leaves are handsome and colour well in the autumn, and when they fall the bare branches are adorned with quaint, spidery flowers in yellow, orange or red. Although the witch hazels are said to need a lime-free soil and shade, I don't think they are as insistent on an acid or neutral soil as they are on shade. I grow them quite well in my limy clay, but I do plant them in shade.

Hamamelis mollis is the one most usually grown. It is a Chinese shrub and the flowers are a medium yellow, the narrow petals backed by claret-coloured calyces. There is a paler form, *H. mollis pallida**, but it is still rather scarce and expensive. *H. brevipetala** originated in France a few years ago and the name indicates that the petals of the flowers are shorter. They are straighter too. In *H. mollis* they curl at the ends, rather like strips of carrot coming from a grater, and it gives the plant a softer, shaggier look. *H. brevipetala** is harder in colour too, being a deep ochre-yellow. It has the same maroon calyx, in which the stamens, looking like four little yellow eyes, are embedded. I have always firmly refused to consider any witch hazel except a yellow one, but some of the red forms can be lovely with the right background, one that is tender green and not rich earth: the pale blotched leaves of *Geranium punctatum*, or the finely cut foliage of *G. atlanticum**, which has such lovely blue flowers in the spring. It is worth looking into the flowers of *H.* 'Ruby Glow'* with a magnifying glass. The petals are delicately waved at the edges and softly shaded with greeny yellow. *H.*

'Hiltingbury Red'*, a form of the Japanese witch hazel, *H. japonica*, has flowers of rich mahogany red. The flowers of *H.* 'Adonis'* are burnt umber in colour, and those who like orange can plant *H.* 'Jelena'* or *H.* 'Orange Beauty'*.

After such fiery subjects it is restful to turn to *Garrya elliptica*, a symphony in grey-green when the long catkins swing from the grey-green leaves, which are leathery. The long strings of flower start almost grey and finish as cream and green tassels of surpassing beauty. This, of course, is the male plant, for the female plant is not so often seen, and yet it too has great beauty. It has small berries which are at their best in winter and lovely in a quiet way in shades of green and purple, with a sheen that looks like silk. *Garrya elliptica* really does best against a wall, as a hard winter can blacken its more exposed leaves, and then the problem of pruning does not arise. I grow mine against a north wall in front of the house, and it is a lovely sight when the fringes of catkins hang on both sides of the wall. But it takes light from the house when it grows too tall, and as it flowers on mature wood heavy pruning can ruin next year's display.

There is not much danger of the sarcococcas growing too tall. Most of them remain neat little bushes; in fact they are not very conspicuous and I always think they show great wisdom in flowering in the winter, when they get the attention that they might not receive at any other time. Even if one passed them without admiring the tiny cream flowers and good evergreen leaves the scent would proclaim their presence, for it is very strong and haunting on the wintry air. I have never decided what it brings to mind—honey, vanilla or some subtle Eastern perfume (the sarcococcas come from China). They belong to the euphorbia family and they grow very happily under trees. It seems unfair to saddle them with such an unwieldy name, which means "fleshy berry", and isn't really very apposite anyhow, as the berries aren't very fleshy. They are either red or black, and remain on the shrubs a long time. The lower branches of *S. humilis** are still heavily laden with small black berries in the winter when the top branches are trimmed with the little tufted flowers, which are little more than bunches of stamens. In *S. hookeriana digyna** the flowers have a pink tinge and the leaves are rather narrow. *S. ruscifolia* has box-like leaves and bright red berries follow the flowers.

The scent of *Chimonanthus fragrans** is much more distinct than that of the retiring little sarcococcas and in some kinds even stronger. A small sprig will scent a room and no one disputes its high quality although there are some who consider the flowers dowdy. To most of us there is something rather fascinating about the translucent claw-like petals, the colour of straw, but given warmth by the circle of small maroon petals at the base. I have seen this wintersweet looking distinctly dull when growing in a front garden near a busy road and without the sun behind to give it sparkle, but it gets quite gay on a bright day, particularly with the sun behind it. *C. fragrans** should now be called *C. praecox*, and certainly it is the earliest to flower. *C. grandiflorus** has flowers that are a little brighter yellow and seem to have a brighter crimson for the basal petals. This plant is scented but not as strongly—or so it seems—as the more ordinary plant. The real charmer of the family is *C. luteus**. The first time I saw it was in the Savill Gardens in Windsor Great Park and it was trained against a wall. There had been heavy rain and every flower was sparkling with diamond drops, which shone brilliantly in the wintry sunshine. It is one of the things I shall never forget as long as I live. I don't believe the scent is as strong in this plant as in the others but it has a great deal to offer without it.

The only daphne that flowers in January—according to the books—is *D. blagayana*, with deliciously scented cream flowers, and it does best in shade. With its questing habits it needs plenty of room, and many flat stones above it; in fact if one keeps putting stones over the stems it will go on seeking fresh territory. Not always a long-lived plant, it needs to be left severely alone. Those stems which seem to be so nicely rooted under their stones don't take kindly to removal and replanting elsewhere, and I have killed off a plant by lopping off its extremities and hopefully planting in other places. It is said to prefer lime, but in my garden the only way I can keep it is in greensand.

There are rhododendrons that flower in January for those with acid soil, but they are not the most spectacular and their early flowering is probably their main claim for recognition. *R. dauricum* has very small magenta-pink flowers, in *R. parvifolium** they are dark magenta, in *R. arborea** vivid pink and crimson and in *R. eclecteum* yellow, white or pink.

January is certainly not a dull month in the garden. It is a time of hope and promise, the days are getting longer and precocious little primroses and violets are promising spring. There are fat buds among the great coloured leaves of the bergenias, and new leaves are pushing through the ground everywhere. Things are happening above the surface and below, and for the gardener another year of thrills and adventures is beginning.

~ 2 ~
February

There are quite a number of gardeners who put away their tools at the end of October and don't reckon to get them out again until March. I would like to take them for a walk round my garden on the first day of February.

A week ago I couldn't see a single crocus and now the cheerful little *Crocus tommasianianus* has come up all over the place and there are flowers from the palest lavender to deep pinky lilac. I plant them in the grass round trees and I don't really want them in flower beds and rock garden, in paving cracks or troughs where I grow treasures. They are prolific seeders but they must also be very quick workers to produce so many flowering bulbs in all parts of the garden. Unfortunately they root themselves deeply so that to extract them often means disturbing other things. I wouldn't mind leaving them in some places, but this year's singleton will be a clump next year—or so it seems—and the attendant foliage is too untidy to accept. I am assured that it doesn't hurt the bulbs to take out the leaves by handfuls, and I am afraid that is what I do now. But all the disadvantages are forgotten when the sun shines on a February morning and hundreds of little flowers open their petals to reveal the colours glowing within and their bright orange stamens.

Snowdrops seem to come up overnight too. The large *Galanthus elwesii* has been out for several weeks, but the little *G. nivalis* which grows in the grass under the apple trees weren't showing at the beginning of the week. Now they are flowering on all sides, singles and doubles, and they are all lovely. The double *G. n.* 'Green Tip'* with green tips to its outer petals is fascinating, and so is the single snowdrop with outer petals marked with green, *G. nivalis viridapicis**, which grows to 8–10 in.

The handsome *G. nivalis* S. Arnott isn't one of the very early varieties but it comes out before February is far advanced. It has round flowers on stems that can be 12 in. high. The different forms of *G. plicatus* are many and even the extra width in their folded leaves can give them individual status. Many of these came to England from men serving in the Crimean War, and take their names from the gardens of recipients, *G. plicatus* Warham being one of the best.

Although I don't really like the "yellow" snowdrops as well as the green ones, I should be upset if they did not reappear each year. The double form of *G. lutescens** ('Lady Elphinstone') does far better in my garden than the single one and one or two bulbs growing in a trough have become a flourishing colony. The single one is in another trough and there are anxious moments until it appears, which it always does when my back is turned. But it doesn't increase and there is still only one little snowdrop with a yellow petticoat.

The snowdrop called 'Straffan' gets its name from the house on the River Anna Liffey where the Hon. Mrs Barton was living in 1856. She received some bulbs from her brother, Lord Clarina, who was serving in the Crimea. One bulb had two flowers and was so much better than the others that it was picked out and from it all those grown today were raised. It is easy to distinguish with its habit of producing two stalks from each bulb. Slight variations have crept in over the years; the one that Mr Bowles grew at Myddleton House goes under that name and there is the 'McMarney Straffan' and others, for collectors get excited over the slightest difference, an extra touch of green or different length of petal or stem. Magnet has a long, curved pedicel, so that it swings gracefully in the wind, and it too produces two stems from each bulb. The peculiarity of G. nivalis scharloki* is the divided spathe, which stands up above the flower-like ears. It is one of the few snowdrops that has a temperament.

Some of the double snowdrops are delightful, and if possible they should be grown above eye level for their charm lies in the neatly arranged petals, which are really a work of art. Our little double form of nivalis always has a few extra crumpled petals which spoil the symmetry (as well as golden stamens nestling in the rather untidy centre), but such charmers as G. 'Poe'* and 'Miss Hassell's' are exquisite in their workmanship.

The more green there is on the petals the more interesting the snowdrop. In Merlin the inner petals are all green, and in Colesbourne, which opens a little later, an edging of white finished the all-green inner petals. And so it goes on, with G. virescens* having green both inside and out, a miniature which Mr Bowles called Norfolk, and many others.

The little woodland snowdrops, plain G. nivalis, look lovely growing in grass but the named ones must be labelled, and these I can study best in little colonies growing in pockets on the shady banks of my ditch. The brilliant crimson leaves of Bergenia delavayi* and purpurascens are attractive with the snowdrops, the large shiny foliage of Fatshedera lizei* is lovely with the large glaucous leaves and glistening flowers of G. elwesii, and the spotted leaves and little blue and pink flowers of pulmonaria seem to go with snowdrops, and so do the small ivies, some of which are variegated. The silver-leaved pulmonaria (which I call P. argentea* to identify it) makes a good companion for G. ikariae, which has green leaves.

The snowdrops have an aloofness and purity against the voluptuousness of the spring snowflake, Leucojum vernum, with its glistening, green-tipped flowers. The snowflakes, too, grow in pockets in the ditch garden and have as a background the large marbled leaves of *Arum pictum* and the fluttering, colourful leaves of the epimediums. There are two less usual versions of the spring snowflake, *L. v. wagneri** with two flowers to each stem and *L. v. carpathicum** with yellow instead of green on the flowers. This may be less usual but to me is also less beautiful.

I hadn't noticed the little bronze-green ruffs of the late aconite, *Eranthis tubergenii**, pushing through the grass, but there are dozens of the tiny golden goblets on this February morning.

Though *Iris stylosa** has been flowering off and on since before Christmas the effort has been spasmodic, but now there are many flowers and plenty of buds to follow. I still marvel at the beauty of the pale variety named after the late Walter Butt. The flowers are very large and a good shape; it is one of the first to start flowering and the one clump I have in the front garden has many more flowers than larger clumps of the ordinary form. It is always a surprise when a rare plant does better than the commoner one. Two of my several varieties of the smaller, narrow-foliaged *I. s. angustifolia** also do extremely well. They both have very dark flowers and make wonderful contrast with the delicate shade of 'Walter Butt'. The blotched flowers of 'La Sainte Campine' form are not very frequent; *I. stylosa speciosa lindsayae**, with its goffered edges, is reluctant to flower and I have never had a bloom on *I. creticum**, although it blooms well in small gardens in a nearby town. I used to get many flowers on plants of white *Iris stylosa**, but too many people wanted bits until my plants rebelled and practically disappeared. Although they have been left unmolested for a year or two they continue to sulk and won't even produce new leaves, let alone flowers. To be honest I do not think that in this case the white form is as beautiful as the coloured. The white of the petals isn't a good white and the yellow beard is rather dingy, but because it is rare and difficult we esteem it more highly than the ordinary plant, which is more beautiful and certainly much easier. Two other less usual varieties which do not flower well for me are *I. s.* 'Mary Barnard', with slender, deep violet-blue flowers, and *ellisii**, which has the bluest flowers of them all.

I counted five different types of pulmonaria blooming this February morning. The two with coral-coloured flowers have been flowering on and off since before Christmas. The common *Pulmonaria officinalis*, with its pink and blue flowers, is as pretty as any when it flowers, and *P. saccharata* has the same colouring but bigger leaves. Usually the varieties with the best leaves are less attractive than the common one when in flower, probably because the small heart-shaped leaves of the common variety don't vary, whereas the silvered, heavily spotted or blue-grey leaves of the superior types look shrivelled and insignificant when the plant flowers. There is one exception and, as may be guessed, it came from Mr Bowles' garden. I have not had this variety long and it has not yet been moved from a nursery bed to a permanent position. But its first flowering shows that it is no ordinary plant. The leaves are long, narrow, a soft blue-grey and not so heavily spotted as some. The flowers are deeper in their shades of blue and pink and come in tight little bunches held above the leaves.

Here and there are early primroses. *Primula altaica grandiflora** is one of the first to flower and its pale lilac flowers peer out under dark hedges. A little cream primula called Dorothy has a tiny crinkled flower to show and the rich blue of 'Blue Ribbon'* makes one think of Mediterranean skies. One that comes from a garden in Craddock I call Craddock Pink, and I can feel quite sentimental about 'Wanda' when it makes a neat clump covered in flowers nestling at the bottom of a wall. I try to keep the wild primroses on the banks outside the garden because they seed so freely that little wildings are likely to come up among the aristocrats. But I grow the large-flowered 'Evelyn Arkwright' and another that tries very hard to produce double flowers but never quite manages it. Another is almost a new 'Jack-in-the-green'. Some years there are enlarged calyces and I think I am getting a new variety, but so far it has always changed its mind. The first primrose spells spring; though I love all the little coloured primroses, none of them is so artlessly lovely as the wild primrose.

How I wish I could grow *Primula bhutanica**, one of the most lovely of all primulas but also one of the most difficult. The petiolares primulas are really not happy south of the Border, although they will grow occasionally for some gardeners. In two parts of Devonshire they flourish but I never keep them for long. From six sent to me from Harrogate only one remains, and I cannot be sure I shall have it next year. Wedged under a stone on a bank of the ditch, its soft blue flowers nestle in rosettes of grey-green leaves. Each flower has a white centre to add to its appeal. A north site and constantly pulling up the bed clothes (packing with peat round the crowns) seems to be the treatment they like.

Heathers are a great standby in the winter and I am ashamed I don't like them better. In some way they are connected in my mind with the little potted plants one gets at Christmas and which shed their leaves the moment they come into the house. But *Erica carnea* brings many flowers into the February garden. Drifts of the pinky mauve flowers under a blue-grey conifer on the rock garden are lightened by the ferny leaves of *Centaurea gymnocarpa**. One that cheers me on dull days has golden leaves and white flowers. It crouches under a large stone on the rock garden; near it the gold and green mottled leaves of the tiny daisy *Bellis aucubaefolia** brings more brightness among the stones, and the mottled leaves of *Lonicera japonica aureo-reticulata** above are tinted with crimson as they tumble among the crimson leaves of a dark antirrhinum that put itself in the wall behind and decided to stay. My favourite heather is a form of *Calluna vulgaris* called 'Mrs Pat'. It has silver and bright pink variegations and is such a lovely symphony of delicate colour that I would not mind if it never flowered. It has to be grown in lime-free soil, of course, and it fills the space between two stones that raise a bed of greensand under a north wall. Behind it the dark, shining leaves of *Pyrola rotundifolia* and *Rhododendron repens** show up the soft colours of the heather.

~ Part Two ~

Just as *Iris histrioides* is for me the iris of January, February is the month for *Iris reticulata*. I have been watching the angular green spears of its foliage for many weeks, then one day in mid February I come face to face with the first purple flower, without having noticed a sign of a bud. Bulb enthusiasts are always extolling the charms of other forms of *Iris reticulata*, the brilliant blue of 'Cantab' and the rich red-purple of 'J. S. Dijt' and the bronzy violet of 'Hercules'. 'Cantab' has no scent at all and doesn't compare in colour with the brilliance of *I. histrioides major**. The different purples and wine shades of the new reticulatas are exciting but I don't believe they smell so sweetly of violets as do the ordinary ones, and I am not sure if they are so reliable. Over the years I have bought several of them, which I have planted with extreme care, labelled methodically and have never seen again. The ordinary reticulata never disappoints me and comes up regularly year after year, but I know that everyone does not have the same experience. I wonder if it enjoys the lime in my soil? Some of my friends who are far superior in skill and soil complain that it will not "do" for them, and we wonder if it is one of those rather rare plants that really dotes on lime.

It was in Mr Norman Hadden's well-known Porlock garden that I saw *Helleborus sternii** in bloom for the first time. I do not know if there is anything different in this hybrid from the *corsicus** x *lividus* cross, of which seeds are regularly offered. *H. sternii** is a cross between *corsicus** and *lividus*, and I have heard that the good form of *corsicus** called Bauer's hybrid* has the same parentage. There is very little evidence of *lividus* blood in the flowers of *H. sternii**. At first sight one would, I think, take them for a rather neat form of *H. corsicus**, but knowing the cross it is possible to see a slight mother-of-pearl sheen on the flowers, though nothing more. There is something reminiscent of *lividus* in the rather looser growth of the flower trusses, and in the shape of the leaves, which are lined with red.

Helleborus cyclophyllus blooms in February if they are old-established clumps but not always just after they have been moved. This is, I think, one of the most beautiful hellebores, with perfectly formed large green flowers, deeper than *corsicus** or *foetidus*, though not as dark as those of *viridis*. Like all the hellebores they look best, I think, as a single clump and not massed in a drift. Grown like this the graceful silhouette of the plant can be seen topped with the proudly held flowers.

One of the finest of the hybrid hellebores, 'Prince Rupert', is in flower this month. This is one of the largest, showing its connection with *H. guttatus* by the heavy maroon stipplings inside the pale greenish cream cups, which makes it one of the most striking hellebores in the garden. 'Apotheer Bogren' blooms the same time and is as dark as 'Prince Rupert' is fair. This hellebore, indeed, is one of the darkest of all that I grow. I have been given 'Black Knight' from several gardens, both full-grown plants and seedlings, but not all are as dark as the true plant. The seedlings, in particular, vary very much, and though they are extremely beautiful with rather small hanging heads in viney-purple infiltrated with green, they are not all as dark as the best forms of 'Black Knight'. 'Ballard's Black' varies considerably and some are very, very dark with a soft bloom.

H. torquatus is one of the mystery hellebores, for according to the experts it is not a true species but a hybrid and with some uncertainty about its parentage. This probably accounts for the variation in the flowers one sees. I have at least four plants of *H. torquatus* from different sources and they have slight variations but all are bluish-purple, with rather small and lightly waved flowers. Some are darker than others, but all have the "bloom" that makes the dark-coloured hellebores so lovely. Usually the outside colour appears as a rim to the inside of the cups.

H. abchasicus* varies slightly too. I have plants from various sources and, though the colouring is mainly deep reddish purple with traces of green, it can be lighter or darker with more or less green, and the size of the flowers varies too, though most are rather small.

I read recently that "Lenten Roses" should be grown in a position well sheltered from wintry gales, but I think one can take more liberties with them than with other hellebores. In one garden I know they are growing very happily in a raised bed, constantly tossed by the wind. No doubt they are growing in good soil, and are not allowed to dry out in summer; there are trees nearby so that they get some shade, and so perhaps with all those requirements satisfied they can put up with a certain amount of wintry wind. These particular hellebores seed themselves in a most satisfactory way. Some gardeners get many more seedlings than others not only of *H. orientalis* but of *H. corsicus** and *H. foetidus* too. I am not one of the lucky ones and wonder if I weed too much. I put a mixture of sand and peat round the plants I want particularly to increase, but even that does not always help. I used to cut my hellebores but now I leave them to flower and—I hope—to seed.

*Clematis balearica** (*C. calycina*) flowers in the winter and though I suppose we wouldn't look twice at the rather nondescript flowers in the summer they are pleasant at this time of year. Usually greenish parchment in colour with crimson spots inside, they have a papery texture. The fernlike foliage is bronzed and makes a good background for the flowers. There is a form with finer, greener flowers which is worth seeking. I grow this clematis on the north side of the wall near the gate and it makes a thick tangle on top of the wall and over the beech hedge, and occasionally seeds itself elsewhere.

It always distresses me to see the leaf-buds forming on the *jackmanii** forms of clematis, for when I see them I am tempted to break my fixed rule of cutting these clematis down on 15th February. Reason, however, always wins, and on that day all those promising buds are consigned to the bonfire. The lower 2 in of the clematises have become thick and gnarled by this time and there is no difficulty in seeing where to make the annual amputation. At the first hint of spring new growth appears and gets away quickly. Sometimes these thick old lower stems get broken, either by a gale or a careless human, but clematises are resilient and usually break again from the bottom, right at ground level. 'Ville de Lyon' and others of the *viticella* group are cut down in the same way, but 'Blue Gem', *henryi** and others of the *lanuginosa* group merely have the dead wood removed. Some of the species receive the same drastic treatment; *tangutica*, *orientalis* and *rehderiana* cut to ground level will race up the wall again each spring. *C. macropetala alpina** I do not touch and I merely restrain the montanas to keep them to their allotted space, defined by wire netting nailed to the wall.

Cornus mas is a good shrub for a small garden for it grows slowly and has something to offer at all times. Mine is the variegated form with delicate green and white foliage; there are red berries in the autumn and in February puffs of tiny yellow flowers attached by magic to its bare winter stems.

Mahonia japonica is still flowering but the spikes of scented flowers are getting shorter and, to make up, the leaves are turning crimson.

Although the first flowers of *Prunus subhirtella autumnalis** may open as early as September they go on flowering till April. A cold spell and the flowers disappear, but when milder weather returns there are more soft pink flowers against the blue of a winter sky. A standard with wide-spreading branches can be very dramatic, but the outline of a bush with flowers on the bare branches from the ground upwards is more intimate. In a garden I know which is made on a steep hill, a shrubby *Prunus subhirtella autumnalis rosea** has been carefully posed on a bank which is carpeted with *Lamium galeobdolon variegatum**. This queen among ground cover plants likes to send its long trails of grey and silver leaves in all directions. Here they are smothering the lower part of the shrub and have left the ground to festoon the lower branches of the prunus. The effect on a sunny February day is quite entrancing. I have spring snowflakes, *Leucojum vernum*, growing round my prunus shrub but the lamium makes a softer picture and is there for a year instead of a few weeks.

Two green-flowered shrubs are lovely in this month. *Ribes laurifolium* is a low-growing plant and the first time I saw it was in an inspired mixed planting round a house. There was a wide border all round the house and it was filled with good evergreen plants that spilled over the stone path. I can't remember now all the shrubs that were used but I know they included foliage of every shade, *Senecio laxifolius**, rosemaries, the bronze *Veronica hectori*, 'Jackman's Blue Rue'*, and the ribes. I visited the garden in February and the pale green flowers were lovely against dark, glossy leaves. It has rather a sprawling habit and is ideal for this kind of planting. I grow mine under a north wall with hostas and hellebores and the blue and ferny *Acaena ascendens**. This is rather a robust plant that likes to swirl over paths and softens any hard corners or stonework.

Garrya elliptica gets more beautiful every day and it drips with long, grey-green tassels, reminding me of the eerie swamps in the Southern States of America where the giant trees are hung with "Spanish Moss".

Also with green flowers but not so spectacular, *Daphne laureola* is a good evergreen shrub for growing under trees. Its small green flowers have scent which is particularly noticeable late in the day. *D. odora* flowers towards the end of the month. I grow the form with margined leaves, which is hardier than the type, and of course the white as well as the purple *Daphne mezereum* will fill the air with rich fragrance this month too. The colour of *D. mezereum* varies from a washy lavender to a deep crimson-purple and this is the one I try to grow, but less worthy offspring appear in different parts of the garden and have to be snubbed. *D. grandiflorum album** is a finer plant than *D. mezereum album**.

The long strings of primrose pearls that hang from the bare boughs of *Stachyurus praecox* and *S. chinensis* look graceful but are actually rather rigid. But the shrub has reddish bark to add to its plumage and grows well in the shade of tall trees.

Although I can't grow them myself I love the camellias that flower in other people's gardens. I have tried them in greensand and in soil that is mostly peat, but they soon turn sickly yellow and then quietly leave me. It used to be thought that they weren't hardy but that myth has been exploded. They do best on a west or north-west wall, so that the early-morning sun is kept from their flowers and the roots are kept cool.

I grow the deep pink *Prunus mume* 'Beni-shi-don'* against an east wall and interest is given when it is not in flower by a large patch of the golden variegated ivy, *Hedera helix* 'Jubilee Gold Heart'*, growing on the wall. The Chinese plum is sweetly scented and the small flowers are heavily stamened. Cut in bud the flowers soon open in the house.

Most of the forsythias flower later but the dwarf *Forsythia ovata* and the taller *F. giraldiana* flower in February. And so does the delightful twiggy little plant, *Abeliophyllum distichum*, which has white flowers opening from pink buds.

Not all the enjoyment from the winter garden comes from flowers; skeletons can be very telling. My garden is peopled by the bare stems of perennials and all the grasses, many of which are bleached to old ivory. In winter one can appreciate every twist and turn of the "Wiggly Willow", *Salix matsudana tortuosa**, and the twisted stems of the corkscrew hazel, *Corylus contorta**. This always looks rather hump-backed when it has its leaves, but the intricacy of its twisting branches shows up in the winter.

Leaves can be lovely with bare stems; the great leaves of *Bergenia cordifolia* turn crimson in winter and are striking against the bright brown seed heads of *Sedum telephium* with the silver *Stachys lanata** beyond. The shining leaves of *B. crassifolia* are gold and orange and lovely with *Santolina incana**. *B. schmidtii** has smaller, dark green leaves, but it is the first to flower and tight little bunches of pink flowers are opening close to the ground. The rich crimson leaves of *B. delavayi** and *B. purpurascens* are lovely with the cream and green striped leaves of *Iris foetidissima variegata*, or the tough silver leaves of *Senecio laxifolius**. *Senecio monroii** is not so silver although its grey leaves are white below, but it shows up well against the rich red-brown stems of *Physostegia* 'Summer Spire'*, which are so bright that I cannot bear to cut them down. The white leaves of *Olearia mollis** complete the picture. In another place the white stems of *Perowskia atriplicifolia** are behind the ruddy seed-heads of *Sedum spectabile* 'Autumn Joy'*.

I don't keep only the stems that have good colour; some herbaceous plants look almost like deciduous shrubs when they have finished flowering and those bare stems add height and interest all through the winter. The branching stems of *Alcea cannabina** reach 8–10 ft, *Eupatorium purpureum* grows to 6–8 ft and more, and makes a splendid thicket of dark stems, after its flat purple flowers. *Serratula coronata* has purple thistle flowers on stout stems which reach about 5 ft and are quite well-keeping. Teasels are even more beautiful for their heads are as lovely when brown as when they are soft shades of pale lavender.

This month is to me the month of promise. The garden isn't awake yet but it is stirring. On all sides I see plants that have been sleeping below the surface pushing their new shoots through the cold, uncomfortable earth. Pink tips of paeonies, the fresh green of veratrum and the blue-grey of mertensia and the closely packed buds of the mandrakes. We don't expect much of the damp days of February Fill-Dyke, but it is an exciting month all the same. If gardening doesn't teach us anything else it should teach us faith. All the time we are shivering and complaining nature is working miracles underground. I die a hundred deaths until I see all my friends coming back to greet me, but I needn't worry; nearly always they come through safe and sound, but I never feel completely safe till I see those thrusting shoots of pink or green or grey.

~ 3 ~

March

Now I expect great things of March, and I don't often get them. Just as we know that February means rain we fear a certain amount of bluster in March. There have been years when we've had sunshine and warmth in this month, but not often. We ought to be able to enjoy the daffodils which come up in their hundreds, but so often there's a fiendish east wind waiting to smite round every corner, and sometimes keen frosts and even snow can spoil all enjoyment in the garden and ruin the fresh beauty of the flowers, but luckily that is not usual.

It always surprises me when I see *Iris tuberosa** so early in the year. I believe *Hermodactylis tuberosum* has always been its correct name but it has always been known as *Iris tuberosa** to most of us. Now that there is a determined effort to tighten up on nomenclature the higher-ups have decided that we mustn't take the easier course any more. I don't think, though, that they'll be able to stop the easy familiarity of the "widow iris", because no one could chat casually about the "widow hermodactylis". Another easy name is the "snake's-head iris".

I am not quite sure which is the best position for this iris. It comes from Mediterranean regions and I imagined it would like the same position as the Algerian iris, *I. unguicularis*, with perhaps better soil, so I planted it in front of the rock garden near the gate, as warm a position as any in the garden. It flowers regularly each year but it doesn't increase. I have seen it grown in an ordinary flower bed, among plants of its own height, to give its slenderness support, and in one garden I know it does well in a sheltered place under trees. But the most magnificent colony I have ever seen was thriving and multiplying under a tall west wall in a garden a few miles inland from Weston-super-Mare. The only way to find out is to plant small groups in different places in the garden and see how they get on. I would prefer a background of green as those delicate green flowers with their velvety-black markings don't show up well against hot stones. Also I would like them to increase so well that I can cut as lavishly as I want. They are lovely with other spring flowers, and I notice that arrangements in which they are used always get good marks.

I enjoy many green flowers at this time of year. There are still waxy-green flowers of our native daphne, *D. laureola*, and for those with bigger bushes the flowers are delightful indoors. I saw a wonderful arrangement at a meeting in Dorset, where branches of the daphne had been cut from the roadside and the leaves removed. I have never found this daphne growing wild, but I do find it seeds itself mildly in the garden and I replant the seedlings where I want good winter foliage. Position does not matter; it is a good plant for under-planting trees, loves a north wall and will grow in the open. Later on it will merge into the landscape, so the position to consider is the one where it looks best in the winter.

Some of the large euphorbias open this month. For weeks I have been watching to see if the leafy stems are turning over at the top, which means they are going to flower. The private life of the euphorbia is a little confusing, and I am often asked by disappointed owners why they don't get flowers on those beautifully foliaged stems. I don't think you ever do the first year and it is in the second that they should be crowned with foot high busbies with orange, brown or black "eyes". The stems are cut off after flowering and in a well-organised plant there should be more stems coming on so that one has flowers every year thereafter—until the plant has such a stubble of cut stems that there is hardly room for the new ones. In some gardens some varieties flower only every other year. Not everyone agrees about the names. My contention—from endless browsings in botanical gardens—is that *Euphorbia wulfenii**, with orange eyes, is the largest, *E. sibthorpii** comes next and is brown-eyed, and *E. characias* is the smallest and neatest with beady black eyes, but I often hear it stated that *characias* is the biggest, finest plant, with leaves more grey than green. For most people it doesn't matter what they are called, they all have most beautiful evergreen blue-green leaves, and those great lovebird-green heads last for many weeks. They cut well too, but the ends must be sealed with a lighted match or hot wax—they bleed profusely. After I have been cutting off the old flowering heads the stones round the plant are white with all the milky-white "latex" that has poured out. This is said to be very poisonous so it is treated with great care.

The largest types look best in a corner with walls or hedge behind as the stems can grow very long and it is difficult to keep them symmetrical. The dark green of cypress or the bright yellow-green of golden privet make excellent foils. Quite by accident a seedling of the biennial yellow-green *E. stricta* came up behind a plant of *E. characias* that was growing in a niche beside some stone steps, and for a season I enjoyed a striking colour contrast. In another place *Helleborus corsicus** has large euphorbias as a background, and the hellebore, with its grey-green leaves and green flowers made luminous by golden stamens, is even lovelier than usual. The euphorbias that I had planted in this sheltered corner are large ones not often seen—*E. androsacinifolia** and *E. valdevilloscarpa**, collector's pieces for the euphorbia addict.

Anchusa myosotidiflora (*Brunnera macrophylla*) is often highly praised, and I agree that it is a good-natured plant that produces its sprays of bright blue flowers all through the year, but some thought is needed when planting so that it isn't too obvious in the winter. It is not a good winter plant, for the big leaves are black and tattered and cover the crowns like dirty rags. Of course, they can be removed in the autumn, but I never like to take away what is undoubtedly nature's protection. But in March they can be cleared away to reveal the neat little crowns of grey-green leaves with tiny blue buds all ready to spring to life. It is always recommended that this plant should have shade and some moisture, but I notice it puts some of its innumerable seedlings in the open as well as in the shade. I grow it with *Epimedium sulphureum** and a white geum, both of which make enough foliage to hide some of the winter shame of the anchusa.

The flowers of omphalodes are bigger than those of the anchusa and not quite so keen a blue but they are produced just as freely. The foliage of *Omphalodes cappadocica*, however, never gets out of hand. It may need a little attention after the winter, but most of the year the pointed leaves are bright glossy green. There are two other omphalodes very similar; *O. nitida* has leaves that are more grey-green, and in *O. lojkae* they are much narrower. Any shady, rather moist place suits them; growing between stones at the edge of a narrow bed under a north wall with cyclamen or lavender primroses, they soon make large tufts, which are easily divided as each stem can be pulled off with plenty of roots to make a separate plant.

Omphalodes verna flowers earlier than *cappadocica*. I often see a little blue eye peeping out from a dark leaf in February or earlier, and in March there are usually plenty of flowers. It is rather a straggling plant, with long stems with tiny leaves at the end. Each of these tufts will root but one needs a lot of them to cover the ground. The white-flowered form is quite pretty to have as well as 'Blue-Eyed Mary', but not instead of. This plant gets rather lost in a big bed but is very good for a narrow bed under a wall with anthericums or pink dentaria. The aristocratic *O. luciliae* flowers later in the year and is not so easy as the others. The very blue leaves and porcelain-blue flowers look best hanging down from rock crevices, and though it is usually recommended to grow it in sun my best results have come from plants grown in shade.

Every day one discovers more primroses in bloom. I like to come on them unexpectedly, in dark corners and tucked between stones at the bottom of walls. It is the custom to sneer at *Primula* 'Wanda', but only because it is so often grown in full sun in an open bed, where the magenta-purple of the flowers does look hard and glaring. But a clump at the bottom of a shady wall is quite a different matter; the flowers look rich purple and the tiny leaves have a purplish tinge. I am sure the way to grow 'Wanda' successfully is to grow it in the shade under trees or walls; it comes out very early, never gets scorched by a hot sun and takes on an added beauty with its background of green. It multiplies quickly and the rich purple of its flowers is very different from the garish tint it appears to wear in the open. Whenever I see 'Wanda's in the shade I am reminded of a little group of them which were planted in a narrow bed in my sister's garden in Buckinghamshire and were quite happy but never spectacular. One winter, builders took possession of the garage and a temporary shelter of canvas was constructed for the car during operations. The bed in which the 'Wanda's were planted was inside the canvas and I have never seen primroses enjoy themselves so much. Never before or since have I seen such luxuriant clumps. There was hardly a leaf to be seen so numerous were those large and laughing flowers, brilliant but not gaudy in the gloom of the canvas shelter.

Many of the lavender primroses are very beautiful and they are easy to place because they look nice with everything. 'Mrs McGilvray' has mauvy pink flowers on polyanthus stalks and its leaves are large and crinkled and easily distinguished. It would be easier if one could tell all the primroses from their leaves. The tiny 'Mauve Queen' has small, rather fragile leaves, those of 'Fair Maid' have a faint blue haze and purple 'Jill' has very flat, dark, crinkled leaves with stems that root, so they are easily recognised. The pink 'Kinlough Beauty' has heart-shaped leaves with a prominent mid-rib and it too is stem-rooting. The tiny cream polyanthus 'Lady Greer' makes such tight little rosettes that they are hardly visible before the flowers come. The leaves of the pink form look just the same, so one has to wait for flowers to make sure. 'E. R. Janes' is another of the tiny ones, but when happy it will often produce its brick-red flowers in autumn and winter; but it can be difficult and I think does best in full sun. Frost doesn't affect the colour of its flowers, although it does strange things to the deep purple of 'Julius Caesar' and 'Tawny Port', and the crimsons of 'Dinah', and 'Betty' and 'David Green'. The paler colours are not affected, nor are the pastel-coloured violets. I grow a lot of red, pink and purple violets: they seed themselves and come in all shades and variations, but though they are quite hardy they don't look happy in very severe weather. Pink violets turn blue with cold, and the reds and violets turn slate-coloured. Luckily they soon respond to warmer weather and seem to change back to their original colour.

To get plenty of flowers on the double and semi-double violets they should be grown in frames or covered with cloches. I can never see much difference between 'Duchesse de Parme' and 'Marie Louise'*; both have lilac flowers, and even 'Mrs J. J. Astor', which is supposed to be pinky lilac, is very little different. The other that grows easily is the white 'Conte de Brazza'*. All the double violets have more yellow, rather small shiny leaves, and in the white one all these characteristics are more noticeable.

Many of the periwinkles start to flower in March. I am not referring, of course, to the big and obliging *Vinca major*, which flowers all through the winter. How I wish I had a place where I could make proper use of this most useful and worthy plant. We take it so much for granted and yet where else would one get that luxuriant glossy foliage that takes no notice whatever of seasons or weather? It has been used very sensibly in a garden near me. There a shrubbery screens the house from the road. At one corner, where the bank meets the wire fence, *V. major* has been given its head. Instead of untidy rough grass here are waves of dense shiny green, which poke through the fence and start tumbling down the bank, and are decked with clear blue flowers all through the winter. I pass this corner on my way to church and it is a treat to which I look forward each week.

Though we may grow *V. major* for its flowers as well as its leaves, the main attraction of the variegated form is its foliage. It is as good as a flower in the winter and the cream-splashed leaves are always sleek and glossy. I often go out of my way in the winter time to see the variegated periwinkle in a most successful growing arrangement. The garden in question is above the road and a brick wall holds up the garden. Many plants that are attractive in the winter have been planted behind the wall, in particular *Cotoneaster horizontalis*, winter-flowering heathers in wine and pink and crimson, and to give contrast large clumps of the variegated periwinkle are planted between, to fling themselves over the wall and work slowly behind the shrubs on the level ground above the wall.

There are always a few flowers on the small vincas during the winter but they open in earnest in March. Brilliant blue *graveana* ('La Grave') will open a sample flower very early in the year, and often there are flowers on the best small white. I used to call this Mr Bowles' white *Vinca minor*, which caused some confusion because there is a blue one that is attributed to Mr Bowles. This special white one was given to me as one of Mr Bowles' pets, and another friend gave me one which he said was Miss Jekyll's small white. I planted both presents as carefully as I knew how, but Miss Jekyll's little friend never took hold and petered out after a few weeks. I was racking my brains how I could get hold of another piece without telling my generous friend that I had lost the first when I discussed vincas, in particular *Vinca minor*, with another gardener. He referred to my special white as Miss Jekyll's form. I knew he was talking about mine because particular mention was made of the foliage which has a different manner of growth from most forms of *Vinca minor*. Instead of making long trails with leaves rather far apart, Mr Bowles' (Miss Jekyll's) plant has the pairs of leaves at much smaller intervals and makes a much thicker carpet. I enquired about the difference between those attributed to Mr Bowles and Miss Jekyll and was told—for the first time—the truth behind the story. The vinca was Miss Jekyll's first, she gave it to Mr Bowles and, when he passed it on, it became his perquisite unless the recipient was paying a lot of attention and heard that it had first come from Miss Jekyll. I am overjoyed to have got to the bottom of the story and even happier to know that I have not lost Miss Jekyll's famous little periwinkle. There is another very small white vinca, with tiny leaves and small flowers, which is good for small spaces.

The wine-coloured *V. minor rubra** flowers better than the semi-double form, known as *V. m. multiplex**, or the double blue, *V. m. flore plena**, with its little blue rosettes. I grow the variegated forms for their leaves and it always comes as a surprise to find a blue flower on the end of a silvered trail or a white one on the golden variegated small periwinkle.

~ Part Two ~

In spite of the north-east winds and constant frosts of late March scillas and chionodoxas are opening every day, some in the places where I want them to be and where I planted them and a good many in spots they have chosen for themselves. The first of all is the pale blue, very dwarf *Scilla tubergeniana**. The chionodoxas, with their white eyes, flower next, then the ordinary scillas. I know there are many more interesting scillas that one ought to grow, but I get great enjoyment from the common squill, surely one of the bluest flowers we have and so kind in seeding itself about that I think it is the most satisfactory of them all. The chionoscillas, which are paler and bigger, are lovely too. They are a cross between chionodoxa and scilla.

There are several paler scillas that flower later. *S. messenaica* is daintier and paler than the common squill and has great ideas about colonisation. In Mr Hadden's garden at Porlock it is turning large areas of the undergrowth into sheets of blue in April, and looks lovely with late winter cyclamen. *S. bifolia* is rather darker in colour and flowers in March and seeds itself well. *S. azureus** is not very different in shade but more akin to the bluebell.

I have one little clump of white scillas, the albino form of the common squill. I must have bought more originally, but only one little planting has survived. It comes up every year but doesn't appear to seed itself, which is a pity because there are not many white flowers in March. In a good year my fat white crocuses, Snowdrift, are lovely, but we sometimes get late frosts which ruin their beauty.

For years I have grown the summer snowflake, *Leucojum aestivum*, which was given to me as a Bermuda snowdrop. I don't know why it is called "summer", because although it comes after *L. vernum* it is still spring when it flowers. It goes very pleasantly with small daffodils and is a graceful plant to grow among shrubs. I had a clump in rather a prominent place near the house. This was a good idea in early spring when that graceful clump of green was very welcome, not so good when a late frost bent the stems and ruined the outline, and not at all good in early summer when it was untidy, turning yellow but not decayed enough to be removed. Now I have transferred the ordinary *L. aestivum* to the front garden and have clumps between the hydrangeas and behind the "Lent Rose" hellebores. Here I hope it will escape damage from late frost and the other plants in the small beds will screen somewhat the last ugly days of its yearly span.

The superior form of this snowflake, *L. aestivum* 'Gravetye Giant', I have planted between stones in the ditch with other tall and graceful plants. It is here that I put the variegated and the double 'Solomon's Seal'* and double camassias, the bronze-leaved montbretia, solfaterra and libertias. The plants that hang their heads on arching stalks get the highest places so that one gets the full beauty of the plant as a whole. The flowers of the snowflake are small for the long stems and thicket of leaves, so they look best with a leafy background.

But if March has a flower all its own I think it is the daffodil. We have daffodils in February, and there will be many still in April, but for the greatest display March is the month.

When we plant daffodils I think we should observe how nature does the job. Wild daffodils grow in grass and usually in clumps so that one can enjoy the outline of the flowers against a background of leaves. Many daffodils grown together need the backing of green if they are not to look garish as they do when spaced in serried rows in bare earth. The most ordinary types grown in their individual clumps with grass as a background are far lovelier than the rarest bulbs grown in a flower bed with nursery neatness. We are all grateful to the people who grow them like this under their apple trees, in their grass banks, at the sides of their drives or even in the grass outside their houses.

The first daffodil to flower for me is the little Tenby daffodil, *Narcissus pseudo-narcissus obvallaris**, only 8 in high, but a perfect miniature of a trumpet daffodil. Coming so early one is not critical of its yellowness. It is rather a deep colour and later in the season I feel it is a little garish. By then the white *N. p.-n. moschatus** is in bloom and the poor little Tenby daffodil doesn't stand up to the comparison.

In the same way we think the bold 'King Alfred' a fine fellow until the white 'Beersheba' and 'Mount Hood' start to bloom. White daffodils can be grown in a flower bed, but the yellow ones definitely need to be toned down by grass. 'Thalia', which has two pale heads on one stalk, is lovely nodding under the shade of a tree and so is 'W. P. Milner', in palest sulphur.

One reason, I think, why we like jonquils is that the flowers are small and delicate and they have as background many dark, narrow leaves. In Captain Berkeley's garden at Spetchley, near Worcester, there is a long narrow bed planted to the brim with jonquils, filling the air with fragrance and the eye with grace.

The really tiny daffodils, N. *cyclamineus*, *bulbocodium* and other miniatures, need a really safe place where they can grow and hold their own. I have found a good place to plant them is in the peat garden among heathers, where they can be left in safety to come up year after year with a good background of foliage.

It always comes as a surprise when I see big buds swelling on the dwarf *Iris chamaeiris**, buds almost as tall as the leaves. These little irises grow well in gaps in paving and are a lovely sight when the flowers in blue, purple, primrose or gold open among the 3-in leaves. The white 'Bride' is a little taller and a little later. It looks lovely thrusting up its grey leaves at the edge of a stone path. Two others about the same size are 'Green Spot', which has blotches of green on its white flowers, and another green and white dwarf called 'Green Eyes'.

Some of the flowers that flower early in the year are gold with a definite hint of green, and they seem to go particularly well with early spring flowers. Later on the dome of green-gold that is *Euphorbia epithymoides** might seem a trifle overpowering, but early in the year it is the embodiment of spring. *E. myrsinites* also flowers in March but its greeny yellow flowers have glaucous foliage to set off their beauty. A large clump of colchicums happened to be planted close to this euphorbia and when the euphorbia flowers the handsome glossy leaves of the colchicum are at their best.

Dondia epipactis (*Hacquetia epipactis*)* would hardly be noticed if it flowered later in the year, but there are not so many flowers in bloom when the first green-gold flowers with conspicuous stamens appear low on the ground, like scattered petals from a yellow-flowered plant. The stems grow slowly, but by the time the flowers are at their best they are 4–5 in from the ground and have a backing of shamrock-shaped leaves. After the colour of the flowers has quite gone there still remain attractive green calyces and the green centres of the flowers, rather dark by now, but pretty among the leaves.

I have no business to write about the beautiful *Adonis dahurica** (*A. amurensis*), which also has green-gold flowers and blooms in March. I have had it half a dozen times but so far have failed to keep it for long. I gave it the rich soil I understand it likes and a place in the sun, and once planted took great care never to disturb it, but there must be other attentions it requires. One is warned that it takes a little time to settle down and so its non-appearance is not so depressing the first time but becomes a challenge later. This member of the ranunculus family is said to have been one of Farrer's favourite flowers, and I do not wonder, for the flowers are round and glistening with a background of feathery foliage not unlike that of an anemone. There is a double as well as a single form, and if there is any choice I think the double variety is more beautiful. The Japanese use it in miniature gardens, and in English gardens it looks best in a rather informal woodland setting, where it gets some sun. I have tried it in peat and ordinary soil without any success.

Plants that flower in March sometimes need careful placing. By the time they come they have a right to expect a little warmth and sunshine, but March can be a beast when it catches all the trusting things that have been making growth in February. I sometimes wonder if *Bergenia ciliata* ought to have a little protection in the bad years. The flowers are lovely when they grow as they should, with delicate apple-pink flowers, little round buds and red stems and calyces. When things go well the flat, hairy leaves, green with a reddish tinge, are a wonderful background for the pink and white blossom, but I have known seasons when the poor flowers have to struggle to open without a scrap of leaf behind them, and the flowers instead of being delicate pink are seared and browned by frost. Some bad years there is hardly a flower on any of the bergenias except the easy, ordinary *B. schmidtii** and *B. cordifolia*, both of which flower well and give no trouble. I certainly don't despise those chubby pink flowers, but I would like to see what some of the others can do. After collecting bergenias busily for a long time it is heartbreaking to have the flowering season pass by without a single flower and to know that one has to wait another year to see what they are like. I have the white *B. milesii** but I haven't yet seen its face; one that is supposed to grow very tall has never flowered, nor a miniature I have grown for twenty years. But really, I suppose we collect bergenias for the beauty of their leaves, and the flowers are an added delight when we get them. All the same, I should like to know how to make my reluctant plants produce flowers.

The ordinary kingcup, *Caltha palustris*, is one of the most perfect spring flowers, with its lacquered globes of gold on thick stems, and magnificent glossy leaves. Each stem, with its flowers, buds and wonderful foliage, is a work of art, but unfortunately it grows rather big and is better in a damp meadow unless one has a very big garden. But the double marsh marigold, *C. p. flore plena**, is a much neater plant, and when a clump is fully out makes a dazzling display. After the flowers are over the leaves get big and make good ground cover. The white king cup is even neater and so unusual that not everyone realises what it is. I have never seen a double version of this plant; it would be a beautiful addition to the early garden if it should exist. Although these plants delight in moisture they will grow in an ordinary bed if it is not too dry, and like other plants that really need moisture will get on without it if they are grown in the shade.

Forsythias come into their own in March—the rich *F. intermedia spectabilis** and the slightly less strident *F. suspensa*, which I have trained against the seat wall of the malthouse, and which would be just as good against a north wall. The dwarf *Forsythia viridissima bronxensis** is a useful little shrub for the rock garden, with lemon-coloured flowers. I have it in the front of one of my terraced beds where it makes a welcome splash of colour early in the year and 18 in of useful foliage for the rest of the season. *F. ovata* is dwarf and bushy and can be used to bring early colour to a mixed border.

The searing winds and bitter frosts that can wreck the March garden don't bother the forsythias much, but in many places the birds do. Devonshire seems to be unlucky in this respect. I have heard the sad tale from Sidmouth and Tiverton, and friends near Chudleigh are so tired of losing every forsythia bud every year by ravaging tits and bullfinches that they have admitted defeat and removed most of the forsythias and put in other trees.

The cream flowers of *Osmanthus delavayi* are small but very sweet, and to get the best from them I think the bush should be planted in not too exposed a position. My osmanthus is in rather a bleak place and sometimes those delicate flowers at the top of the bush are seared by frost or wind. I recently saw a very tall bush in a Worcestershire garden planted against a summer-house and with taller shrubs behind it, and I was told that each year it produces a crop of perfect flowers.

~ 4 ~

April

In a normal year April is a balmy month, with gentle showers that leave the sky clear and blue, and furtive sunshine, which heartens without scorching. February should have brought enough moisture to stop anxiety for many weeks, the angry winds of March should have dried up the surface of the soil and made it workable, all ready for the gentle play of shower and sun in April.

Of course it doesn't always happen like that. We don't always get rain in February, and March winds do not always know when that month ends and April begins. But worst of all are the years when we have weeks and weeks without rain, sometimes even into May. This can be disastrous for plants that have had to be divided or replanted rather late in the season. Some years April doesn't live up to its reputation in any way. It can be cold and sometimes things seem to take a long time to get going. I have been more disappointed in April than in any month because we expect so much. I always remember, in the days when we divided our time between London and Somerset, with what eagerness I dashed out to see what had come out while I had been away, and it was usually very little.

In a good year *Viburnum utile* is a pleasant sight early in April. I have this shrub trained against the east wall of the malthouse. There are odd flowers as early as February and in April it covers itself with flat flower-heads of pale pink, enhanced by deeper buds. I know that many people do not consider this viburnum worth growing, preferring the product of its mating with *V. carlesii* in *Viburnum burkwoodii**. I grow *V. burkwoodii** as a bush and it soon makes a very big one and is practically evergreen. Compared with *V. utile* it seems to have more foliage than flower. The "thinner" utile is so covered with bloom early in the year that the stems and sparse foliage hardly show. I often think how lovely it would look grown against a white wall. The grey stone of the malthouse is not the best background for pale flowers, but even that disadvantage cannot detract from the beauty of *V. utile* at the height of her glory.

*Prunus subhirtella autumnalis** is still flowering and I can think of no other tree that has a six month season. There are not so many flowers now, of course, and it doesn't now give the impression of a snow-storm against a blue sky, but there are enough flowers to make it worth picking. Even without the flowers I should pick it because the leaves alone are lovely in tender green, with a pink tinge, and very welcome at this time of year.

One would think there would be plenty to pick just now but with the exception of bulbous plants and little things like primulas, anemones and rock plants the picking cupboard is really rather bare. The good old standby, *Mahonia aquifolium*, is still in full spate but it drops its petals very early and though the young foliage is glossy and almost crimson the old leaves can look rather frost-bitten.

The pink-flowered, purple-leaved sloe (*Prunus spinosa rosea**) is a lovely little shrub for the small garden. It is a double form of wild sloe and the light reddish foliage is rather unusual. It is a shrub that really needs a place all to itself and I wish I could have placed mine as well as a friend of mine has planted his. The garden in question must have been a quarry at some time because in several places there are high walls of natural stone, and it is in the little garden sheltering at the bottom of one of these walls that the sloe has place of honour. To come round a corner and see it smothered in pink blossom almost takes one's breath away. One day, I remember, it was raining softly and the little sloe was mysteriously shrouded in mist.

Another shrub that delights me in April is *Cytisus kewensis**. Some plants can be put anywhere but this prostrate broom needs just the right position if it is to show what it really can do. Not all gardens can supply a flat bed behind a wall, where it can spread and pour down over the wall, like rich cream. After it has finished flowering it is still attractive as a thick, neat mat, which melts into the landscape. The only attention it needs is a light clipping of the ends of the stems after flowering.

There are still hellebores in bloom. *Helleborus lividus* is getting towards the end of its day but that isn't surprising when we remember that the first buds were showing in January. The present worry is whether there is any hope of seed; and that unfortunately is not likely. Something seems to discourage *H. lividus* when it has been in bloom for a few weeks: the stem becomes black and dwindles, the flowers turn black too instead of opening wide with their faces to the sky to give room to the swelling seedpods. By this time fresh young growth is usually starting from the ground and one cuts off the old stems and hopes for better luck next year.

*Helleborus corsicus**, although it opened in January, is still lovely. It is not a long-lived plant, but luckily it sets a great deal of seed and the moment one can burst the seedpods by slight thumb pressure I cut off the stems to ground level to give the new growth a chance. The new leaves of all hellebores look very shiny and healthy, and the young growth of *lividus* and *corsicus** is the most encouraging of all.

There seem to be three distinct forms of the *lividus* x *corsicus** cross. For years I grew Bauer's hybrid*, which I was given as a good form of *H. corsicus**, improved by a touch of *lividus*. There is another form which doesn't boast a name, just calls itself *H. lividus* x *corsicus**, and lastly there is Sir Frederick Stern's cross of the same two, *H. sternii**. The *lividus* blood isn't very noticeable in any of them. The flowers have a faintly luminous look which may have come from the lividness of *lividus*, and the flower bracts are tinged with pink. The leaves are certainly greyer and more spiny and have a rosy lining, but none are really robust.

It is quite impossible to distinguish between the different forms of *H. orientalis*. They seed promiscuously and parentage is very mixed. I have one very good greeny cream one that flowers very late. I have noticed for several years that it is the last to open and lasts in flower for a very long time. I collect the seed very carefully and call it 'Greenland'* to distinguish it. It has been distributed widely and I get nothing but good reports of it.

Some of the euphorbias are just as difficult to sort out and I wonder if we all mean the same thing when we talk about a certain species. *E. wulfenii** is the name under which I was sold the big one that does so well in the paved terrace, but I think, if one were to be exact, its correct name would be *E. sibthorpii*, because the eye is dark brown, and the real *E. wulfenii** has an orange eye. I even heard it called *E. characias* by an expert recently, but I think most people agree that *E. characias* is the dwarfer, bluer black-eyed beauty, which has rather pink stems and a very distinct crook on its flower buds, which take some time to straighten out.

There is confusion too between *E. biglandulosa** and *E. myrsinites*, and some forms of the latter that are finer than others are called *biglandulosa** but are still *myrsinites*. I am sure about one euphorbia, and that is the busy little ground coverer, *E. cyparrissias*. Kind friends warn me when they see it in the garden, but so far I have not found it a nuisance. It is definitely very active and likes to get about but it is by no means a common plant and I find a lot of people want it. In its early stages it makes neat and attractive ground cover and when in full growth its 12-in stems mingle pleasantly with plants nearby. In some gardens the bracts turn soft crimson in the late summer, and I am sorry they do not do it for me. I used to think there were two distinct plants but when I see good autumn colour in gardens where I know only the usual one would be grown I don't think there can be. I noticed in Austria that some of the native plants turned well in autumn.

I wish *Euphorbia polychroma* increased as readily as *E. cyparrissus*, the clumps do get bigger each year but not much bigger. I have never seen seed on the plant, nor found a seedling near it, and cuttings are not dependable. Some years early shoots will root at once, in another they won't root at all and one has to try the autumn growths for cuttings. When it is possible, division is always a good way of increasing one's plants and I have divided *E. polychroma*, but it is a woody plant and a certain amount of brutality is needed to get many divisions.

There is sometimes confusion about its name but I think it is now established that *E. polychroma* and *E. epithymoides** are identical, but *E. pilosa major** is different. Both are beautiful in early spring, making rounded domes of greenish gold which are gay but by no means garish. *E. polychroma* has a long flowering period but it has no autumn season. But *E. pilosa major** is never unattractive, and in the autumn many of its leaves turn soft crimson and it produces more heads of green-gold on 2-in stems. Even after this there will be new growth so that it gives all-the-year service. It makes a big plant by the end of the season, so should not be crowded in by other plants. In one part of the garden I have *Veronica gentianoides* growing near it because for most of the year it makes a carpet of glossy dark green and the 12-in spikes of pale blue flowers do not last long.

I am always glad to see the leaves of *Euphorbia hibernica** which come up in a forest. I think there are several forms of this plant but the one I regard as the true plant grows in the Exmoor area of Somerset. When a friend offered me a plant from her garden I thought the tuft of delicate green I was to take belonged to a nice little plant. But not a bit of it. Those tender little leaves belonged to a great root as big as a young tree trunk and after trying to get it out with several tools we were at last driven to use a tyre lever; we managed to prise it out with that. It needs a place on a shady bank with such plants as hostas or *Brunnera macrophylla**.

Euphorbia sikkimensis is a lovely plant to use as a "filler" in a shady bed. I mean by a "filler" that it should be given a free hand in an empty space between shrubs or under a hedge. It grows to 2 $\frac{1}{2}$ in –3 in in such a position and is lovely at every stage of its life. I love the brilliant red shoots when they appear in January and February and later the typical green flowers are a fitting climax.

The more recent *E. griffithii* reverses the colouring. The foliage is good, like that of all euphorbias, but it is for the flower bracts that we all covet it. They are orange but not a harsh or piercing orange. The colour varies somewhat. As is usual with seedlings there is no certainty that every one will have the excellent qualities of its parents and I have seen some rather dowdy plants of *E. griffithii*, which suggests that we ought to see our plants in flower before we buy them. It is safe, however, to order the variety 'Fireglow'.

Every spring I notice how many ordinary aubrietias have come into the garden although I have put in nothing but good ones. And far, far too much of the deep yellow alyssum. I always mean to mark the best coloured aubrietias and take cuttings in the autumn. Some text-books advocate taking cuttings directly they have finished flowering, but these do not succeed with me. Far better, I find, are the fresh young shoots that spring up after the plants have been drastically cut down to ground level. Some of the new aubrietias are magnificent, large flowered, deep coloured and often double, so there is no excuse for keeping the small flowered, washy mauve plants that sow themselves so industriously.

The deep yellow alyssum is just as determined to keep its foothold in the garden. It sows itself in a mild way, and increases in girth at a great rate. Every year I put in as many of the pale form as I can, either by raising them from seed or by taking cuttings of my few pale yellow plants. But very few seem to survive. I often wonder if the paler flowers have a paler constitution to go with their delicate colour; certainly *Alyssum citrinum** hasn't the constitution of the deep yellow form. I have noticed the same thing about the other variations of *A. saxatile compactum**. I have had the soft biscuit-yellow flowered 'Dudley Neville'*, and the double-flowered form, but they seldom last more than a year or two, while the ordinary golden alyssum becomes more buxom every season. I sometimes wish I had the courage to remove every scrap of this alyssum, which is really too strident a tone for civilised society, but I know I shouldn't have enough of the delicate lemon-yellow to take its place, and I couldn't face the villagers if I banished all their beloved "gold dust".

I also feel I ought to be firmer with white arabis, and could doubtless find other more worthy plants to fill the walls and paving (and beds and rock garden when it gets a chance), but I always feel a little sentimental about it. For one thing it was growing in the walls when we bought the house, and when I had little else I used to pull out bits and plant them in bare places. For another it does appear very early, and the patches of glistening white are very effective early in the year. I admire the way it packs itself so neatly into the smallest crevice and the grey-green foliage is pleasant all through the year. But it overdoes things and has to be removed in vast quantities every year. Unfortunately, the various pink forms are not so vigorous, nor is the really lovely double form, which comes late. If only the double white arabis was scented it could be as good as a stock. It needs drastic trimming and renewal by cuttings from time to time.

The deep red-purple *Arabis blepharophylla* is not a long-lived plant, but it is a most effective little plant to grow in a wall, with good foliage and rounded flower-heads on stiff stems.

Some of the later daffodils are particularly beautiful. It is a happy day for me when the buds of Inglescombe begin to open. This is quite an old daffodil but it holds its own. The lemony-primrose of its double flowers, with their slight green tinge, could be taken for a primrose-coloured gardenia. As a general rule I do not think that double daffodils have the beauty of the single ones, particularly those with two coloured effects, but Inglescombe is an exception as it is completely double and not just a double centre with perianth.

I hoped to have erythroniums flowering in the grass with other spring bulbs. I have seen them grown most successfully in this way and when I found great packed clumps of seedlings coming up in the peat garden I felt I could risk some under the tree on the lawn. I pictured the hanging pink heads coming after the crocuses and I thought they would make a good foil for the ordinary blue muscari, but so far all we have had are leaves, nice spotted leaves, of course, but not so good without the flowers. These are the ordinary *E. dens-canis*; the others grow in raised beds, the bright yellow *E. californicum* and 'Rose Queen'* which is the best of the pink dens-canis type. The rich yellow *E. tuolumnense* has good light green foliage, as does the pale 'Cream Beauty'*. All the erythroniums do best in shade and I have used santolinas to give them shade with good effect until they get too big and then they or the erythroniums have to be moved, usually the latter, for it is very easy to keep removing all plants that get a little big but it has a very levelling effect on the garden. Everything small, neat and ordered may please some people but it makes a dull garden, however well tended.

It is a great temptation to buy some of the exciting bulbs and corms that are shown at R.H.S. fortnightly shows but not all of them take kindly to my heavy, limy soil. Some 'Juno' irises I bought one year are quite satisfied and reappear with faithful regularity ever since. These irises are about 12 in high, they flower in April and bear their flowers in the axils of the leaves. I think *I. bucharica* is the most striking of those I chose, with satiny white and yellow flowers and soft green leaves. In *I. graeberiana* the flowers are a pale cobalt-blue, and *magnifica*, which is the most robust of them all, has white flowers faintly tinged with blue.

The chamaeiris always flower before I expect them. They are good plants for sunny paving or growing in crevices in front of the rock garden, with outsize flowers amid tiny leaves. Pale and deep yellow, blue, violet or white, the flowers do not last very long, but there are many of them. Another dwarf iris that flowers in April is the smoky-red *I. mellita**, only 4 in high.

Most people can grow *Iris japonica*, with its fresh green leaves, but it is not so easy to make it flower. And the beautiful variegated form is even shyer. It seems that there is more chance to get flowers if the plant is left undisturbed for several years. I know one garden where the iris grows against a shaded west wall, and every year there are myriads of fragile-looking flowers, which might be orchids.

~ Part Two ~

Gardeners are becoming more bulb-minded because they realise how easy they are to please and what interest they can bring to the garden. Fritillaries are almost as popular as snowdrops and many of the more usual ones can be bought quite easily. There are others that can be grown from seed as more and more enterprising collectors are bringing back new varieties. The trouble with this is the time it takes. I have several friends who have greenhouses filled with pots of fritillary seed and these have to be kept weeded, watered and housed for several years before they flower. When I see all these pots year after year I hope fervently that the flowers will be worth the long wait. And I expect they will, for I have never seen a fritillary that was not attractive or interesting.

Having no greenhouse and an impatient nature I content myself with buying what is available. *F. pallidiflora* has large creamy flowers, spotted with sienna brown inside. In *F. persica* the hanging bells are smaller and their slaty blue colour is like a thundery sky. *F. pontica* is a very delicate shade of sea-green, with a hint of dull rose, and it is certainly one of the fritillaries that should be grown above eye level because the inside of the flowers is glowing green with black nectaries. *F. pyrenaica* is another that keeps much of its beauty inside the flower and looks best in a raised bed. The rather dark brownish exterior hides a green lining with most exquisite markings. The colouring of *F. ruthenica* is rather similar, but the flowers are carried on 2-in instead of 15-in stems. *F. acmopetala* is also 2 in, with bronze as the outside colour and greenish yellow inside. *F. pudica* and *F. citrina** are both pale yellow.

Fritillaries like a moist, leafy soil but need good drainage as excessive moisture may make them rot. I grow mine in troughs or raised beds, or in pockets on a shady bank, where the beauty inside the flowers can be enjoyed.

The only one of these I have seen naturalised in grass is *F. pyrenaica*, and in this instance it had increased well and was a lovely sight growing in quantity.

Of course, our native snake's-head fritillary, *F. meleagris*, will thrive and multiply in damp grass and the white-flowered variety is particularly lovely naturalised with pale narcissi and *Anemone blanda*. I grow all sorts of bulbs in the grass under a variegated sycamore—erythroniums and muscari, aconites and snowdrops, with jonquils and such narcissi as 'Thalia' and 'W. P. Milner'—and I thought fritillaries would look lovely too, but I think it is too dry for them. They exist but do not increase.

I wouldn't plant the named varieties of *F. meleagris* in this position, because with their bigger, more exquisitely marked flowers they deserve V.I.P. treatment in raised beds. 'Charon' is so dark a purple as to be almost black, 'Orion' also is purple and 'Artemis' a chequered greyish-purple. The pale lavender and white 'Poseidon' is perhaps the largest of the named varieties, but I foresee we shall get others even more exciting. One has only to wander in a damp meadow where these lovely flowers grow to notice how many variations of the theme there are, and what infinite possibilities there are of exciting hybridisation.

The primroses and polyanthus which have been coming out in small numbers for the last few weeks are a sheer delight in April. Like other enthusiasts, I take great trouble over my primroses, but I often think they would do just as well if I did not fuss so much. What they really enjoy is a wet summer and all the mulching, dividing and watering does not really make up for it. After adequate rain it is a joy to see those swelling buds and crinkled leaves. And when they open I go down into the ditch several times a day to bury my face in the cool fragrance of *Polyanthus* 'Barrowby Gem'*. This is a very old plant and we should be grateful that it has survived, because I would not really call it an easy plant. It doesn't increase with the robust vigour of some of the polyanthuses and its roots are inclined to rot. But there is nothing more spectacular than a well-grown plant, with its large, clear yellow flowers, each with its pale green eye, and with the most delicious scent imaginable. All primroses and polyanthuses have a typical primrose smell; they smell of themselves just as babies do, and cows, and even little dogs, but not many have the strong, heady perfume of 'Barrowby Gem'*.

'Bartimeus'*, the eyeless polyanthus, has no particular scent, but it is rather a striking plant, nevertheless. The flowers are so dark that they look quite black in the rain. Sometimes I imagine I can see an eye and wonder if I have lost the true plant and have been fostering an interloper instead, but it isn't there next time.

Growing primroses can be an exciting hobby because one never knows what new charmer will appear. I am not very good with seeds, but I know if I were there would be some very unusual flowers among the seedlings. One year I knew at least two gardeners who had magnificent green polyanthus among the packets of mixed seed, and some of the variations in laced and mottled polyanthus are most surprising.

I am always hoping that some of the rare doubles and hose-in-hose will appear among my plants. One year there was a double flower on the low-growing purple Jill. I carefully removed that part of the plant and replanted it in a place of honour and have watched it ever since, but there has been no double flower since. Another time I was given a very fine bright blue polyanthus. The friend who gave it to me was taken with the colour but had not noticed anything else particular about it. Some time after it had been growing in my garden I noticed the flowers were hose-in-hose. I could hardly believe my eyes and could hardly wait for the spring to come so that I could see it again. I had never heard of a blue hose-in-hose and thought I was about to make history. But when the next spring came round my hopes were dashed to the ground. The flowers were very fine, the calyx of each of them was rather loose, like a man with a collar too big for him, and there were touches of blue at the edges, but no hose-in-hose flowers.

Anemones are lovely in April. If you let them, *Anemone blanda* or *apennina* will take possession of the whole garden. They do not really do any harm, because you do not think of them after they have had their season and, though they may be growing thickly all through the beds, no one would know they were there until they turn that area into sheets of blue. There is a good dark blue form of *A. blanda atrocoerulea**. *A. blanda* 'Fairy' has dazzling white flowers, *A. blanda rosea** is a clear pink and *A. blanda scythinica** is white with blue inside.

We all love to see wood anemones growing in the hedges and banks and I always feel they are good enough for any garden. The double-flowered form, *A. nemorosa alba plena**, is an enchanting little plant, *A. alleni** has soft blue flowers and *A. robinsoniana** large lavender blossoms.

New pulsatilla anemones are appearing every day. I think there is nothing more lovely than a shining white pulsatilla, and now there is a new red, 'Red Clock'*. Some of the best pulsatillas I have ever seen grow in a large paved rock garden and come up regularly from between the stones, a little more buxom each season. I have planted some in gaps in the paving on my terrace, but they don't do so well as those in ordinary flower beds.

Most gardeners are agreed that the ordinary grape hyacinth known as *Muscari* 'Heavenly Blue' is beautiful when in bloom, but very untidy before and afterwards. We can't do without them, but it is not always easy to find a place where they won't be a nuisance and where their seeding ways won't bring them into worse disfavour. I once saw the problem successfully solved by planting them between a yew hedge and a gravel path. They made a most colourful border and when they weren't in bloom the tangle of leaves wasn't an eyesore.

There are different forms of the normal grape hyacinth. *Muscari neglectum* has flowers in two colours, deep blue and such a dark blue that it is almost black. *M. viridis* isn't very green; in fact it is more sea-green but charming none the less, and to add attraction it is scented. *M. moschatum flavum** is scented too. It opens purple and turns yellow. I have grown it for several years and it hasn't increased much, nor does it flower. I have just learned that the instruction I was given, to plant it in a shady spot, was wrong. It needs a hot, dry position, and now I have replanted it I hope I shall get flowers.

I like the small *M. azureum* in bright Cambridge blue, which is neat and brings and takes its leaves with it. The white form, *M. azureum album**, is even more enchanting, but they are both too small to be let out into the garden and are more suited to rock garden pockets and special little beds.

Daisies are at their best in April. My favourite is still *Bellis* 'Dresden China'*, so well named and so lovely when it is happy. It isn't as easy as its innocent look would lead one to expect. I am often told by gardeners that it won't grow for them. It needs good soil and regular division, and if it is just planted and forgotten it probably will quietly slip away. I have never managed to keep the white counterpart, 'The Pearl'*, but luckily I was given another, rather larger double white daisy and that is a bouncing beauty, which soon makes a tight carpet of shining leaves. So far I have had to call it by the name of the friend who gave it to me. It might easily be the white form of the crimson 'Rob Roy'*, which is inclined to get dessicated if it is forgotten and undivided. It does best in light shade and its colour is better under a canopy of leaves. 'Alice'* is the pink version of 'Rob Roy'* and I think she too is difficult judging by the difficulty I have had to run her to earth. I had this daisy once, and in spite of all my attentions I couldn't keep it. The speckled 'Bon Accord'* isn't easy either. It is a little bigger than 'Rob Roy'* but it doesn't increase and it doesn't always stay. The "hen and chickens" daisy, *B. prolifera**, is as easy as any of them if it has rather moist, rich soil and is divided as soon as there is anything to divide. It is exciting when the flower is surrounded by baby daisies hanging on slender stalks.

Daisies look well if grown in bands at the edge of the path or in blocks between perennials at the front of the border. As a rule they do best in soil to which manure has been added.

As a general rule I am not fond of plants which disappear completely after flowering. If by chance the label disappears there is danger of damaging them with a fork. Also it is very easy to plant something else where they are growing. By now I ought to know that a bare space in the garden means something lurking underground, as the garden is as closely planted as any cottage garden. Some things disappear and are never seen again. For some reason platycodons, arnebia and adonis won't grow for me, although I have given them different positions and special soil. But quite a number of plants come up year after year, regardless of frenzied scratchings above their heads. The deciduous members of the corydalis family are very faithful. I have had the soft lavender *Corydalis solida* ever since I have had a garden, because it was growing in a cottage garden nearby and I was given some. Although that cottage has changed hands, and been modernised and the garden remade, the little lavender corydalis still appears every spring. It does the same thing in my garden, and though it occasionally gets moved to a better place and is not always labelled, it reappears without fail. The leaves come through first, and when they have made a ferny forest of blue-grey the flowers appear. *C. cava* is so named because it has hollow roots, and the flowers, which are bigger than those of *C. solida*, can be white or lilac. It is faithful in its reappearance and looks attractive coming up among the heathers 'Springwood White' and 'Springwood Pink'. I know it is safe beneath their spreading stems. *C. densiflora** is like *solida* but has more tightly packed flowers and *C. farreri* is distinguished with black markings on its yellow-green flowers. The two aristocrats of the family are *C. cashmiriana** and *C. wilsonii*. I never succeeded with the icy-blue *C. cashmiriana** until I grew it in a greensand bed under a north wall, but I have never managed to keep *C. wilsonii*, which makes a flat rosette of delicate blue-grey leaves, and has canary-yellow flowers. It is not quite hardy and is often grown in an alpine house.

The easy corydalis I grow in the ditch garden, in pockets on the banks. Plants that like moisture grow at the bottom of the ditch. In one place I widened the channel to make a miniature pool. That was before the water disappeared, but I am still left with a damp bed which is shared by lysichitum and *Iris kaempferi**. Both these plants like to grow in shallow water, but if the site is shady make do with moist soil. The yellow-flowered *L. americanum** is more robust than the Japanese *L. camschatense**, with its white flowers. The great golden spathes that surround the flower spikes of *L. americanum** appear before April is out and they make a dazzling show, needing nothing but green as a background, and certainly should not have *Primula rosea* as a companion, as one so often sees. After the flowers are over there are enormous glaucous green leaves as background for the purples, pinks and lilacs of the iris.

The Virginian cowslip, *Mertensia virginica**, is one of the loveliest spring plants, but risks its life by disappearing completely after flowering. Its grey-green leaves are smooth and look almost purple as they come through the soil, to be followed by graceful sprays of violet-blue flowers which open from pink buds. The flower trusses are heavy and rise above the leaves and usually need a little support. A fairly loose soil suits this plant best, and a happy symphony is made by planting it with *Lathyrus (Orobus) vernus praecox**, which has soft pink and white pea flowers in neat clumps which are lower than the mertensia. As the lathyrus keeps its foliage, to grow it nearby protects the sleeping mertensia.

Other plants that can be grown near the mertensia and need the same cool woodland conditions are the epimediums, which have most beautiful foliage as well as little fairy flowers on wiry stems. *Epimedium rubrum** has mahogany-tinted leaves in spring, in *E. perralderianum* the flowers are yellow and the leaves toothed, *E. pinnatum colchicum** and *E. versicolor sulphureum** are also yellow. The aristocrats of the family are 'Rose Queen'* and the white or pink *E. niveum**, but they are slow to increase and cause anxiety by losing their leaves after flowering.

Blood root, *Sanguinaria canadensis*, does the same thing and it also likes moist, light soil and shade. Its lovely blue-grey leaves would make it worth growing without the snowy flowers with their glowing golden anthers. Some plants lose something when they have double flowers, but blood root becomes even more beautiful for the flowers have such narrow petals that they look fringed. These plants hate to be disturbed and are happiest among deciduous shrubs.

Reineckia carnea likes the same cool, shady conditions but it makes life easier for the gardener as it keeps its leaves, which are long and narrow, and sometimes develop pleasant variegations. The flowers are lilac-pink, rather like small hyacinths, often half hidden in the foliage. The plant makes roots on its horizontal stems and is very easy to increase—I use it among pulmonarias, *Arum italicum pictum** and bergenias.

Many of the bergenias are at their best in April, particularly *Bergenia cordifolia,* Miss Jekyll's form, which has deep magenta-pink flowers on 18-in stems, and *B. ciliata*, with apple-blossom flowers enhanced by red calyces.

~ 5 ~

May

By this month the garden has really come to life. It seems only yesterday that the ground was bare and nothing had started to grow. Now, without our noticing it, a miracle has happened. Delphiniums are 18 in high and should be staked, heleniums and michaelmas daisies are growing fast and the world is suddenly green and leafy. There should be flowers in plenty soon. I read somewhere that the garden would be bare in May without tulips, but I have never found mine lacking in interest. Of course, June and July look after themselves and no one can help having plenty of flowers then, and May is nearly as easy, with all the beauty of young leaves and breaking buds. I still have the clumps of white and pale yellow tulips I put in when I made the garden, but beyond thinking longingly of gay parrot tulips and the dusky beauties of Dutch flower paintings I leave it at that.

Asphodeline lutea is at its best in May, but it is a good all-the-year-round plant because its foliage never varies. I like to plant it in bold groups for this very reason; it makes welcome height at all times and the grassy, glaucous foliage is good in the winter. I used to feel rather irritated with this plant because it is so disorderly in its flowering habits, but have now got used to it. Most spiky plants open either from the top or the bottom, but they do it systematically. Our friend the asphodeline has no method; it opens an eye here and another there, there is never a perfect spike, but it keeps up our interest for there are asphodeline flowers for several weeks. The general effect is quite good, and never too yellow. The flowers themselves are tempered with black markings and the general effect is more old gold than young gold, the buff-coloured bracts helping to soften the glitter, also the dark lines up the stems. If I had room for a gold and silver border *Asphodeline lutea* is one of the plants I would choose.

Asphodeline capensis is much less usual and a more refined plant. Stems, leaves and flowers are all smaller and instead of making one straight spike it has a branching habit. In one part of the garden *Geranium* 'A. T. Johnson'* is growing round its feet; the veined, blue flowers and the finely cut leaves of the geranium contrast well with the asphodeline. In another place its companion is *Achillea serrata* 'W.B. Child'*. I recommend this plant to gardeners who suffer from the exuberance of *A. ptarmica*, with busy little white roots. Instead of running, 'W.B. Child'* increases by making larger clumps, its foliage makes bright and ferny tufts and the flowers are little single daisies, with large white centres, instead of double-flowered buttons.

Asphodeline capensis has to be companioned by something delicate in colour and shape, and I have let the dwarf variegated grass *Holcus mollis variegatus** make a solid cushion of delicate white and pale green round one clump.

Polemoniums have been with us for a long time. Every cottage garden has its Jacob's Ladder, but I have always been rather disappointed with this ordinary *Polemonium caeruleum*, because the lower flowers are invariably fading before the top ones have opened. The white form behaves a little better, but the improved version of the old cottage-garden plant, named *P. richardsonii**, is much more satisfactory. The flowers are bigger and the lowest ones manage to stay awake until the top ones have had a chance to open. The plant is altogether sturdier and finer, but unfortunately does not seed itself as liberally as the old-fashioned plant.

I have several dwarf creeping polemoniums which I find most useful but are not often seen. Many nurseries catalogue *P. reptans*, which is blue, and I imagine had something to do with the new and dwarfer 'Blue Pearl'*, an excellent little plant for the front of the border. It increases by creeping like *reptans*, but the leaves are more like those of *P. caeruleum*, so I imagine these were its parents. Though I am devoted to *P. reptans*, with its mat of ferny foliage, I like even better a pinky mauve form which I was given years ago and have increased so that it is now in the gardens of all my friends. The flowers are larger and looser than those on the blue form, and they go on for most of the summer. For my own use I called it 'Lambrook Pink'*. At first I called it 'Pink Pearl', but that was wrong because that would make it a pink form of the smaller 'Blue Pearl', which it isn't. Although I call it pink it is really a pinky lilac and a taller one of the same type, which I call Lambrook Mauve, is lavender.

P. carneum is more flimsy in growth and its flowers are a real flesh-pink. I once grew some from different seed and they were a pale washy pink without any flesh tones.

Polemonium foliosissimum has been illustrated in the *Botanical Magazine* and I hope it will induce more people to take an interest in this family. It makes a fine bushy plant, about 18–20 in high with flowers of soft violet growing in loose panicles. There seems no end to its season, for right into November there will be odd flowers. I believe this is the polemonium that was once called *P. archibaldae** and is sometimes called *robustum*.

And that isn't the last of the polemoniums. There is the tiny *P. humile**, only about 6 in high, and the even rarer *P. pulchellum**, also tiny and rather pale in colour. Various polemoniums are sold under these names but not all are correct.

The new hybrid *P.* 'Sapphire' is deep in colour and makes a fine solid clump; I grow with it the old-fashioned *Erigeron philadelphicu*s with small, pale pink flowers. I have never made up my mind whether it is worth growing the biennial yellow polemonium, *P. flavum**. It seems to seed better in some gardens than in others. *P. pauciflorum* is also yellow and is listed in seed catalogues as a perennial.

As a cottage gardener I have to keep one plant of the double kerria, Jew's Mallow, but I don't like the colour of the flowers or the straight lines of the bush and much prefer the graceful single form, with its paler open flowers on slender arching stems. Unfortunately it flowers for a short time only and doesn't come and go for months like the other. The single form with variegated leaves is even lovelier and an excellent plant to grow among herbaceous plants.

The overpowering scent and rich pink flowers of the Garland Flower, *Daphne cneorum*, are worth any amount of trouble, and usually it needs trouble—or luck—to establish it. I understand the form *D. c. eximea** is easier, as well as being a better plant. I have established this form in a bed of greensand under a north wall, and the ordinary type in a south-facing rock garden, and the treatment in both cases is to cover the stems as they grow with pieces of flat stone. The dark blue *Brodiaea laxa**, which is equally happy in sun or shade, has the strong, deep colour that the daphne needs.

There are plenty of shrubs in May; lilac and deutzias, and the "pearl tree", exochorda, dripping with strings of white flowers which look like pearls. *E. racemosa* is the one usually grown, and it makes a very pleasant spreading tree, but it doesn't like a shallow chalky soil, and if one has to garden in soil of this kind *E. serratifolia* is the one to choose. It grows up to 12 in and *E. giraldii wilsonii** is even taller. Weigelas flower in May and June. I think the queen of the tribe is *W. middendorffiana*, with sulphur-yellow flowers which have dark orange markings in the lower lobes. It is a good shrub for shade and needs rather a sheltered position. Of the others, being a variegated addict, I like best the variegated form of *W. florida*. It makes rather a spreading bush and can be kept compact enough to put among the flowers. As weigelas flower on the previous year's shoots the best time to prune them is directly after flowering.

As mine is a cottage garden, of course I have to grow a guelder rose, and it is one of the shrubs I should not like to be without. *Viburnum opulus* may be a common tree, but those greeny flowers are most attractive as a cut flower for a dark background and they last quite well if the woody stems are hammered. Mine is just the ordinary form, which, incidentally, colours well in the autumn, but there is a neater form, *V. opulus compactum**.

I have a laburnum too. A well-grown laburnum, standing by itself, can be very beautiful. I once lived near one in London, and I used to go out of my way in May and June just to see it. It was the only tree in a little garden and probably, like mine, just the common laburnum, *L. vulgare**. If one wants something less ordinary there are several others to choose: *L. vulgare aureum** with golden leaves, or *L. v. autumnale** with flowers on and off all through the summer and early autumn, or *L. v. quercifolium** with leaves that remind one of the oak. But whatever laburnum is chosen it looks better if it can be planted where its silhouette is not spoilt by other things. Some people use laburnums as host trees. I know one on which a most healthy clematis, 'Nelly Moser', is clambering up to dizzy heights.

My favourite spring shrub, *Cytisus kewensis**, is past its best in May but the upright 'Cornish Cream', which is just as good as it sounds, is still beautiful, and so is 'White Pearl', also rather tall. For a dry, sunny bank there is nothing more generous than *Genista hispanic*a. It makes solid mounds about 2 in high and is covered with fresh yellow flowers in May and June.

There are still a few narcissi. Every year I panic because I think I must have dug up by mistake my pheasant-eye narcissi, *Narcissus recurvis**. Though it is very old I don't know any newer one that takes its place. The flowers are not very big but they are beautifully made and they have a most heavenly perfume. The foliage is rather flabby and gets untidy, so it is best grown between shrubs where it is not too obvious. I like to enjoy them in company with the fluttering leaves of very young beech. I can remember them years ago when my mother arranged them with the young leaves of copper beech and a few doronicum.

Another late narcissus that worries me by its non-appearance is the old gardenia narcissus. I ought to know by now that it flowers long after most of the others have finished, but again I panic and look among its leaves to see if any buds are hiding there. *Narcissus plenus odoratus** is the double form of white *Narcissus poeticus*, and I have no idea how old it is. It has rather flat flowers and does look rather like a gardenia. It is sweetly scented too and sometimes there are little flecks of green on the back of the flower, which is an added beauty. I see nurserymen recommend it for naturalising in grass, but I was advised when I was given it that it is best grown in a flower bed. Even so it does produce a number of empty buds, and I am often asked by other gardeners what is the cause. I wish I knew.

The shaggy heads of the plume hyacinth, *Muscari comosum plumosum**, open this month; they are out for a long time and again they cut well. It surprises me that more people do not know this easy but rather unusual flower, with fine feathery plumes of violet-coloured filaments. One used to see the little green and white flowers of *Ornithogalum umbellatum*, 'Star of Bethlehem', in most cottage gardens, but somehow it seems less in favour these days. To me, green or green and white flowers have great fascination and I'd always find a place for this modest little plant. I read recently that it was called the 'Star of Bethelem' because it grows on the hills in Palestine and is the plant called, unromantically, "doves' dung". The bulbs are used for food and when they are in bloom the hills look as though they are white with the droppings of doves.

Another ornithogalum that is worth growing and does best in shade is *Ornithogalum nutans*. It has hanging bells on foot high stems and the flowers are translucent which makes them look as though they had been frosted. There is green on the outside of the flowers but a green so soft and indeterminate that it looks almost grey.

The leaves are the best part of *Allium karataviense*, which flowers in May. They are wider than any other allium I know and the blending of blue, orange and red gives an extraordinary metallic effect. I never think the flowers are worthy of such splendour. In bulb lists the colour is given as pink to rose, but to me they are rather a washy lavender-pink. There are two tall alliums with good purple-lilac flowers which look well growing among rhododendrons or other shrubs. *A. afflatuense** is 3 ft and the flower-heads are densely packed. *A. rosenbachianum* is even taller and has even larger heads.

'Solomon's Seal'* reminds me of cottage gardens. It is not a bulb, as one might think, but has rhizomatous roots, like an iris. There is nothing more graceful and lovely than those arching sprays of drooping green-tipped bells, with delicate leaves above, especially if planted above eye level. I realised I didn't get half the fun that I should from my *Polygonatum multiflorum major** growing at the bottom of the ditch. So I dug them all up, or I thought I had, and put them at the top of the bank, where they would look down on me. But they must have been very busy while they were living at the bottom of the ditch, for I still have a forest there although I have parted with hundreds and replanted many more. These are the splendid giant strain, which are good for a bold colony; in some places they are rather too big and there I use the smaller, more delicate variety which may be minor, or just the wild strain. Then there is the double flowered 'Solomon's Seal'*, halfway between the two in size but not quite so vigorous nor so beautiful, although it is interesting and unusual.

I wonder why we fuss about double flowers, because on the whole I don't think they compare with the single-flowered forms. But many of them have the charm of the unusual. I wouldn't cherish an ordinary buttercup, however magnificent a specimen, but I check up regularly to see that no zealous friend has removed my precious double buttercups which look just like common weeds when not in flower. I have three. The one I like best, because it makes solid clumps and has large glistening golden flowers with green centres, I fondly hoped was the rare *Ranunculus bulbosum fl. pl.**, but an expert named it for me as *R. speciosus fl. pl**. The meadow buttercup, *R. acris*, has a double form (*R. a. fl. pl.*)*

but the flowers are small for the 2 $^1/_2$-in stems and it is such a straggling plant that it is best planted among shrubs. The double form of the creeping buttercup, *R. repens**, is also rather small and it too grows on 2-in stems which need the support of other plants to make them look at all attractive.

Again, I wouldn't give hospitality to the single red campion, although I love to see it in the hedgerows, but I think the double red campion, *Lychnis dioica fl. pl.**, is a most friendly little plant. It is a real woodlander and needs an informal setting and light shade, such as is found under shrubs. The foliage is small and neat and it increases quite quickly, so that it is ideal for covering empty spaces. It would probably hold its own quite well in the rough grass of a dell.

The double cardamine is informal too. I have always had a soft spot for "milkmaids" as they were called when I was a child. Another old name is "lady's smock", and though I think they are good enough for any company with their delicate lavender flowers, I try to keep only the double ones. The trouble is that they look alike until they flower. They propagate themselves by leaves, I understand, and quite a number of single plants appear from my double plants. The nearest I can get to a damp meadow for my double milkmaids is in the ditch, but I don't think they mind an ordinary bed.

Paeonies grow in popularity every year because they are perfect for our present style of gardening. They cost rather a lot to begin with, but they save money in the end because once you have planted them they will need no more attention. Nothing could be better for growing among shrubs and in other permanent plantings. They like to live well, so they need feeding, but they don't have to be lifted and divided every year, and the foliage is good even when they are not in flower.

The first paeony that flowers for me is *Paeonia tenuifolia*, with its feathery foliage and deep red flowers. Mine is the single form and I keep meaning to get the double one, because this paeony is so easy to grow and so seldom seen that it always excites interest. It has a different way of growth; it doesn't actually run but it spreads quite reasonably and it is quite easy to get pieces off without digging up the whole plant.

Also early to flower is *P. mlokosewitschi*, with its lovely single flowers. I have one complaint only to make about this lovely pale yellow paeony, and its delicate pink counterpart, 'Perle Rose', and that is the short time the flowers stay with us. One waits all the year for those glorious globes of pale loveliness, but they come and go in less than a week; so much of one's enjoyment is anticipation but the foliage is good, turning crimson in autumn—and the bright cerise seed-pods with black seeds are beautiful.

The delightful small paeony *P. cambessedesii* has the same brilliant linings to its seed-pods. It also has most beautiful foliage, almost metallic, with a crimson sheen underneath. *P. corallina** is a single pink which grows on the island of Steepholme and is often called the Steepholme paeony, although it is not considered to be a native. Other single paeonies which are beautiful but short-flowered are *P. potaninii** and *wittmaniana*. I really must time my paeonies one year to see whether it is only imagination that the single ones have a shorter season than the doubles.

The old cottage paeonies keep their flowers for a longer time. Of course there are never enough to balance the plentiful supply of leaves, and I always think the right place for these paeonies is among shrubs or in a wild garden. Although the deep red form is the one we usually see, there are white, pink and shaded white and pink forms of *Paeonia officinalis* and a delightful anemone-flowered variety.

～ Part Two ～

If the old May-flowering paeonies are plants of the cottage garden so is that delightful old plant *Dicentra spectabilis*, sometimes known as "bleeding heart", "lyre plant" or "lady-in-the-bath". One can judge its popularity by the number of names it had, from the days when it was found in every garden, large and small alike. I am surprised that the flower arrangers have not made a dead set at it, so graceful are its arching stems. It might have come right out of an old Dutch painting. Whenever I show a picture of this old plant on the screen there are appreciative Oh's and Ah's, but we hear more about the new varieties of the dwarf dicentras. I agree that *D. eximea** and its exquisite white form, the slightly taller *D. formosa* and the new and better form 'Bountiful' make excellent ground cover under shrubs and trees, but they haven't the grace or colour of *D. spectabilis*. The grand old plant, of course, looks best grown where it can be admired from all sides, against a wall in a shady garden or in a corner where it has shade, moisture and safety from disturbance. Its brittle roots are vulnerable, and I never know how nursery men propagate it. The only plant I would grow with it is 'Solomon's Seal'*, which also needs to be grown where its arching loveliness can be seen in its entirety.

In May one can still feel friendly towards *Anchusa myosotidiflora** (*Brunnera macrophylla* as it is now called), for it is still showing its pleasant side with endless sprays of intensely blue flowers and leaves that remain neat and fresh. It is when the foliage becomes coarse and rusty and out of proportion to the delicate flowers that I wonder why I grow this plant. It makes sure that I do because it seeds itself far too generously.

There must be something appealing about blue flowers. Forget-me-nots have the same effect on me. When I see them coming up everywhere I don't feel at all loving towards them because I know I shall never have time to deal with them. Every year I make up my mind I will be ruthless and will let them remain only in the places where I want them and not in all the awkward spots where they sow themselves, often on top of precious treasures. Of course I never do, and instead of having properly planted patches at reasonable intervals my garden turns into a haze of blue at forget-me-not time and looks as lovely as a bluebell wood. It is so beautiful that I forget I am having a private war with those innocent-eyed spreaders. Some people take great trouble to grow only the very deep form with new seed each year, but I think I prefer my common little plant, which prevents monotony by producing white and pink children as well as blue.

Getting rid of the forget-me-nots after they have flowered is quite a big operation in my garden and takes several days. I never do it early enough because there is rather a naked look about the beds when all those barrow-loads of blue mist have been wheeled away, and of course the plants take advantage of this reprieve and sow themselves frenziedly—to my autumn annoyance.

I don't pull out the perennial forget-me-not, *Myosotis dissitiflora*, unless they are mildewed and unsightly, but I often have to replant some of the seedlings as they are just as irresponsible in their seeding as their common cousins. I wonder we don't see the perennial forget-me-not more often. The flowers are bigger than those of the annual plant, and flatter, and though they are a little paler their bigger clusters on longer stalks makes them more showy. The leaves are a little different, longer and less hairy, with a somewhat shiny look about them. It is quite easy to distinguish them from the common type.

The cool greenish flowers of my late-flowering hellebore (a particularly good form of *Helleborus orientalis*) make a restful contrast to the gaudier colours. This hellebore seems to have the gift of perpetual life and I am glad I have some growing in the front garden opposite my desk, not far from *H. corsicus**, which inspires me for so many weeks early in each year.

The pale green spikes of *Tellima grandiflora* are also restful and make a good background for the bright pink of poppies and the cool lavender of *Thalictrum aquilegifolium**. The flowers of *Heuchera viridis* are very similar to tellima but they are more fringed and do not have a tinge of pink after they have been out for some time. The leaves are easy to distinguish. Those of the heuchera are a darker green, very hairy and have not the dark markings on them which make tellima such an attractive plant. Nor do they turn so readily to lovely shades of crimson in the autumn as do those of tellima. There is another form of tellima called *T. purpurea*, with bronzish leaves, and this is even more striking in the autumn when it becomes dazzling crimson. I have a heuchera with scented buff flowers and this too makes rich autumn colour.

There are dwarf irises still flowering. 'The Bride' is always later with me than the purples and yellows, but it is obviously neither a *pumila* nor a *chamaeiris**, being taller than either. I think it may be a form of *Iris lutescens* although paler, or of *I. virescens*, which has smoky grey-green flowers, and also flowers after the early dwarfs. Some of the June irises start flowering in May and I notice that the whites and off-whites are usually the first to open.

In modern gardens it is difficult to find a place where lilies-of-the-valley can be left to multiply and flower. Those old walled kitchen gardens had ample space where they could have a quiet existence, but where can we grow them now? Wherever I put them they soon get in the way of plants nearby and I spend most of the year cursing their precocity. Of course, when they flower and fill the garden with the most wonderful of all scents I wish I had been kinder. Every lily-of-the-valley is lovely, but if one is growing them it seems sensible to have the biggest flowers on the longest stems. 'Fortin's Giant'* used to be the biggest but now there is an even better strain sold as 'Mount Everest'*. Lilies-of-the-valley get on for a good many years without attention, unless they are being grown commercially. When they do become so congested that something has to be done about it, the usual way is to dig out the bed, or part of it, and replant the lilies in a fresh place. And the result of that is that they don't flower well until they have settled down. Admittedly, this is the best thing to do, and it is what commercial growers do except that they do it more often and they add special soil and bone-meal (or something like it) to encourage the plants to get back on the job as quickly as possible. The Victorians were not always so drastic, for, according to old gardening books, their plan was to cut out small pieces of soil and plants all through the bed and fill up the holes with special sifted soil.

One of the joys of gardening is the occasional unexpected success after consistent failure. I felt very dashing when I bought two pleiones, *Pleione pricei** and *P. formosana*. Most people put these near-hardy orchids in a cool house, but I have no cool house, or any other greenhouse, and I thought my climate was mild enough for a gamble so I planted them in the peat garden. I cover them each winter with a pane of glass because I understand it is winter wet, not cold, that they dislike. Each year they have thrown up leaves and it seemed that they were increasing satisfactorily, but after one very wet winter I could see no sign of the green pseudo-bulbs, which cluster like a nest of eggs just above the ground.

Gentle proddings brought no comfort so I feared I had lost my gamble. Then one day I was strolling along the bank opposite my little peat garden when I suddenly saw an exotic bloom poised self-consciously among the heathers and azaleas as if it had slipped off the ample bosom of a magnate's lady. Since then I have these delightful little orchids in several other places, in greensand under a north wall, and on an easterly ledge of a rock garden in ordinary soil, and I have added *P. limprichtii* to the other two. I don't get as many flowers as my friends who grow them in pans in the alpine houses, but I always get a few and they increase steadily, and I could divide them if I had the nerve.

I suppose *Arum creticum* should not be put in the same category as pleiones, but for some of us it has the same fascination; in fact I like any arum. The one that grows on Crete has yellow flowers—not the bright yellow of lysichitum but a luminous, very deep cream. I was told to put this plant in the hottest, driest place I had but I now discover this isn't necessary. In one garden I know it blooms equally well in a hot, sunny position and in the damp shade under trees.

It was in the same garden that I met the pretty pink and white form of *Orobus* (or *Lathyrus*) *vernus*. It is called *O. v. albo-roseum** and makes a delightful foot-high clump for the spring rock garden. I have had the other forms of orobus for some time. The ordinary one has vetch-like flowers in violet-blue, *O. v. cyaneus** has very bright blue flowers and there is also a good white. With them I grow the dwarf silver plant, *Dorycnium hirsutum**, which has silky leaves and tiny pink and white flowers all through the summer. This likes a hot, dry place and the orobus will grow anywhere.

Another plant that makes a happy companion for the orobus is the perennial *Cheiranthus mutabilis**, with flowers that can't decide whether they are purple or rose madder. The bronze and primrose wallflower 'Miss Hopton'* (or Wenlock Beauty) goes with almost anything and so does the very pale *Erysimum capitata**. I find *Cheiranthus* 'Moonlight'* the most difficult wallflower to place as the flowers are deeper than the name suggests and they open from glossy brown buds. 'Harpur Crewe' doesn't need companionship; those neat, bushy little plants should, I think, be planted by themselves in key positions where something attractive is needed all through the spring. This provides scented double blossoms in soft yellow from January to June, and off and on after that. Even without any flowers it is a shapely little bush with good foliage.

The "Prophet Flower", *Arnebia echioides* (*macrotomia*)*, is an unusual member of the borage family, with yellow flowers with a deep purple spot on each petal when it first opens. I have never succeeded with it and I wonder if it dislikes lime. I notice that nurseries charge up to 5s. 6d. for it so it can't be as easy as most herbaceous plants.

Another rather different plant that is scarce and expensive is "Fair Maids of France" (or Kent), *Ranunculus aconitifolius fl. pl.* * I find this easier than arnebia but it doesn't increase very fast, and as it disappears completely after flowering there is always the danger of it being damaged or disturbed. It is a delightful plant, about 12 in high with white button flowers and dark, well-cut leaves.

Incarvilleas are other plants that go to ground and have been known to be put out of action while hiding. Incarvilleas are like nerines, so exotic-looking that one is always surprised to meet them in an ordinary garden. The incarvillea most usually seen is *I. delavayi*, with large orchid-pink trumpets and delightful foliage. In *I. grandiflora* the flowers are more deep pink than orchid. These flowers having disappeared from the garden a good many times, I now grow them in a raised bed with special snowdrops and fritillaries.

The dentarias have to be well labelled if one is not to damage their "coral" roots, which do look exactly like coral. *Dentaria pinnata*** can have either white or pale mauve-pink flowers on 9-in stems. These plants need a cool woodland position and so does *Gillenia trifoliata*, an 18-in charmer with graceful foliage and butterfly flowers in pink and white all through the summer.

I find the running oenothera, *O. speciosa*, does best with a little shade. It is unfortunately not completely hardy in a very hard winter, but quite dependable in ordinary weather. The large white flowers, with their prominent styles, do not shut during the day. They open pure white and fade to pink.

Trilliums, the "wood lilies" of North America, are not at all difficult to please if they have shade and a leafy soil. I grow mine on a bank under the shade of willows in ordinary soil and they come up faithfully every year, but I do not find they increase very quickly. They would do quite well between shrubs if the soil is enriched by humus and not allowed to dry out. The most beautiful is *Trillium grandiflorum*, with large, three-petalled white flowers on 9-in stems. The dark crimson *T. sessile* is scented, and has mottled leaves, the white or pink flowers of *T. cernuum* are nodding, and they are also nodding in *T. stylosum***, the Rose Trillium, which has pink flowers. The painted trillium, *T. undulatum*, has white flowers with claret markings. Trilliums take a little time to settle down but once they start they flower regularly every year. Good cover is made by *Mitella breweri*, which has small flat leaves and tiny green flowers.

The plants that like shade have a subtle charm that grows on many gardeners, and that is one of the reasons why shrub borders become more popular. They certainly save labour in the garden, but they also give one a chance to grow many plants that do well between shrubs. Hostas do not flower till later but in May their furled leaves are coming through the soil. The young leaves of *Hosta albo-picta*** in pale yellow with a pale green edge are among the most beautiful sights in the May garden.

~ 6 ~

June

June is the month that takes care of itself. Even the dullest garden can't help being colourful in June. When the cow parsley reaches shoulder level in the hedgerows and the roadside is scented with honeysuckle and wild roses the garden too seems to grow up overnight. This is the time when one discovers if one has planted too closely, and I always have, and if one has staked sufficiently and efficiently, and I never have.

June is the month when roses tumble over the walls, the tall spikes of delphiniums tower above the jungle of the borders, at the mercy of the gales that nearly always turn up some time in June, to humble our pride and challenge our foresight. The farmers take the "June drop" in their stride. Though it flattens the corn and brings violent rain to devastate the hay, it also thins out the apples for them. The poor gardener has no such compensations for his shattered hopes.

I have some really lovely white 'Pacific'* delphiniums and when we have a wet May they outdo themselves in height. The taller they get the more brittle are their hollow stems and nothing can save them if we have a good rousing gale. I know if I had time to give each tall spike an individual cane they would be safe, but that I'll never be able to do. Peasticks might work if I could ever get them in sufficiently deep, which I know I can't unless my heavy clay soil changes its form overnight. My iron half-hoop supports are magnificent for most occasions, but they are too unresisting for tall delphiniums and other hollow-stemmed perennials, and in a bad blow the fragile stems are broken or crushed against the iron.

I wish there was some way to keep delphiniums within reasonable proportions. Michaelmas daisies, heleniums and goldenrod can be cut down when they have reached about 12 in and they will grow again, but only to half their normal height. I am afraid it wouldn't work with delphiniums because the stems of the second lot of flowers are often nearly as tall as the first ones. Nothing will stop plant breeders producing bigger flowers on taller stems, and all we can hope for is that there is some way of producing stronger stems to carry the weight of blooms.

I have a double delphinium with flowers like little blue roses, and that towers up on its slender stems. But the 'Tibetan'* delphinium is a low bushy plant with arching sprays of dark blue flowers. It doesn't need staking but it is not very striking either, being attractive in a subdued way. I grow it in pockets in the ditch garden and put it near the bright pink *Dianthus callizonus*, which looks like a mule because it has green leaves, but is, of course, a species. The double primrose Orchid Pink usually flowers when the others have finished and is good with dark blue and so is the dwarf *Dicentra formosa* Bountiful, which has deep pink flowers and blue-grey foliage, and flowers on and off throughout the season. The intense red of the single *Paeonia lobata** needs either a green background or something so dark that it does not distract, and this the delphinium would not. It is a pity that paeonies have such a short flowering period, this one particularly, for its large flowers are pure scarlet, without a trace of orange. It is usually recommended to plant it in sun but I like to see it shining out from under trees or on a shady bank, which is where I grow the delphinium from Tibet.

I was asked recently which climbing rose I would choose if I could have only one. I said Albertine, which may surprise some people. I know the flowers are not the most shapely roses we can have, nor do they last for more than a day or two. Another drawback is that it has only one flowering, but what a job it makes of it! Whatever other roses are grown, I think there should be at least one Albertine in every garden for its luxuriant growth and rich shining foliage which never has a trace of black spot. Its cuttings strike with all the ease in the world and those delightful deep salmon-pink roses, so sweetly scented, are produced in such profusion that one can cut and cut during the weeks they are in bloom. At no other time am I so prodigal with flowers in the house. Bowls of Albertine appear in every room and I have no conscience in sacrificing buds as I have with other roses. As a matter of fact it is impossible to cut Albertine without a few buds, but they open in water so it is not really wasteful.

My next choice, I think, would be the China rose. We were lucky in finding a healthy China rose growing beside the door into the garden. There was one of these roses in the first garden I remember, but we always called them "monthly" roses in those days. The flowers haven't the colour, the shape or the strong perfume of Albertine but they bloom in every month in the year. I have picked them at Christmas, and I enjoy the sight of the tree in June when it is covered with blossom. We prune our old rose drastically and spray it when it is attacked by greenfly, and it remains strong and healthy. I think it must have been growing by our garden door for at least a hundred years. A friend in the next village was born in this house; she is now over eighty and says that the rose was there when her parents came to the house a good many years before she was born.

Rosa mutabilis* I grow as a bush, a slender, graceful creature that looks well in a corner that is not too important but where its colourful single flowers are pleasant all through the summer. It doesn't flower as generously as the other

China roses but one wouldn't want as many of its brilliant blooms. The buds are scarlet, they open to a mixture of coppery yellow and pale salmon-pink and finish as a dull crimson.

I know that not everyone shares my love for the green China roses, *R. chinensis viridiflora**. People who enjoy most green flowers are quite rude about it, and say it isn't like a rose at all. It is queer, I agree, and never quite as wonderful as I think it is going to be, but I enjoy its crumpled harmony of dull green and faded crimson and would always want it in the garden. Sometimes it has a very late flowering which it would be wise to do often for, without the competition of other flowers, we realise that it is beautiful as well as being queer.

June is the month for irises, but there are so many of the large flowered June irises that it is difficult to know when to stop. Every year more and more are produced, each one lovelier than anything we had imagined, so what are we to do? I, for one, can't scrap all my old friends, but I usually end by buying several new ones each season and then don't know where to put them. The first move is to scrap all duplicates and reduce large clumps so that I can grow three kinds where I had a big patch of one before. Then I weed out those that are very similar and keep the best. And what happens next? I have been told that there are many better irises than the old-fashioned *Iris pallida*, with its delicate colour and haunting scent, but I still want it and its variegated forms, one with golden variegations and the other with silver stripes on the leaves, so lovely and so very slow to increase.

It is a good thing that the species irises don't take up much room and are content, for the most part, to grow in odd corners and in narrow slits between stones. Two yellow ones, *I. kerneri** and *I. forrestii*, look fragile but are quite tough. *I. kerneri** likes a hot, dry position and I grow it in the open surface of an old wall. *I. forrestii* can stand a little shade but it won't flower without some sun. The American irises seem to do better in shade. I have various members of the douglasiana group under the willow trees in the ditch and they bloom quite well in shades of lavender, pinky mauve and purple. Their informal way of growing makes them ideal for growing in the ditch, but they take time to settle down as they hate disturbance. Here too I grow *I. chrysofar**, a hybrid of *chrysographes* and *forrestii*. It is a curious mixture of yellow and purple, with not very big flowers, and is not as good as either of its parents.

Iris graminea, with its exquisite little flowers hidden in its leaves and rich scent of greengage, is happy anywhere but takes a little time to settle down after division. Are there two forms of this I wonder? One I have is bigger in every way but identical otherwise.

Among the damp-loving irises *I. setosa* seems easy enough, and the red form particularly so. I have too much lime to please *I. laevigata* and *I. kaempferi**, but all the forms of *I. sibirica* increase almost too fast. My favourite is still 'Snow Queen'*, with the crimson 'Eric the Red' as a close second.

The tall *Iris ochroleuca* flowers towards the end of June and is useful when the June irises are almost over. The yellow variety is very striking but less beautiful than the one with white flowers and yellow markings. Both are useful for picking, as the flowers go on opening down the stalk after they have been put in water, and they can be kept attractive for over a week with a daily grooming, in the same way as our native pseudacorus. I used to grow the ordinary yellow flag but it gets too luxuriant and seeds itself everywhere, so now I harden my heart to the ordinary type but encourage the one with pale primrose flowers and the form with golden variegated leaves. I wonder if other gardeners suffered a shock as I did the first year I grew this. I did not know that it lost its variegation in the middle of the summer and went back to green, and thought I must have dug it up by mistake.

June is the month when veratrums flower—if they are going to. I haven't yet discovered what they really like. The best flower spikes I have ever had were one damp summer on *Veratrum album* which was growing on a shady bank. It was so magnificent that I put a dark-flowered *V. nigrum* nearby, and *V. viride*, which has green flowers. But I do not think it matters if *V. album* grows in shade or in full sun, which, of course, is where it grows in its native Austria. There the great ribbed leaves do not get ruined by slugs and snails as ours do. We grow veratrums for the handsome clumps they make, with broad leaves and towering spires of dark velvety brown, white or grey-green, but it is worth looking into the individual flowers which are exquisitely formed. Though veratrums are so common in other countries they are scarce in gardens, probably because they are usually grown from seed and develop slowly.

It is curious how things come and go in a garden. I used to have many large clumps of the sticky *Lychnis viscaria fl. pl.**, with its brilliant little rosettes of wicked magenta. It was always a problem where to grow them and I found the soft blue flax, *Linum perenne*, one of the best plants to choose, also the dwarf form of *Campanula lactiflora*, which is called Pouffe and makes a dome of palest blue against light green.

The problem has been solved for me because most of them have gone from the garden, although the single form remains. Once I had many single white and some in delicate pink, but they have disappeared too.

The same thing must not happen to the dwarf form of *Lychnis coronaria*, with its rose-pink flowers. I have always known it as Cottage Maid, but I think its correct name is *Lychnis flos-jovis*, and it is sometimes called "The Flower of Love". It doesn't, unfortunately, seed itself freely as does the old *L. coronaria* 'Abbotswood

Rose'*. There is no danger of losing that, but who would want to? From the big silver rosettes that cheer us in the winter to the relays of rich red velvety flowers on jutting stems all through the summer it is always welcome, and strangely not ignored by more choosy gardeners than I am. I was pleased when a very great gardener asked me for a plant of my lychnis because he thought it was a better colour than his. And in return he gave me a white one. There is also a white with a pink centre which is a cottage-garden plant, if ever there was one.

June is the month when oriental poppies flaunt their great heads of colour. I have one very good deep pink which is so lovely that it is allowed to occupy a fairly large area. It flowers over quite a long period, but there is an awkward period after flowering until the foliage dies down. I cut it down by degrees to prevent too big a blank and hope that the potentillas I have planted between will come up and cover the maimed stumps. 'Mt Etna' is good for this purpose, because it is a quick grower and its long arms and generous silver-lined foliage can be trained upwards and supported to mask the blank spot. 'Perry's White'* is the best white poppy I know, with its maroon-blotched centre, but my favourite of all is 'Watermelon'*, the most luscious deep pink which is just the colour of the green-skinned watermelon, but without the black seeds. There are several plants that are happy growing with this poppy and they have different form as well as colour. *Thalictrum aquilegifolium** is an easy plant but not a common one. It has aquilegia-like foliage in blue-grey and fluffy heads of flower in pinky mauve or cream. Even without its flowers the leaves are beautiful and I never cut down the plant until late in the year. The seed-heads are attractive too.

*Amsonia salicifolia** is another plant that has quiet charm and is in no way aggressive. Small heads of slate-blue flowers are carried on 2-in leafy stems, and the plant increases to a thicket by strong underground stems. Sometimes it is erroneously called *Rhazia orientalis**, which is a much rarer plant and is seldom seen.

Aquilegias always strike me as "thin" plants, to be used incidentally between heavier subjects and never as a big planting. My garden is overrun with self-sown "Granny Bonnets", which I prefer to the stylish long-spurred varieties. They are often in deep old rose and various shades of blue, and even if they are in the wrong places I let them flower before I pull them up. In one part of the garden the deep blue 'Hensol Harebell' (a form of *Aquilegia alpina*) sows itself about but generally keeps to one place. It should be a vivid deep blue but varies slightly. *A. coccinea** has small red flowers on 2-in stems; in fact it makes rather a big plant for the size of the flowers, but there are so many of them that it holds its own growing among tall perennials towards the back of the border. The little flowers dance on their long stalks and are good next to the very pale blue *Veronica exaltata* or either form of *V. virginiana**. This veronica is different from other veronicas with its leaves growing in whorls up the straight stems. The flowers can be either white or pale blue and they grow in such slender spikes that the effect is subdued colour. In *V. michauxia* the spikes are thicker and deeper in colour.

The gold and red of *Aquilegia canadensis* needs white flowers to tone down its brilliance. By accident I planted *Anthericum liliastrum** nearby and its small, delicate flowers near the aquilegia made light relief. The larger-flowered species, *A. liliago* (St Bernard's Lily) and *A. algerense**, have larger flowers and would not look so well.

There are many smaller columbines but I have not been successful with them, although the green columbine, *Aquilegia viridis**, is doing well in a trough. The flowers are sea-green, and being rather a small plant compared with the others it is safest to grow it in the rock garden.

Nearby I have another little green flower, *Ixia viridiflora*, almost the colour of verdigris, with black spots to make it even more impressive.

Green flowers are restful in a flowery month; in *Bupleurum angulosum* they are small with pin-cushion centres and again the colour is sea-green. The pale green bells of *Galtonia princeps* are the colour of alabaster. This galtonia is smaller than *G. candicans* and has to be used in a different way. It looks lovely growing on a bank or at the bottom of a wall in a narrow bed and needs nothing with it but a low-growing plant such as the tiny *Viola* 'Haslemere', sometimes sold as 'Miss Nellie Britton'. This has small flowers of lavender-pink and flowers all through the summer.

The dwarf jack-in-the-pulpit, *Arisaema triphyllum*, is a woodland plant and looks right with a background of tiny ferns or the dwarf *Mitella breweri*, with 3-in spikes of microscopic green flowers. Not everyone likes aroids but some of us find them very fascinating. This one is rather comical, rather like a greeny brown pouch, with a prominent spadix and three prominent leaves as a background. Even smaller, *Pinelia tubifera** has a very narrow green tube for a flower with long black spadix, like an attacking cobra. It likes to grow in shade, in a moist, damp position, and with me it shares a narrow pocket in the ditch garden with the little mitella, which is about the same size but evergreen.

I never know quite what to grow in the bed where *Arisaema candidissima** should make its appearance in June. This plant shows no sign of life until midsummer, and when the sturdy spike pushes through it very soon opens to a dazzlingly beautiful white arum, about 8 in high, with green and maroon shadings. The flower is followed by large and handsome leaves. So far I have used no ground cover here, although I suppose the arisae ma would push its way through anything, but *Euphorbia robbiae** makes a border on one side and an epimedium is growing on the other side.

~ Part Two ~

June is the month for dianthus. There may be a few odd flowers in May and many of the carnation-type flower in July, but it is in June that one has sheets of white and pink and crimson, filling the garden with scent. One of my favourites is a deep red single I call Brympton Red because it was given to me by Mrs Clive of Brympton d'Evercy. Though the flowers come on long stalks they never straggle, and it is a most satisfactory plant for walls, paving or borders; in fact any place in the garden. The flowers are a glowing crimson, how glowing I discovered only this year when some I had planted in front of a huge smouldering clump of black fennel came into flower. This dianthus is greatly admired and has found its way into several nursery men's lists as Brympton Red. I now learn that it has no right to its name. Lady Lilian Digby of Lewcombe, near Evershot in Dorset, saw it growing in a workhouse garden in Beaminster and was given cuttings, and it was she who gave it to Mrs Clive.

I wish the double-white form of the 'Musgrave'* pink, 'John Gray', had as good a habit. I like its large flowers, although the green centre isn't as distinct as in "Musgrave'*, and it has long stalks, which make it ideal for picking, but it needs careful planting as it doesn't stand up well but lies down when it gets a chance. I try to plant it on the top of a wall with plenty of space on both sides. It has a particularly strong scent and the flowers are compact.

I have grown mule pinks for as long as I have been gardening, but I discovered only recently, when reading an old book on gardening, why they are so called. It never occurred to me they had any connection with the cantankerous quadruped of that name. But both are produced by the mating of different species which have no business to marry at all. In the case of our flowers it is a Sweet William and a carnation. They have the green foliage of the Sweet William and dianthus flowers, but alas no scent.

Mule pinks 'Emile Pare' and *multilflorous* are quite easy to propagate and soon make carpets of dark green foliage. But the new and most floriferous 'Casser's Pink' flowers so prolifically that there is hardly any "grass", and if I want to get a lot of new plants I sacrifice some flowers. But even that is not as difficult as one very old mule pink. 'Napoleon III' is a bad-tempered old gentleman and I disagree when people suggest that 'Casser's Pink' is one and the same thing. 'Casser's Pink' has the disposition of an angel compared with the crochety old aristocrat. At his best Napoleon III is rather a delicate creature, with thin, pale leaves, and far too many crimson flowers for his limited strength. Sometimes I see dianthus labelled Napoleon III, but if they look strong and happy I feel pretty certain they aren't the real thing.

The old laced pinks fascinate me and I grow every one I can. Most of them are rather spindly and look their best growing in walls or at the edge of a stone-edged path. I used to grow many named ones, but it was difficult to keep so many varieties separate and now the only two that I keep named are 'Argus', a good white with a deep maroon centre, and 'Pheasant's Ear'* which has the same colouring but is double. One of the best of the recent introductions is a bright salmon-pink called 'Doris'. It is easier to please than 'Day Dawn', which is an even better shade of pink but not such a satisfactory plant. Many people grow the salmon-pink dianthus with silver plants and though the effect is very good, I also like a mass of *Campanula portenschlagiana* as a background. Sometimes called *C. muralis**, this campanula makes a sheet of blue when in full spate, but it potters on all through the season and as it has real evergreen foliage it is useful to show up flowers of bright colour. In several places in my garden it is growing with *Geranium endressii* and the two together are pretty for a long time. One form of *G. endressii* is particularly dwarf and very free-flowering. The flowers are not all the same shade of pink and the effect is unusual and attractive. I was given this particular form from a garden in North Somerset and I have since seen it in other gardens in Somerset and Dorset but I have no idea what form of *endressii* it is.

One of the first plants I put in the rock garden was a tiny dianthus, 'Mme du Barri'*. It is very pale pink and very sweetly scented. Over the years it has become a vast mat of blue-grey, and in June is covered with flowers. Above it grows the blue flax, *Linum perenne*, which flowers for the whole summer. When the dianthus is at its height, it is lovely with the flax. Later *Cosmos atrosanguineus* (which smells of hot chocolate) opens nearby and the smouldering deep red flowers are as perfect with the flax as the dianthus. The cosmos isn't quite hardy and some people lift it every year as they would a dahlia. I find it will come through even severe winters if buried under a pile of peat.

I have never thought of growing the soft pink *Astrantia helleborifolia** nearby but it would harmonise well with the soft blue of the flax. Of all the astrantias I think this is my favourite. Its dull pink flowers are pale green on the outside and have the usual cushion centres. It increases by means of white running roots and so is easy to propagate as every bit grows. The only thing I have against it is the fact that it flowers once only (where as *A. major* goes on till Christmas). It used to be easy to remember the name of this astrantia because it has three lobed leaves, like a hellebore. Now it has been changed to *A. maxima* and I can never understand why. It is certainly not as big as a *major* and not nearly as big as the giant form of *major*, which has large shaggy flowers, heavily shaded with green. This grows to about 3 ft and so far no one has a name for it, and it is not in general cultivation.

There are several green, white and pink astrantias so like *A. major* that it is difficult to tell them apart. Some have a little more green or a little more pink but they are all very much alike. One is *A. biebersteinii**, another *A. carniolica* and a third, which seems a little smaller, is *A. gracilipes**. There are two others that are distinct, *A. carniolica rubra**, which has deep crimson flowers and is much slower to increase than the others, and the tiny *A. minor*, about 6 in high and with small button flowers. The astrantias are such good mixers that they fit in anywhere and go with everything and are particularly useful for growing between violent colours that might otherwise clash. With the dense red astrantia I like the very pale, almost washy, pink of *Dianthus caesius** or its double form.

Another very good mixer is a very plebeian plant, *Pimpinella major rosea**, which is nothing more than a pink cow parsley. Ferny leaves and rather dull pink flowers are a good foil for any strong-coloured or bold plant. I happened to plant it near the deep blue *Campanula glomerata*, with its clustered heads, and both plants are better for the association. I have never given much thought to the cow parsley and was rather shaken when a visitor from a distance who spent a long time doing the garden, told me at the end of the tour that seeing the cow parsley had made his day and he would have come any distance to see it! It made me feel I had been unappreciative and I went back to look at it spreading its delicate leaves under the Judas tree, and in another place where it was growing with *Polemonium caeruleu*m and the striped grass, *Phalaris arundinacea variegata**, with a blue cedar as background.

It is always a great pleasure—and surprise—when you happen on just the perfect place in which to plant some special treasure. Quite accidentally I planted the little single green-leaved pink, *D. callizonus*, which looks like a mule but is a species, between two stones at the top of a bank. It liked its new home immensely, nestled down with satisfaction and flowers on and off all the summer. The flowers are pink and speckled and remind me somewhat of a Sweet William. A grey-leaved dwarf veronica, *V. colensoi**, grows nearby.

Years ago friends in Dorset gave me a clump of *Orchis maculata** from their spinney. It settled down with me and sowed itself mildly in various parts of the garden. Later I was most generously given a plant of *Orchis elata**, which I think is the most handsome orchis I know. It makes strong 18-in spikes of bright purple and a small planting makes a brave show. It likes a fairly moist, rich position, and after that doesn't seem to worry about soil. But it likes some gardens better than others.

Nurserymen are beginning to cultivate some of the easier terrestrial orchids and so far I am finding the greater butterfly orchis and some of the marsh orchids are reappearing regularly. The marsh orchids seem happy in the peat garden, and *Epipactis palulstris* in a little piece of garden made of greensand and lime-free soil under a north wall. *Pleione pricei** growing in the same place looks better than the plants growing in peat.

On the whole olearias don't like me. I had *O. oleifolia** for some years and enjoyed its grey-green foliage and old ivory flowers, but one bad winter it died and I never replaced it. Later I was given a small plant of *O. gunniana**, and this time I had learned my lesson and planted it in a sheltered corner. When my little bush covers itself with white flowers it is often taken for a nice clump of michaelmas daisies. I don't know what you do when you hear one visitor say to another, "Look at the michaelmas daisies flowering in June". If anyone asks me a question I answer it as best I can, but I like people to enjoy the garden in their own way and don't bother them with information and long names unless they want them. I often feel that gardeners can be very tiresome with their long names; in fact I wonder sometimes how ordinary people put up with it. We shouldn't think much of it if doctors peppered their light conversation with all the longest medical terms they could think of.

Veronicas make a good splash of colour when they are in full bloom, particularly the various forms of the rather dwarf 'Royal Blue' and 'Shirley Blue', but these veronicas in particular hold their flowers for a very short time. No sooner are the flower spikes in bloom from top to bottom than they start to drop. I never attempt to pick them and I never rely on them to give me colour in the garden for any length of time.

The taller veronicas, *V. spicata* and *V. longifolia* in their various forms, are just the same and I usually cut off the unsightly stems before all the petals have dropped. The blue-flowered forms have been in the garden since I made it, but the musical series, *V. spicata* Barcarolle, Minuet and Pavane, in various shades of pink, have never seemed really happy.

While on the subject of veronicas, *Hebe cuppressoides* has to be brought in for the ninety-ninth time. I usually extol it for its incense-like fragrance and the soft blue-grey of its foliage which is such a cool delight in summer, but I enjoy its flowers too. In June the whole bush is smothered with tiny lavender flowers, exquisite in themselves and a cloud of pale loveliness looked at as a whole. The flowers are a little deeper in colour than those on the dainty little veronica attributed to Mr Bowles, and they come once only in the year whereas there seem always to be sprays of pale flowers on Mr Bowles' little bush. This hebe is looser in form, and its pale lavender flowers look lovely near crimson flowers. Mine is below a 'Paul's Scarlet'* rose.

I know one shouldn't be much concerned with foliage while there are so many flowers giving their summer display, but I enjoy foliage whatever the time of year. I have two chrysanthemums which I first noticed because of the scent of their foliage. *Chrysanthemum balsamita** smells strongly of camphor, with flowers that are small and white, and to which I paid little attention in the beginning. I suppose my plant is getting bigger or I grow it better, otherwise I would have noticed before what a lovely foil its silver-grey leaves make for the plants around it. Given a little support it makes a nice solid clump about 2 $^1/_2$ in high. The other chrysanthemum, *C. balsamita balsamitioides** is very similar but smells strongly of spearmint and is the plant sometimes called costmary or alecost. Its small yellow flowers are much later and come on 3 ft, rather limp, stems.

Skimmias have lovely foliage, always shining with good health but sometimes rather more yellow than green, particularly in the summer. My hibiscus, too, take on rather a yellowish tinge in June, which is just before they flower, but when the shrubs are covered with their blue, crimson or white flowers I don't notice it. *Elaeagnus pungens aurea**, of course, gets deeper in tone as the season advances. The new leaves, in early spring, are almost green (a cause of great concern the first year it happens) but by autumn they are really golden, and in winter the gold is burnished and shining. It is a reliably good-tempered plant that remains unruffled and unblemished throughout the year.

Escallonias are good shrubs for mixed borders, *E. virgata* a good white one for any but a chalk soil, and the newer 'Gwendoline Anley'* or 'Apple Blossom' are good pinks to grow with it. For an acid soil I have seen the dwarf *Moltkia petraea* (which has pink buds opening to violet-blue flowers) looking lovely below *Kalmia angustifolia*, with deep pink flowers.

Two particularly good ericas for summer flowering (and lime-free soil) are the deep pink 'Mrs D.F. Maxwell'*, which is low and spreading, and 'H.E. Beale'*, which has 8-in spikes of double silver pink flowers. The bright blue of the dwarf *Anchusa caespitosa** makes a foil for 'H.E. Beale'*, and the very pale blue spikes of *Veronica gentianoides* make 'Mrs D.F. Maxwell'* look even deeper in colour. I have seen 'Mrs D.F. Maxwell'* covering a square yard or more and it lasts in beauty for several weeks. In one garden I know a bed of ericas was raised in places by split tree trunks and various small plants used near the front; large deep-red sempervivums had packed themselves against one piece of log; in another place the blue-green giant echeverias, which of course have to be wintered in a greenhouse, were an unusual and very striking idea.

Viola cornuta has small flowers which are as graceful as butterflies, and if it gets next to a taller plant it rises to the occasion and works its way through the other plant. The white form of this viola is particularly pretty; then there is the deep lavender-blue one and another in a paler blue. This is the one that looks lovely with *Euphorbia cyparissias* or *Alchemilla mollis*. For a pastel planting the pinky lavender *Erigeron* 'Quakeress' makes a good background. Both it and the white form are veteran plants but still very good ones, flowering throughout the summer, which is more than the newer ones do.

Though the tall sedums flower in late summer the new hybrid, 'Ruby Glow', flowers earlier with me. It is a cross between *S. cauticolum* and 'Autumn Joy'*, and even before the flowers the purple-grey foliage is lovely. It is quite dwarf and the long trails of fleshy leaves make effective ground cover. Plants of the red spinach, *Atriplex hortensis**, put themselves behind the sedum and the effect was most sumptuous, particularly in late afternoon, when sun shining through the red leaves of the spinach made them the colour of rubies, even more bright than the red-purple flowers of the sedum. Once the spinach has been in a garden it comes up every year thereafter and gives welcome colour in the summer. Another plant that behaves in the same way is black fennel. This would look well with the sedum, too—as it does with crimson roses or deep crimson pinks.

The fennel makes a particularly rich picture with the floribunda rose 'Rosemary Rose'. This is a wonderful plant if the garden is not too cold and draughty. I have it in a border with a high wall behind and its wide growth makes it ideal for a mixed border. The purple leaves keep their colour, so are an asset even without the roses. If you had a flower of this rose without knowing from what manner of bush it came I think you would take it to be a Bourbon rose, so flat is it with petals neatly packed and quartered. It has the scent of an old rose too, and to add to all these good qualities it flowers again in September or later and is out at the same time as *Penstemon* 'Stapleford Gem', which grows tall and straight and has flowers the colour of an opal.

Another rose I find outstanding is the climbing 'Guinée', with dark, velvety crimson flowers and a very strong scent. It also has very good hips if friends, pruners and helpers can be persuaded not to dead-head it.

It is difficult when visitors automatically nip off dead heads from one's roses. In most cases it is a good idea but I try to steer them from the rugosas, for one year I lost all the wonderful fruit from 'Frau Dagmar Hartop'*. This is a lovely rose on all counts, with delicate pink single flowers, and fruits that are as large and bright as tomatoes. It has a second flowering which coincides with the ripening of the fruit. The Frau is rather low and spreading in growth and is good under a low wall or in a mixed border.

'Roseraie de l'Hay' is another rugosa good for happy associations. The flowers are magenta-purple and lovely with the soft blue of nepeta, and with the rose I like the big Six Hills variety* or the large-flowered 'Souvenir d'André Chaudron'* (Blue Beauty). *Dracocephalum prattii** is the same colour but taller and has the same evil smell. To complete the picture *Geraniun endressii* 'Wargrave'* or the pink form of *G. macrorrhizum* will fill any odd space.

Nature can be very kind sometimes. Ever since I have lived in Somerset I have grown *Ceanothus veitchianus (floribundus)** up the front of the house (although not the same one!). The powder-blue flowers are charming against the faded pink brick of that wall and for years *Gladiolus byzantinus** has made a practice of coming up in front of the shrub with great success. Sometimes this gladiolus is a little too indiscriminate in its seeding, but each flower is a picture, for the soft magenta petals have the iridescence one finds in begonias and other flowers.

If I had to name my favourite herbaceous campanula I think it would be the quite ordinary *C. persifolia*, for it carries its wide, cup-shaped flowers on graceful, wiry stems and produces them throughout the season. The glossy foliage is evergreen and its mats are quite useful ground cover. I know it seeds itself to a certain extent, but the flowers are good for cutting and there are some interesting variations. The pure white form is one of the loveliest flowers in the garden, and one never knows what shades will turn up in the blue seedlings. *C.* 'Telham Beauty'* is a good deep blue and *C.* 'Cantab'* a lighter colour. In this case I don't think the double forms have the same charm but the cup-and-saucer varieties certainly have. I like the white cup-and-saucer particularly and especially when it has touches of green on the petals. So far I have been able to find only a washy blue counterpart, although I feel there must be a better one somewhere.

Some gardeners won't grow alliums because they smell of onions, but many are so beautiful that you don't even notice the smell. The pale pink *A. roseum* is, of course, almost a weed as it sows itself far too generously, but *A. cernuum*, in a much deeper lilac-pink, is more discreet and very pretty with its grey, grassy leaves and tiny nodding flowers. I have always had the good tempered yellow *A. moly*, which has leaves as wide as our native garlic. If I didn't grow it for its flowers I'd welcome the seed-heads, which become the colour of old ivory and manage to hold on to their black seeds even when brought indoors. The wild *A. triquetrum* would be more welcome if it did not seed so freely. I admired it in a garden on Exmoor and was warned that it was not garden trained, but I still like its white and green flowers and triangular stems.

My two favourite alliums flower later in the year and both are tall. *A. siculum** grows to 2 $\frac{1}{2}$ in and carries its buds in an upright transparent case, which might be cellophane. When it splits, the buds come tumbling out, and they should be grown above eye level so that the maroon markings inside the green and cream bells can be enjoyed. When the seeds are fertilised the stems become upright again and remain so until the whole plant is stiff and bleached and good for interior decoration. There is then no smell of onion.

My other allium has large mop-heads of soft mauve-pink on 4-ft stems. It was given me as *A. babbingtonii**, but I don't think it is because it does not make bulblets from the flower. The buds are encased in a peaked transparent cover which is broken round the stalk and sits on top of the opening flowers like a little cap until the flowers are fully open.

Plants that produce their flowers at the top of long bare stalks are often useful for growing in stones or in a narrow bed where their outline is not blurred. How seldom is *Armeria* 'Bees Ruby' grown and yet it is a very distinctive plant for such a position. I have a white-flowered armeria about the same size and which I find does well—and looks right—among the stones edging a circle of grass in the drive. It was given to me as the Cape St Vincent thrift; one expert swears it is *Armeria pseudameria*, another insists on *A. plantaginea*. I know that it is a very handsome plant which flowers from June till December and is very difficult to propagate.

The anthericums also look best as individual clumps but need a rich, moist soil, and are good plants to grow with dwarf shrubs. *A. liliago*, St Bernard's lily, has small starry flowers, and so has the more branching *A. ramosum*, sometimes known as *A. graminifolium**. *A. liliastrum**, St Bruno's lily, is usually listed as *Paradisia* and is a more stalwart plant, with bell-like flowers. It has fleshy, claw-like roots reminiscent of a hosta, and they are easy to disentangle for replanting. *A. algerense** has the biggest flowers of all, and they are like small white lilies. Mr Norman Hadden grows another unusual one, but has no name for it. The bright yellow *Chrysabactron hookeri** used to be called anthericum. This is a New Zealand plant and needs a very deep, moist soil, and would do well in boggy conditions at the edge of a pond.

~ 7 ~

July

Always I am having to guard against too much yellow in the garden. It is easy to over-yellow the garden scheme in the spring, and again in the autumn there is a chance that the golden flowered plants will be too overpowering. And if one isn't very careful there will be too much yellow in July.

Most of the silver plants have yellow flowers. The buds of *Senecio greyii** are as white as snow but they open to strong yellow, and a big bush of this senecio is very yellow when it is in full flower. Cutting off the flower-heads means cutting back the bush rather drastically, but that isn't very serious for in a few weeks it will be bursting out of the bed again. But it will not look very pretty until it grows again, so a way out is to give it a nice green background so that it can flaunt its golden shower without upsetting the colour balance. A background of *Euphorbia wulfenii** will calm it.

The helichrysums can get very yellow and again a lot can be done by careful planting. I have the airy-fairy *H. plicatum* perched at the side of the little crooked path, so that it grows over the low wall that holds up the path above the lawn. At the height of its flowering the bush is a mass of yellow, which I find almost too much so close at hand. It is quite easy to cut off the flat, yellow heads on their long and slender stems, but it seems ungrateful to remove the result of a year's effort. When I am torn between humanity and aesthetics I wish I had a high rocky bank in which to plant this helichrysum. A friend of mine had a garden in Devonshire quarried out of solid rock, and this plant was perfectly placed in a pocket on that rock face which was draped with the evergreen *Clematis armandii*. It is a rather flimsy creature liable to be knocked about by wind or rough treatment, and the wall of rock gave it the protection it needed and the clematis toned down the dazzling display of gold.

That neat little bush *H. trilineatum** also has yellow flowers on every stem, but they are small and of a quiet tone; in fact they look like little clusters of old-gold plush and are short-stemmed so that they nestle in the bush and have the background of silver to temper their yellowness.

There are two helichrysums that smell strongly of curry. The one that is commonly known as the "curry plant" is *H. angulosum** and, as one can guess from the name, has fine silver foliage. The flowers are burnished gold rather than yellow and blend well with the leaves. The foliage of *H. siculum** is wider and pure white. It makes a big spreading bush and after the flat, yellow heads of flower are over tiny sprigs of flower open up the stalks.

Senecio 'White Diamond'* has the whitest of white leaves—and the yellowest of yellow flowers, so when the dazzling white buds start to open they have to be removed. The flowers of Centaurea gymnocarpa* are not yellow daisies but dirty-mauve thistles, so they have to be removed from the luxuriant fern-like leaves, of which they are quite unworthy.

The santolinas have sheaves of deep yellow button flowers and it takes a long time to cut them off. It is easier in the case of the compact S. incana* than when S. neapolitana* has to be shorn. This cotton lavender is the tallest and whitest. I keep two of its billowing mounds but prefer the ivory-flowered S. sulphurea*, which came to me years ago as an achillea! S. 'Lemon Queen'* has grey-green foliage and parchment-coloured flowers.

I thought I had found yet another santolina. I have a very large bush of S. neapolitana* that has spread itself over several plants growing nearby. I noticed one day that its flowers were lemon-yellow, lemon-yellow with a touch of green like an unripe lemon, and I was overjoyed at the sight. But my excitement was short lived, for when I investigated I found that the big S. neapolitana* was sitting on top of a poor little plant of S. pinnata with green leaves and which, though flattened, was not going to be completely squashed and had thrust its flowers up among the silver foliage of S. neapolitana*.

There are two santolinas with green leaves; the one I don't grow because it has the yellowest of yellow flowers is S. viridis*; the other, with its greeny lemon flowers, is S. pinnata, and it makes luxuriant rounded bushes of evergreen foliage which spread attractively over the top of a wall.

Unfortunately, the best of the silver plants are not quite hardy. Senecio leucostachys* has foliage that is as delicate as a fern and as white as anything in the garden. And to make it even more valuable the flowers are ivory and not yellow. Sensible gardeners don't attempt to keep it through the winter but have a good supply of cuttings which they put out in the spring. There are two good ways to grow it. It makes a delightful effect if planted at the front of a raised bed where it will make a wide, horizontal plant by the end of the summer. For a prominent place this silver plant looks well with pink ivy-leaved geraniums or plumbago, which give colour all through the season.

Not being a sensible gardener, I grow my senecio against a south wall in the hope that it will go through the winter—and sometimes it does. Not realising how rampant it could become, I planted the climbing groundsel Senecio scandens near the silver groundsel and it does give it protection, although it almost smothers it.

I fell in love with *Artemisia arborescens* in an Irish garden where it was growing in a bed about six feet from the ground and hanging over the wall. It was summer and the artemisia was in flower, typical artemisia flowers, so that it looked like a miniature mimosa frothing over that grey stone wall. I begged a cutting and have managed to keep it ever since by cosseting the cuttings in the winter. It has the most delicate foliage I know and makes quite a sizeable plant by the end of the season.

The best way to grow another very white plant is from seed. *Centaurea candidissima** makes a large tufted plant by the end of the summer and I usually lift and pot my plants as I am not very successful at growing things from seed.

*Verbena venosa** usually starts flowering in July and goes on till the end of the season. I am devoted to this verbena and I am sorry it has to be planted in places where it cannot receive the admiration it deserves. Many people raise new plants each year and use it as a bedding plant. If it was used in harmony with a soft pink, ivory or even cherry colour it would be most pleasing, but for some reason the arbiters of park bedding seem to fancy it in association with rich orange tagetes, which is a little too Eastern for me. Sometimes it is used by itself to look like cherry pie, but not, alas, so fragrant. People have different ways of growing it. For bedding one must start with young plants each season and these can be either made from cuttings or grown from seed. I am afraid I don't grow mine in such an orthodox way so I can't say which method is the better. I find occasional seedlings near my plants and they start flowering very early and become good plants by the end of the season.

*Verbena venosa** isn't quite hardy. It will come through most winters if it is planted near stones so that its adventuring roots can burrow under them during the winter. It is an ideal plant to have at the edge of a stone path or paving and looks pretty peeping from under the skirts of a deep pink hydrangea.

I like this verbena better than *V. corymbosa*, although some choosy gardeners consider *V. venosa** rather common—I suppose because of its bedding associations—and have nothing but praise for *V. corymbosa*. I agree that a big planting of *V. corymbosa* is very pleasant, with deep lavender-blue flowers on 2-in stalks. It is sometimes likened to heliotrope, but it is more blue than violet and unfortunately has no scent.

It is not a neat plant, being too lanky to hold itself up well, and not the type that can be staked, so it needs placing. As a filler between shrubs it is ideal because it seems to like a little shade.

Verbena bonariensis grows even taller and can easily reach 4 or 5 ft. It is much more rigid than *V. corymbosa* but rather brittle, so a thin iron stake is a good idea. I have never decided if this is a biennial or a perennial, or is perhaps not quite hardy. It looks best when grown in a clump as in the National Trust garden of Hidcote Manor in Gloucestershire. I always get a few seedlings, but not enough to make a big clump. I like to see it swaying above the more lowly plants in a mixed border. It is one of the features of another National Trust garden, Tintinhull in Somerset, where it is planted in a wall border.

*Actaea spicata rubra** would not look right in a herbaceous border. It needs shade and I think is best suited to a woodland setting or in an odd corner. I have it near *Helleborus corsicus** in the north-east corner of the front garden. Its flowers are small and ineffectual, rather like a white astilbe. But it is not for the flowers that we grow this plant, nor for its delicate fern-like foliage, but for the magnificent red berries that follow those miserable little flowers. The berries are big and shining and grow on a spike held high above the leaves. They last for several weeks; the birds don't eat them and when they start to fall I collect them and sow the seed. Always some escape me, but as I have never found a seedling it seems safer to sow them in a box.

If *Actaea spicata rubra** is a handsome plant, *Actaea alba** is staggering. There are two white-berried actaeas, I was told by Herr Wilhelm Schacht of the Munich Botanic Garden. *Actaea spicata alba* is pretty but it doesn't compare with *Actaea alba** which has very large shining berries and red stems. I first saw it in the garden of a friend and it stood out more prominently than anything else in the garden.

Most of the pinks are at their best in June, though there are some that flower in July, but they don't seem to be the strongest members of the family. I am ashamed when I think of all the unusual and entrancing July pinks I have had and haven't got now. There was the 'Holbein Clove', an intense pillar-box-red single flower with two or three small, twisted white stamens that looked like question marks. I managed to keep it a year or two but could never say it enjoyed the best of health.

Another unusual crimson pink is 'Sops and Wine'*, a small double in rather purplish crimson. It did well for me for several years but disappeared in the end. The yellow-flowered *D. knappii* has been renewed several times because I like its pale flowers.

Among the bigger-flowered pinks the old cottage clove is still the best, but it seems to be given a back seat these days. Other crimson doubles are grown but they do not have the scent or the colour of the old flower. I have been given several that are said to be improved forms of the old cottage clove, but they do not flower so freely nor smell so sweetly.

One seldom sees now the bright scarlet 'Grenadier', which is the same intense colour as a guardsman's coat, and makes a wonderful patch of brilliant colour when the garden is beginning to get rather drab. There is a lovely pink about the same size. I was given it as 'Marie Antoinette' and it is just the colour of the panniered frocks of Marie Antoinette's Court.

'Reine Hortense' flowers profusely but doesn't contribute bright colour. This old pink is the softest pale pink. It has a habit all its own because the flower stems are rather long with buds branching off in all directions. When they first begin to flower it is practically impossible to pick any without sacrificing several buds, and that is something that always distresses me. It really needs to be discreetly staked as otherwise the flower stalks, loaded with loveliness, lie on the ground. Because of all the buds it lasts in flower for several weeks, and when I can bear to cut any I find they look their loveliest arranged with silver foliage, particularly the feathery *Artemesia pontica*. I have been chided by more orthodox gardening friends because I don't disbud this pink, but I like the plants to flower in family parties and I much prefer my flowers as they grow, instead of cutting down the number of blooms and getting finer specimens.

I bought and lost *Iris laevigata* many times before I discovered it is a lime hater—at least so I am told—but it may be that it is just a difficult plant. It is the delicate pink *I. l.* 'Rose Queen'* that I tried to grow. It flowered for me once and I was enchanted by her, but I have never succeeded again. For some strange reason one piece of the variegated *Iris laevigata* has remained in the wettest place in my ditch garden for many years. It doesn't increase, and I spend a great deal of time checking up to see that it is still there. Sometimes it flowers and it is exciting to see striped buds opening to soft lavender flowers. The first time I saw this iris it was growing right in the water of a pond in a Hampshire garden. It was evidently extremely happy because it had increased to considerable drifts.

Very tall penstemons need to be grown against a wall or planted among other tall plants where they get some support. Sometimes a little discreet staking has to be done, but it is better if it can be avoided. I find I have to stake *P.* 'Pennington Gem', as its slender stems are sometimes 3 ft high. The small bells are a soft pale pink and it flowers after the others.

Two of my newer penstemons were found at Hidcote. One of them is a medium pink with deeper markings inside the flowers. To distinguish it I called it *P.* Hidcote-laced. The other, I am now told, is *P.* 'Geo. Home'*. It is in great evidence in the red border at Hidcote and also grows at Kiftsgate Court. It has very big, very bright red flowers and fresh green foliage. There is some uncertainty about the name of a good blue penstemon I was recently given. Some people called it *P.* 'Sour Grapes', others 'Unripe Grapes', and both names describe perfectly the soft purple-blue shade with an iridescent bloom.

Penstemon 'White Bedder' always gets much admiration. The colour is cream, not white, with a hint of cherry, and the bells are rather wide and flaring.

I am always preaching penstemon for continuous colour in the summer garden and I add a few to my repertoire every year. For a long time 'Hewell's Pink Bedder'* has been one of my favourites, with its rather small salmon-pink flowers and branching habit. 'George Elrick' is very similar in colour, but the flowers are larger and more flared, which makes them look wider. It has the usual rather sturdy penstemon habit and makes a solid clump.

Penstemon schönholzeri* is a newcomer, at least to me, and I think it must be hardier than most because nurseries which normally do not list penstemon (they are frightened they may not prove hardy, usually because gardeners will cut them down before frosts are over) are now putting it in their catalogues with Penstemon 'Garnet'* and Chelone barbatus* (Penstemon barbatus). The flowers of Penstemon schönholzeri* are almost as intense a red as 'Newbury Gem', but they are smaller and the plant has not the woody, straggling habit of 'Newbury Gem' and makes a neat, compact plant. It has more substance than Penstemon hartwegii, which is rather slender both in flower and form.

~ Part Two ~

Most of us could be more imaginative about astilbes. I know I could. It is not as though they *have* to be grown in a damp place. Of course they do better if one can plant them at the edge of a stream, but if they have shade they can do with less water, and humus added to the soil helps.

Astilbes are long-suffering and flower year after year however much they are neglected. I have had some of mine for twenty years and have done nothing for them. From time to time I am asked for bits and I chisel off odd pieces, which keeps them from getting too big. The only one I can name is the dark red 'Fanal' with bronze leaves. The dwarf, A. chinensis pumila*, makes good ground cover but its lilac-pink flowers don't go with everything. It needs a blue to flatter it into beauty, the strong blue of Lindelofia longiflora, with its hairy leaves, or the soft lavender-blue of Lactuca bourgiae.

There are so many good astilbes listed that it would be difficult to make a choice. A. 'Red Sentinel' stands out because of the vivid crimson-red of its flowers, and A. 'Ostrich Feather' is a tall one with pink arching plumes. A. simplicifolia atrorosea* is a pleasant dwarf, and I see that there is now a form with dark leaves called A. s. a. 'Bronze Elegance'*, and one with filmy white flowers called A. s. a. praecox alba*.

Ever since I have had a garden I have grown the tall Spiraea palmata*. It is a tough, good-natured plant with woody roots and strong straight stems. The smallest piece of root will grow and it increases well. It is rather looked down on these days and I have looked through half a dozen catalogues without finding it included. But several nurseries grow a new dwarf, *S. p. rubra**, which is half the size of the veteran. I understand that, correctly, *Filipendula palmata* is the name for these plants, but many nurseries still stick to *Spiraea*.

Some people are much better at growing plants from seed than others. I am very low down among the others and probably get only one out of every ten I plant. The successful ones tell me that the best way to be certain to have eccromocarpus every year is to bring on a batch of seedlings, but I always hope that the plants I was given one year will reappear the next. So far they have and sometimes produce a few seedlings, but I may be out of luck one year. I put the small plants I was given in stone troughs against the malthouse and offered them the hospitality of *Viburnum utile* and *Viburnum fragrans** as comfortable aerial homes. These are the crimson-flowered form, which I much prefer; the variety with orange flowers goes in less conspicuous places.

I am trying to induce *Cobaea scandens* to come through the winter but so far I have not succeeded. I know it is a half-hardy perennial that has to be treated as an annual, but I have friends who manage to keep it in a very sheltered corner, and it gets bigger and bigger each year. People sometimes complain that it has an unpleasant smell but I have never noticed it, and I don't think it would stop me growing it because I find the flowers extremely beautiful in their form and colouring; nothing could be lovelier than the delicate shade of green with which they open and the soft shade of purple in which they finish their journey.

Flower-arranging friends tell me that the white form of *Cobaea scandens*, *C. s. alba**, is even lovelier than the ordinary one, the flowers being a pearly white, but I have never seen it, although I buy seed hopefully every year. The fruits of cobaea are almost more exciting than the flowers, they look almost like large greengages, with a delicate bloom, and turn from green to yellow, then to soft orange. Seeds of *Cobaea scandens* planted in the open ground in early June will produce flowers by the middle of August—and vast quantities of stem and foliage. It is advised to sow the seeds on edge. This plant is too exuberant for a small space but the perfect answer for a wall or fence that needs a quick summer screen. The annual canary creeper is just as fast in its operations.

Most of the border phloxes start flowering at the end of June and are at their best in July. They usually continue to produce a few flowers for the rest of the summer. To prolong their season a few clumps can be planted rather late in the spring and well watered. There is often a very dry spell in April and copious watering after planting is the only way to be successful. I have two late-flowering species which are very dear to me—the tall *Phlox paniculata*, which some people think is not worth worrying about. True, the lavender flowers are smaller than the average border phlox, and they are in larger heads on rather longer stalks. But it has a refinement and charm that the hybrids do not possess, it flowers late and long and I love the delicate shade of lilac of those small and delicate flowers. I also cherish a white form of this phlox.

Phlox ahrendsii* is a dwarf, with flowers the size of an ordinary phlox and the rather loose habit of Phlox divaricata (but not its temperament, thank goodness). The flowers are lilac-coloured and it is a good subject for a shady border that does not get too dry. Mulch or humus make it happy, and it needs breaking up fairly often, as its roots soon become hard and congested. I have been given a very old white phlox, not unlike ahrendsii* but I don't think the same. It came from Ireland and had been in the family of the donor for some years. It is quite dwarf with very pure-looking white flowers up the stem. Phloxes grow well among shrubs and are good shade plants.

I know everyone does not agree with me, but I find great satisfaction in a well-grown plant of rose plantain*. Many gardeners refuse to grow this old friend which Mr Bowles loved so much, because it seeds nearly as badly as the ordinary plantain. I agree with them and, until I learned to tell from the leaves, I used to get on my hands and knees to scrutinise the little strangers that come up in the paving to see if there was a suggestion of a frill about the tiny flower spike. Rose plantains* seem rather susceptible to mould; in a very wet year, and sometimes in a very dry one, the leaves get unsightly, and then the only thing to do is to dig them up. Luckily there is always a supply of young ones to take their place and these are lovely in their prime, with strong, smooth leaves and great ruffled green heads. For some years we—my gardening friends and I—thought there were two kinds of rose plantain*, those with rounded heads and others in which the heads were long and pointed. We were so convinced about this that if rose plantain* was wanted I always asked which type was required. But I have come to the conclusion that it is just a matter of luck which kind of flower you get. I see that Parkinson says that they can be either flat or long and pointed. For my own part I prefer the rounded heads, which look more like roses, but sometimes find both types on one plant. Rose plantain* is an informal plant and looks best in odd corners or in front of taller perennials. Being completely green, it goes with everything and makes a good barrier between strong colours that do not like each other.

I have been trying for several seasons to grow catananche, but the grown-up plants I have had in the past have not survived the winter. Tap-roots and heavy clay soil don't go well together, and it was not until I was given large seedlings that I managed to establish them. It was worth waiting a season or two for them to get into good-sized clumps, and I am overjoyed to have this plant in the garden. I enjoy the silver buds as they sway in the wind, and the blue flowers are a very happy, soft shade that blends with all colours. I grow it between a pink rose and a deep cream early dwarf chrysanthemum.

July is the month when most of the clematis are at their best. In addition to some of the old ones I have adventured with some exciting new ones recently. 'Hagley Hybrid' is an exciting mixture of shrimp and crimson, and fades to soft lavender. I have tried *Clematis florida bicolor** several times but so far I haven't found the right way to treat it. This is one of the most difficult clematis to establish but it is worth any amount of trouble. The white flowers with their rich purple centres look almost like passion flowers.

The species clematis are often easier than some of the hybrids. *Clematis markhami** in soft blue and *macropetala* in pink are not as rampant as *C. tangutica*, with its yellow lanterns and fluffy seed-heads. *Clematis rehderiana* takes a little time to get started and then it clambers over everything, hanging its trails with small pale green flowers that smell of cowslips.

I planted it on the east wall of the cowhouse, where I already have a *Viburnum fragrans**, the single pink rose 'Complicata' and *Clematis tangutica*. By the time *C. rehderiana* is in bloom, *C. tangutica* is over and the plant is hung with silky seed-heads. They add to the pale beauty of *C. rehderiana* as it swings from rose to viburnum and then festoons the other clematis.

The greatest clematis discovery of recent times is the form of *C. orientalis* which Ludlow and Sheriff brought back from Tibet. The four waxy petals which make up the flowers are as thick as orange peel. To begin with they are pale green, then they turn to yellow and finish real orange colour. With me they start opening in late July and there are a few flowers in November. The foliage is sea-green and as delicate as a fern. I have one plant on a west wall and it frames the kitchen window, climbs up on the roof to smother the wireless aerial and works its way round the corner on to a north wall. When it is heavily laden with flowers in September it would completely curtain the window if we didn't deal with it firmly. The other one is on an east wall and the growth is even more luxuriant because after reaching the top of the wall it has to work forward and has smothered the bed below with tropical luxuriance. I planted the soft blue *C. jouiniana praecox** to cover the lower part of the wall and have great difficulty in keeping it from being swamped. And the finish of the flowers isn't the end of *Clematis orientalis*, for the balls of silky down which mingle with the flowers all through the season hang on until it is time to cut the clematis down in February. I asked Mr Roland Jackman how I should treat this clematis and he told me I could cut it down to about 2 in in mid-February.

Compared with the luxuriance of the orange-peel clematis the other clematis that flower in July are very restrained. The pearly flowered *C.* 'Huldine' is best appreciated if one can look up at the flowers. *C. albo-luxurians** should be at eye level as the green-tipped white flowers have a delicate beauty, and *C. kermesina*, another viticella type, is a strong pink and associates well with *Ceanothus* 'Autumnal Blue', with soft blue flowers.

I have always grown as many bergamot* (monarda) as I could, from the tall mauve to the pinks and reds. The tall leafy stems stand erect and the foliage is aromatic even in mid-winter. *M.* 'Snow Maiden' is a new one and an exceptional plant. White flowers are always needed in the garden, and when they are ruffled with green and make a fine upstanding clump about 2 in high they are particularly valuable. I have it growing with *Solidago* 'Lemore'*, which has greeny yellow flowers and shows up best with white. The monarda blooms for several weeks and doesn't seem as insistent on moist soil as some of the others.

July is the month when regale lilies scent the air, and their delicious fragrance draws me many times a day to the places where they grow. I don't think it is possible to have too many regale lilies and I plant out every seedling I find. Seedlings appear all round the plants, sometimes in crevices between stones and in the path. The best regale lilies I have ever seen were growing in an enormous pot, so I put mine in raised beds, tubs and troughs which they have to share with fritillaries, snowdrops and dwarf daffodils. It is a good idea to plant any spare lilies in pots which can be sunk in flower beds needing interest in July.

There is growing interest in lilies, but those of us with very limy soil can grow only very few. It doesn't worry me because the lilies I love are white and scented and I am content with *Lilium regale*. *L. candidum* grows but not as well as it should. I should like to succeed with *L. longifolium** but it doesn't fancy my soil, but I intend to give it and *L. auratum* the pot treatment. I should like to grow the greeny yellow *szovitsianum**, but the tawny and red lilies, most of them unscented, I willingly leave to others. 'Martagon'* lilies in crimson and white naturalise themselves among shrubs, and the little yellow lily, *pyreniacum*, seeds itself about. No one could call that sweetly scented, but when a plant grows because it wants to one isn't too critical. Even the experts have great difficulty making some of their lilies happy. In one famous garden small raised beds have been made by peat blocks among shrubs. These are filled with special compost and the lilies are carefully seated on sand—and even then they don't always do well.

There is growing enthusiasm for hostas (also belonging to the liliaceae family), but it doesn't reach anything like the thrall that lilies have for some people. I can understand the devotion to plantain lilies because they have wonderful leaves as well as lovely flowers, and the flowers are in gentle shades of lilac if they are not white. Also they are easy to grow if they get moisture and humus. Some experts say they will not grow in limy soil, but I do not think they can be too particular as I can grow them. I always put in plenty of peat when I plant them. Primarily they are plants for shade, but they will grow in sun and usually flower better in a sunny position, though the leaves are bigger in shade. In sun they need more moisture. I have never decided which kinds I like best; variegated plants fascinate me, but for sheer beauty the great crinkled leaves of *H. sieboldiana* come first. They are blue-grey, with a delicate bloom and deeply veined. The flowers are pale lilac and if left on the plants the seed-heads look almost like silver flowers and last all through the winter.

I saw a lovely planting of this hosta in a friend's garden. A small rose garden had the climbing rose 'New Dawn' trained on one side. It was to make a screen and all along the bottom these magnificent hostas were growing. The very pale pink of the roses was entrancingly lovely with the leaves of the hosta and its pale lilac flowers.

Hostas look lovely under old-fashioned roses and are good growing under trees, with perhaps the tall white *Iris ochreleuca* to give height.

This late-flowering iris, in spite of its name, doesn't absolutely insist on moisture. I grow it to give height at the back of a border and I wish I had thought of putting *Anchusa* 'Loddon Royalist'* in front of it. I saw this happy planting in a garden. The anchusa had been left without support and had made a sprawling mass of deep blue and dark green.

The tall *Campanula lactiflora* is a very pale blue and *Spiraea* 'Anthony Waterer', with its crimson flowers, enhances its beauty. Two other plants that vary the theme slightly are *Amsonia salicifolia** and *Achillea* 'Cerise Queen'*. The amsonia, with little starry flowers in slate-blue, is a good mixer. I have it with the magenta-pink trailing *Geranium* 'Russell Prichard'* in front, with silvered leaves, and behind the cerise achillea fades pleasantly to a soft sad pink.

Mr Bowles' Red Rhubarb, *Rheum palmatum*, is exciting from the moment the bright cerise buds come through the soil. The red crumpled leaves slowly unfold to make a yard span, and though they get greener as they age the linings remain crimson. The flower spike can reach 5 ft and the flowers are the colour of ripe raspberries. One of my plants is beside *Anaphalis yedoensis**, the tallest of this family, with silver and ivory flowers on 3-ft stems and green and silver leaves, with the tall *Thalictrum glaucum*, with lemon flowers, behind.

It seems strange that *Senecio smithii* isn't grown in more gardens. Given a damp place there is nothing easier, and the fleshy roots and overlapping leaves soon increase. Everything about it is sturdy, the flowers are white daisies about an inch across on thick stems. Its shining evergreen foliage is quite unperturbed by weather.

Parts of the garden can at times look rather flimsy, and where this happens the giant *Kniphofia northiae* will give substance—great substance, for it is a monster of a plant, with long, wide leaves making enormous rosettes from which the solid flower spikes rise about 3 ft high, shading from coral to greeny yellow. Among the plants I grow with it, *Campanula burghltii** looks particularly well. It has outsize bells in slaty blue and goes on flowering for weeks on end.

There is no difficulty in getting flowers for July, but most of them are tall. There is one polygonum that is good for front line places, *P. emodi*, with narrow bronze-red leaves and spikes of blood-red flowers. In odd corners where they can be enjoyed the summer *Cyclamen europaeum** produces its flowers over many weeks. As they are scented one enjoys them most in a raised bed—I have heard that if it is content this cyclamen keeps its leaves throughout the year. It does with me, I am glad to say.

~ 8 ~

August

This is the month that tests the gardener's skill and ingenuity. The garden can look very tired, particularly after a dry spell, with brown grass and rusty or mildewed leaves. There are flowers that will carry us through the dull period, but they need finding and I bless my mounds of foliage in August more than in any other month. The cream and pale green of *Scrophularia aquatica variegata** is as good as any flower; the silver plants like hot weather and are at their best in high summer. Purple or golden sage is much nicer than the stubble of finished flowers, and there is something very cool and calm about the flat glaucous leaves of othonnopsis, making a carpet of blue-grey. The small shrubs with variegated foliage that I grow in my borders are particularly popular with me in the summer; variegated kerria and the variegated symphoricarpus* are always good value but particularly when there is a lull in garden interest.

The gardens that are really gay in August are usually well planted with annuals (and well-grown annuals can be extremely effective), or they rely on dahlias to keep them cheerful.

I am ashamed that I am not kinder about dahlias because individually I like them very much, and I think a clump here and there in the garden is very pleasant, particularly if there is a good green background to temper the brightness of their flowers, but a bed or a garden crammed with dahlias of every possible colour makes me long for a restful sweep of green grass. Dahlias used sparingly and in gentle colours can be very useful in a mixed border as the season advances.

Pale pink dahlias help washy blue michaelmas daisies, and so does the bright peach colour of D. 'Baby Royal'. Lemon-yellow that is almost green is cool and lovely with white flowers, and if it is green enough can be used with deep crimson.

If only dahlias were just a little more hardy, life would be much easier. For more than twenty years I had two large clumps of dahlias that came up regularly every year and I was glad to see them, although they were not the colours I would have chosen. Both were scarlet, one double and the other single, and I had to plant carefully round them. The grey-blue leaves of purple sage looked pleasant and a carpet of the white and green *Euonymus radicans variegata** made a good background. I could have used *Stachys lanata** safely or variegated artemesia, with its white and green cut foliage. Variegated marrubium or the variegated form of apple mint, *Mentha rotundifolia variegata**, can make luxuriant growth, and the quiet blending of cream and pale green would be good with scarlet.

My problems were solved by a very severe winter and I have not grown dahlias since, although I realise that my summer garden would be more colourful if I did.

Thalictrum dipterocarpum*, with its delicate glaucous foliage and clouds of tiny lavender flowers, is a much easier plant than red dahlias when it comes to companions. Various forms of mallow sow themselves in various parts of my garden; the dwarf *Malva moschata* has flowers of a rather sad shade of pink but they go well with the thalictrum. The deep pink annual *Lavatera* 'Loveliness' would be even more striking but I always forget to grow it. I have an upright form of *M. moschata* which is more effective than the usual type but it has flowers the same shade of pink. I should like the tree mallow, *Lavatera*, better if its flowers were a little brighter, but its general effect is gentle and it harmonises well with the thalictrum. Both do well in shade and the thalictrum needs plenty of moisture if it is to achieve its 5 f stature. The mallow, of course, will go on flowering almost till Christmas, and if cut down in the spring will soon make sturdy new growth. Instead of the thalictrum a buddleia can be its companion. The strong colour of *B*. 'Royal Red'* is effective or the pastel blue and silver of *B. fallowiana** 'Loch Inch'.

Salvia verticillata makes a good carpet for the tree mallow. With its soft woolly leaves and small blue-grey flowers this salvia is rather indefinite in colouring, but it is not indefinite in the way it grows. It sends its prostrate stems out in all directions and soon covers a great deal of space. Its lanky habit is useful to cover the bare ground under a mallow, but is not so desirable in a bed where small and precious plants are growing.

Malva 'Primley Blue'* is still blooming in August and is very pretty in a quiet way. This is a form of *M. sylvaticum* which originated in the garden of the late Herbert Whiteley at Paignton. I first saw it growing as a carpet under shrubs and it needed plenty of room because it has long rambling stems. I thought it would look better if it were planted so that it could work through a low shrub, and I grow mine near a group of the floribunda rose 'Ingrid Stenzig', which has bright pink flowers and grows to about 3 ft. The scheme has worked very well, for the long stems of the mallow wander in and out of the roses with the small, flat flowers and their complement of leaves appearing as they go. The blue of the flowers is rather dull but improved by lines of darker colour. A large clump of *Catananche caerulea* grows near the rose and the blue flowers with their silver buds complete the picture.

Another mallow that can help the garden in the summer is the white form of *Malva moschata*. I have no idea how this mallow got into the garden, but I was delighted to find it one day and admired its cunning for putting itself in front of a pale yellow verbascum. The group was one of the happiest in the garden—and had nothing to do with me—but the verbascum overplayed its hand and grew so enormous that it had to be removed from its narrow bed. Now I am looking for something else of more reasonable proportions to plant behind the white mallow.

I believe that July is the orthodox time for the phloxes to make their most dazzling display, but mine are always at their best in August. And if one can find young plants to put in they will usually be at their best in September. But once the phloxes have started to flower they go on intermittently for months. I find by cutting off the flower-head directly it is over the side shoots develop and flower away quietly for a very long time.

New phloxes appear every year and it would be hard to keep up with them all. For years I have grown 'Leo Schlageter' and I don't think the newer 'Brigadier'* is very much better. Both are that bright salmon-pink that one connects with such plants as begonias, and is bright without being in any way gaudy. I think my favourite phlox is a pure white one, the whitest white I know, and it flowers almost longer than any other. The new 'Mother o' Pearl'* is soft and delicate and 'Fanal' is one of the best reds.

We can be too stereotyped in the way we use phloxes. They are excellent border plants but they also do remarkably well in shade and are most effective planted among shrubs. I was very impressed with the way they were used in the garden of a friend of mine. This garden has no real flower borders, in the ordinary sense of the word, but shrubs have been used to give a simple, furnished look to the garden, and to make the work easy. The garden surrounds an old farmhouse, and there are still evidences of the farmyard. The duck pond is still there, and the old stone farm path, and phloxes are just the kind of plant that can be used with the shrubs to give colour through several summer months. It was pleasant to catch glimpses of crimson and violet, pink and lavender as one wandered on well-kept grass between beds of shrubs.

I have never discovered how a tall and handsome member of the onion family got into my garden. When I first saw the little family among my primulas I thought they were leeks, and I couldn't think how they got there. I grow very few vegetables and never leeks, yet there they were, first a clump, which grew bigger every year, and then members of the family started to break away and I found young stalwarts in odd places round about. I am plagued by the wild allium, with its whiskery green head, and I wondered if another interloper had arrived to add to my work. Of course, they are distant cousins, but whereas I struggle to rid the garden of the troublesome green allium, I cherish the big pink heads of my "leeks" as they tower over a low wall. I discovered, too, that they dry remarkably well and add another shape to my bowls of "deads". They keep their delicate pink hue very well and a suspicion of green makes them even lovelier. A knowledgeable friend thought she had solved one mystery for me. She told me that my outsize leek was *Allium babbingtonii** and for a while I took her word, but *Allium babbingtonii** happened to be illustrated in a book I read and the picture showed heads much shaggier than mine with smaller bulblets growing out of the flowers. Another helpful suggestion was that my allium is one called the 'Lundy Leek', but that is difficult to check too.

Leeks remind me of herbs, and in particular of hyssop, which is one of my August standbys. I have always grown hyssop, because I like its stiff habit of growth, the blue, pink or white of its flowers, and the pungency of its foliage. It seeds itself mildly and usually conveniently; I couldn't have chosen a better place for a huge clump that has pushed its way up between big stones near the garden door. Each year I get a shock because each year I am visited by a professional gardener to discuss pruning to be done in the garden, and each year I have the same comment—how effective a common plant can be if grown in the right way. I had never thought of hyssop as common and, come to think of it, I don't see it in many other gardens. I am often asked what it is and I quote the biblical reference to add interest. There is nothing better when you want something firm and emphatic to break a hard line or add interest and colour in the rock garden. After a few years it gets rather woody and gnarled and then it should be scrapped and an infant put in its place. One can cut and trim for several years, but unless it is grown in a place where size is an asset there comes a time when one can cut no more.

Though hyssop is quite good at providing a few seedlings, it doesn't do to rely on them and it is as well to take cuttings of each colour each year. If this is not done systematically it is quite easy to wake up one day and discover that every plant of one of the colours has disappeared from the garden.

There is a dwarf hyssop (*Hyssopsus aristatus**) which is quite useful for filling in spaces between tall perennials but hasn't, I think, quite the character of the ordinary hyssop, *Hyssopus officinalis*. The stems of the dwarf plant are only 9–12 in high, and are so stiff and erect. It flowers a little later and I have never seen any other colour than blue.

I rely on herbaceous lobelias to give me colour in August. In an average year they do quite well in ordinary flower beds and do not insist on a waterside position, but there is no question that they hate being too dry and if I had a stream

I should certainly plant them near it. But as I haven't, I give them plenty of humus and plant them where the soil is deep and rich. In a wet summer they grow very tall and have large flowers; in a drought they have difficulty in keeping upright. Some manage better than others. The lovely blue syphilitica is often distressed after a long dry spell, but *Lobelia syphilitica* 'Joyce' in bright pink and *L. s.* 'Jean' in violet seem to survive better and I think are hardier. The large violet *Lobelia vedrariensis** is extremely tough and showy.

The crimson-leaved lobelia, which is usually called *L. cardinalis* but is really *L. fulgens*, is a superb creature when well grown. Get it with the early evening light shining through its plum-coloured leaves and glowing red flowers and you will think your garden is set with jewels. It pays to give it plenty of water. I always put a few clumps in the trough beside the garden door. Of course it is quite the wrong place, under a north wall and in a stone trough which should be reserved for small treasures that need cosseting (but most of which flower in spring), but I cannot resist the sacrilege, for the honey-coloured wall behind is a perfect foil for the blood-red flowers, and there they catch the last rays of the sun before it dips behind the trees.

The lobelias that grow in the trough are always the finest I have in the garden because they get more than their fair share of water. There is an old copper on the other side of the door, which takes the water from the roof, and I keep a tin dipper by it so that I can scoop up water for the lobelias with the minimum of trouble.

Mr H.C. Pugsley of Derby has done a great deal of work with lobelias, as with verbascums and many other plants, and he has produced a wide range of hardy herbaceous lobelias in delightful shades, ranging from mauve to reds and cerise, and one really dark crimson, which he calls Old Port. These lobelias start flowering in July and August and go on to October. I try to keep the dead flowers removed so that after the central spike has finished side shoots carry on. By the time they have completely finished flowering, the single rosette we put out in the spring will have made itself into a big clump, to be pulled apart into individual rosettes in the spring.

If I had unlimited frame space I think I should divide my plants in the autumn and leave the divisions in a frame for the winter, as many people do with the not-too-hardy *Lobelia fulgens*. In this way one would have a flying start in the spring, which can be dry for weeks on end. I have at times lifted the large clumps of *Lobelia fulgens* and put them in a frame, but now I leave them where they are and give them a top dressing of peat. Most years this is not necessary, but one never knows, and the peat is good for the soil anyway. Some gardeners like to grow red lobelias by themselves, filling beds with them and treating them almost as bedding plants. In one garden I know a bed at the bottom is first filled with tulips and after they are over the lobelias are planted out. It works in this garden because the bed is in front of a yew hedge which divides the garden, but without this the concentrated colour would be a little overpowering. I prefer to plant them with other flowers in a mixed border. In one bed *L. fulgens* has as a companion *Euphorbia pilosa major**. This euphorbia flowers in early spring and in August is a mound of delicate green and makes a pleasant associate for the lobelia. I used to consider that *E. epithymoides** was the better of these two spring-flowering euphorbias because it was more compact, but I have come to appreciate more *E. pilosa major** because it remains attractive after it has flowered. In fact it is almost more beautiful in summer and autumn because the fresh green foliage takes on shades of crimson and pink which blend with the lobelia.

Bright blue is always welcome, and particularly in August when there isn't much about. I wish I had met the Mexican *Commelina coelestis* earlier in my gardening life because I find it a fascinating plant, not only because of its flowers, which are a real Mediterranean blue, but also for its unorthodox way of growing, with little wrapped leaves, rather like a tradescantia. Commelina doesn't pretend to be a hardy plant (in seed lists it is described as half hardy), but sometimes some plants do come through the winter. But it seeds itself well and once you have it in the garden I am told that it makes sure you have it always. I hope this is so because I fully intend to grow those lovely blue flowers every year. There is a white-flowered form, which I haven't yet seen, but I can imagine it would be almost as lovely.

Commelina is about 18 in high and the small, intensely bright blue flowers can be very telling and give a fillip to a tame planting. It doesn't really need another colour to enhance its beauty although blush pink or lemon-yellow could be used. I prefer my commelina in clumps among iris foliage, which seems to provide just that background to show up colour at its purest.

~ Part Two ~

It is always a red-letter day when the first spray of summer jasmine opens because I know I shall have these deliciously scented flowers till November or even December. One sprig scents a room and a small pewter mug filled with jasmine is my unfailing bedside offering to my guests. Every garden should have at least one *Jasminum officinale*, for there is nothing so ravishing as the scent of the common jasmine. One of my earliest recollections is being taken down the garden path at a seaside cottage to a little house romantically wreathed in jasmine. I believe that jasmine was the popular treatment for such places, and quite rightly. So when I made this garden I planted my jasmine on the north wall of the little stone house "down the garden", which I subsequently gutted and converted into a summer house.

Later I was advised to buy the superior form of *Jasminum officinale*, listed either as *Jasminum officinale major* or *affine*, because its flowers are bigger. I admit they are, and delicately flushed with pink, which is very attractive, but there are not nearly so many of them, and I don't think their scent is so strong. The plant itself is most vigorous, with larger leaves, but it doesn't keep putting out sprays of fragrant white flowers all through the summer, as does my common old plant, and it makes far too much foliage.

There are certain flowers which will always be rare, and will always make our friends envious. I first saw and admired *Alstroemeria psittacina* in the wonderful garden of Crathes Castle near Banchory and I felt I must have it at all costs. It is not a plant for which you ask your friends, and I am quite certain they wouldn't give it to you if you did. I saw it again in Mr Haddon's garden at Porlock, growing beneath his greenhouse wall. I have seen it in other gardens but never in large plantings, although I suppose it does increase in time. I was able to buy some eventually from a private garden which sells superfluous plants, and I managed to get two plants. One plant was put in a sheltered corner between west and north walls where the soil is damp and rich, and I never saw it again. The second plant I put on the top of a rock garden against a south wall, and that was the right place. Every year since I have had a few flowers. In a wet year there are not so many; when it is hot and dry the long, fragile flower stems keep coming up, even though the leaves are yellowing and dying off. I love those red and green tubular flowers which give it its name of "parrot lily" and look as though they had come straight from a Dutch flower painting. I have never succeeded in inducing the beautiful Ligtu hybrids to grow for me, whether from seed or as small plants, and I wouldn't invite the ordinary alstromeria to take possession of any part of my garden, but the romantic, sinister *A. psittacina* is one of the compensations for August.

Lysimachias are not a very striking family, but they are useful in the garden, and give no trouble so long as they are not allowed to dry out. I even like the irrepressible *L. punctata* for a place which needs quick and luxuriant results. In the spring its artless yellow flowers and generous foliage are very welcome, and it is easy to control.

For wide bare spaces the ordinary wild lysimachia, *L. vulgaris*, is very pretty and not as invasive as many plants used for such places. It has a more branching habit than *L. punctata*. *L. ciliata* has orange centres to its flowers, and *L. verticillata** is not dissimilar.

I wish the little pink-flowered lysimachia, *L. leschnaulti**, was as easy as the others. It is a very attractive little plant but it is quite frank in letting me know that it can't stand my garden, and nothing I do will induce it to change its mind. I have struggled to please it for years and now I shan't bother any more—unless I happen to see it doing really well in someone else's garden, and then I know I shall try again, for the challenge is irresistible.

Now "creeping jenny" (*Lysimachia nummularia*) is only too anxious to help, and if it were not so easy I think we should make a great fuss of it. The little round leaves shine as though they had been lacquered, and the open yellow flowers have a simple loveliness that is hard to beat. It is a magnificent ground coverer, especially in a damp place, where it creeps along in all directions, pegging itself down as it goes. The yellow-leaved form is even better, for the fresh colour looks like a flower from a distance. It is just as easy as the green-leaved form and a most useful plant for bringing sunshine into a dark place. I see it is being used at Hidcote in the yellow garden, and in another garden it has been planted on a ledge above an archway, where it gives that needed gleam of sunshine as one comes out from the dark of the arch.

Lysimachia clethroides shares the family dislike of very dry conditions and looks its best when it has plenty of moisture. It has the same ruffled stalks of *L. punctata*, but the flowers are white and come in a curving spike at the top of the stem. I was once told that it got its name because the shape of the flower is like a shepherd's crook, but I can't find any justification for it. Reference books say that the name clethroides comes from the fact that the flowers are like those of clethra. Whatever the meaning of its name it is quite an effective plant, especially if it can be planted with its back to a wall or hedge. Then all the graceful flowers point the same way, whereas if it is grown in an open bed they don't really know which way to look. The leaves of this lysimachia turn crimson in autumn and it associates well with the herbaceous *Clematis heracleifolia*.

The aristocrat of the family is, I think, *L. ephemerum,* with its glaucous leaves and grey flowers. It is definitely a moisture lover and I have seen it grown most effectively beside a stream, although I have never had complaints from it about the position I give it in my mixed borders. It has a tall and stately habit, and is one of the most useful summer plants because it fits in with any summer scheme. Occasionally I find an odd seedling, but never many, which is a pity, because it doesn't increase very rapidly and one needs to treat the divisions with great respect. They are rather fleshy and sometimes rot away in a very wet autumn.

Although I wouldn't call penstemon an August flower it is certainly most useful in this rather difficult month. By this time one has cut off the first flowering spikes and is enjoying the next batch. I think penstemon really need

1.Striking red tulips and other bulbs in April under
Acer pseudoplatynus 'Leopoldii'

2. Snowdrops and *Crocus tomasinianus* naturalised in the Old Nursery

3. *Crambe cordifolia* about to display itself in the Terraces in late May

4. *Cistus ingwersonii* in the Silver Garden in late May

5. Wisteria flowering on the Malthouse in June

6. *Geranium pratense* and *Iris ocholeuca* in the Sundial Garden

7. *Philadelphus* 'Belle Etoile' with *Crambe cordifolia* in full bloom in July

8. Narcissus and leucojum on the Top Lawn under the mature
Judas Tree *(Cercis siliquastrum)*

9. May flowering of *Rosa anemenifolia* in the Silver Garden

10. Snowdrops in the Ditch in February

11. *Rosa mulaganii* magnificent in late June

12. *Digitalis orientalis* has a long flowering period

13. *Tellima grandiflora* and polyganum in the Ditch

14. Various iris plantings give continuous flowering for many weeks

15. View across the Ditch in early June

16. Leaf drop from *Rhus potaninii* at the end of October

17. A magnificent Judas Tree *(Cercis siliquastrum)*
at the end of May

18. *Astrantia* 'Shaggy' *(Astrantia involocruta)*
Photo courtesy of Jack Keogh

19. *Bergenia* and variegated bramble (*Rubus* 'Variegata')

20. The bird cherry tree *(Prunus padus)* in full bloom in mid-May

21. *Cornus controversa* 'Variegata' grown as a standard gives months of pleasure

22. The Terraces with mixed plantings (the *Cornus controversa* 'Variegata' in the background) are at their best in May and June

23. The Terraces with the Pudding Trees (*Chaemycyparis lawsoniana* 'Fletcheri'), which are clipped only once a year in August

24. The Terraces from the Silver Garden at the end of May

25. A planting of *Astrantia* 'Shaggy' splendid in July

26. The Terraces in early July

27. White Tulips give interest in the Long Border in April

28. The front door with wisteria and *Rosa banksia* in early Summer

29. *Watsonia beatricia*

30. *Morina longifolia*

31. *Clematis* 'Perle d'Azure'
flowers for most of July

32. Valerian in the Terraces can give
pleasure for many months

33. The Terraces before a storm in August

34. Cambrian poppies between the Pudding Trees
flower throughout the summer

35. *Helleborus orientalis* in the front garden in early Spring

36. *Mahonia japonica* flowering during the winter

37. *Primula vulgaris* 'Alba Plena' flowering in early Spring

38. The old rose 'Great Maiden's Blush' on the front of the house

dead-heading more regularly than almost any other flower if one is to keep up a continuous flow of flowers. Also the flowers themselves are so much more attractive if there are no finished spikes among them.

I don't know if it is imagination, but it always seems to be that the pink and red varieties of penstemon are at their best late in the year, or it may be that they reach a special brilliance in the late sunshine. Though I admire them all in their first appearance, I do not think 'Castle Forbes', 'Newbury Gem' and the pinks like 'Hewell's'* and 'George Elrick' are nearly so colourful when they first open. The tall lavender 'Mrs Hindley'* and the rich bloom of Purple Bedder are often good late in the year. 'Mrs Hindley'* in particular comes into her own in late summer and looks particularly well growing near deep cerise roses such as 'Independence' or 'Rosemary Rose'. 'Rosemary Rose' often blooms late and the flat cherry-red flowers are lovely with the slender spikes of the penstemon. Even without flowers the rose makes happy contrast because its dark purple foliage keeps its colour throughout the season. The opalescent bells of *Penstemon* 'Stapleford Gem' are more blue than lavender, but they are so indeterminate in colour that they combine well with the colouring of 'Rosemary Rose', although this penstemon is rather stiffer in growth than 'Mrs Hindley'* and not quite so tall. *P. heterophyllus* never approaches the luxuriance of its first flowering but it potters along pleasantly all through the season, and when there aren't so many of the pink-flushed blue flowers one appreciates more the dark bronze foliage. The spreading stems are brittle and need trimming from time to time as each plant makes wide growth by August.

The tall coral and tubular isophyllus is a good later flowerer. I always try to grow this against a wall and by accident I discovered a very happy combination. By the time this penstemon has grown really tall the small plant of *Senecio leucostachys** I planted nearby has become a sizeable bush. Both like the comfort of a south wall and the coral spikes thrusting through the silver filigree of the groundsel is really charming. Probably another year it won't be nearly so good, but at least I have had a pleasing picture for one long season.

Though the individual flowers of *P.* 'Garnet'* are small, the plant tends to get quite big by midsummer and can be untidy if not tidied up from time to time. In front of it *Alchemilla mollis* makes a froth of tiny green flowers with beautiful grey-green leaves. I don't know any flower that is not improved by having *Alchemilla mollis* nearby. The lucky people who can grow alstromeria, particularly the Ligtu hybrids, have discovered how lovely they look with *Alchemilla mollis* planted in front of them.

Every gardener has different ideas about flowers and colour. I love the pastel shades of the penstemon and do not care for the harsh yellow flowers of early autumn, and because I try to avoid an over-abundance of yellow in the garden I am rather half-hearted about the many varieties of goldenrod. Individually they are all beautiful, and it pays to look closely into the structure of all those tiny flowers, but all the same I don't want too many of them in my garden. I rather agree with the Americans in this. In their country goldenrod is one of the most rampant wild flowers and it is never allowed in a garden. There are many new and beautiful solidagos to choose from and I grow only one, S. 'Lemore'*, because it has that pleasant greenish tinge to its lemon-yellow yellow that makes it a very good mixer. The large mop-heads are carried on fairly dwarf stalks and are very soft and pretty. They dry well too and are almost as lovely in death as they are growing. The golden michaelmas daisy, *Solidaster luteus**, is very similar. Many people prefer a really deep golden variety called 'Goldenmosa', a name which describes it well. It is conceivable that its hard, egg-yolk-yellow might look well against a background of white or green but it needs careful placing. I am quite attached to a very old goldenrod called *S. caesia*. It has whippy black stems heavily encrusted with small yellow flowers, which makes it different and graceful as compared with many other goldenrods. It too looks well with *Alchemilla mollis* or white *Bergamot* 'Snow Maiden'*.

Green eryngiums always excite a lot of curiosity. Certainly the foliage doesn't look much like an eryngium although the flower-heads have an eryngium look. *E. bromeliifolium** is the first to flower. It is smaller than the others, with fine, sword-like foliage which is not so heavily spined as the others. The flower stalks are from 3 to 4 ft high, well clothed with small green "bobbles", and it keeps up a succession of such spikes for two to three months. *E. serra* is dwarf too, a much more stocky plant than *E. bromeliifolium**, with wide, spiky leaves and green teasel heads on stout stalks. It looks like an agave, and I do not wonder that even in some botanic gardens it is labelled *E. agavifolium,* which is a bigger plant and between *E. serra* and *E. bromeliifolium** in size. *E. pandanifolium* is the giant of the family, with long, narrow, spiked leaves, and flower spikes that reach 8 or 10 in. These spikes are widely branched and are decked with myriads of tiny round mushroom-coloured flowers. This handsome plant looks truly magnificent silhouetted against a deep blue sky. One needs gloves, however, to handle it, and after the winter it does need a certain amount of grooming. Many of the outside leaves are tattered and brown and have to be removed, and later in the season it needs some sort of support if those majestic spikes are to keep upright and beautiful. They are not at their best until late in the year and must be protected against autumn gales.

There is great fascination in green flowers, and I would like to make a "Green Garden" where I could assemble all the plants with green flowers. The trouble is that some of them need different positions and soils. Eucomis I grow in the front garden which faces south and where they do well with the house behind them. *E. punctata** has lovely hanging bells in alabaster-green. The stems of the leaves are heavily spotted. I like it better than the more spectacular *E. bicolor* with violet centres to the flowers and a tinge of violet on the transparent bracts.

Another delightful green flower, *Bupleurum angulosum,* does best for me in greens and so it has to grow in a special bed under a north wall, where its small sea-green flowers and narrow foliage are lovely for several weeks.

Nor could I risk *Galtonia princeps* in an ordinary flat bed. I have grown it on the flat and it wasn't a success. Slugs are particularly fond of the glaucous leaves and brittle stems of this lovely green "snowdrop", and they are not so tiresome if it is grown in a raised bed where it gets good drainage.

The hardy *Watsonia beatricei** needs sharp drainage and a southern aspect too. In a normal season it does very well but a really severe winter means no flame-coloured flowers the next summer and two very severe winters no watsonia, so it is not really hardy after all.

Strangely, the members of the ginger family we all try to grow are much hardier than we thought. *Cautleya robusta** has flowered after two of the most severe winters in living memory and *Hedychium densiflorum* not only survived in Somerset but in gardens near London. Even without flowers the smooth stems and wide leaves make the plants worth growing. I am experimenting with *Hedychium gardnerianum* now to see if I can leave it out too, covered by peat.

It is in August that *Selenium carvifolium** flowers. This British native, sometimes known as Cambridge Parsley, is still found in one or two Cambridgeshire fens. It is a lovely plant for the woodland garden, with its flat, fern-like leaves and flat heads of frothy white flowers, made more spectacular by their red stems. It needs to stand alone. Mine is near a lime-free bed where I grow *Cornus canadensis*, and the flat rosettes of leaves on 5-in stems, with white flowers in the middle of each, make a charming carpet in the shade of the wide leaves. The flowers of the cornus are sometimes followed by red berries and the leaves turn crimson.

Moisture rather than shade is needed for the little Japanese plant *Houttuynia cordata*, with its dark leaves and small white flowers with their prominent centres. There is also a double form, perhaps not so beautiful but certainly interesting. The plant runs slightly but not enough to be a nuisance.

An interesting aster that would be a welcome addition to the summer garden if it did not run so much is *A. macrophylla**. It has large heads of pale lavender flowers, which are composed of narrow petals and have a stiff structure that is quite unusual. Large, hairy, heart-shaped leaves on sturdy stems complete the picture, but it is a picture that has to be constantly checked. I grow it next to a small pink floribunda rose called Radium and the two plants together look very pretty.

Nearby I have to contend with another runner. I sometimes wonder why I struggle with, *Achillea* 'The Pearl' because its running white roots seem to be everywhere. I try to control it by sinking wide drainpipes and planting it in them, but it manages to get over the top. But in August, when there are not too many flowers in the garden, I am grateful for the small white daisies which last for such a long time in the garden and are so good to pick. In front there is a large plant of white gypsophila perched on the edge of the low wall that holds up the bed. I always grow gypsophila at the edge of a wall. The plant looks better grown in this way and there is no awkward gap after it has finished flowering as most of its mound of blossom billows over the top of the wall. Behind the achillea, phloxes make good colour in the summer. Variegated *Phlox* 'Border Gem'* combines good colour with lovely white variegated leaves; the violet of this phlox is lovely with the pink of *P.* 'Sweetheart' and the deep crimson of *P.* 'Joan Elliott'.

Artemisia ludoviciana is another runner, and again it is too good a plant to do without. I grow it behind *A.* 'Lambrook Silver'*, and the tall and slender spikes of the artemisia contrast well with the filigree foliage of the more woody artemisia and the two together make a patch of white and silver as a contrast to brighter plants.

The monk's-hoods are plants we are inclined to take for granted and yet they are most varied in their types and times of flowering. *Aconitum lycoctonum* may not have enough colour for everybody, but some of us enjoy the greeny cream narrow flowers, perched like birds on rangy stems. It is not a compact plant and likes to behave in our gardens as it does in its native Austria. It doesn't take kindly to restraint, so the thing to do is to grow it with perennials with which it can intermingle and make a pleasing picture. I have it in front of the tall species *Phlox paniculata*, which has soft lavender flowers, and behind that is a big clump of *Achillea* 'Gold Plate'*. All these have to be supported but I do it loosely so that they don't keep themselves altogether to themselves.

The climbing monk's-hood, *Aconitum volubile latisectum**, is a most original plant but one seldom sees it. I first met it in the famous Valley Gardens at Harrogate. It was growing in the rock garden and had travelled quite a long way above ground by attaching itself to plants growing a foot from the ground. As a conventional climber it will make a large patch of soft blue on a wall, or it can be planted to grow with other twining plants, as at Wisley, where its soft colouring shows up the scarlet brilliance of *Trapaeolum speciosum* and the clear blue of *Codonopsis vinciflora*. Its first station in my garden is the scented *Artemisia tridentata** and it shows up well among its small silver leaves. Clematis come and go throughout the year and August's offering is one of the most exquisite. *C.* 'Countess of Onslow' has warm pink urn-shaped flowers, each with a deeper central band. I have trained it along the top of a descending wall and the first white blooms of *Anemone japonica** rise majestically behind it.

C. flammula is almost a glorified wild clematis but it grows a different way and is deliciously scented. The clouds of tiny white flowers smell strongly of almonds and greet me every time I open the garden gate. A large pink hydrangea of the hortensis type has its head almost in the cloud.

After the earlier clematis are over it is pleasant to have the soft blue *C.* Perle d'Azur pouring over my high wall, with the delicate *Alcea cannabina** towering up behind. This small-flowered hollyhock was one of Mr Bowles' favourites. The soft pink flowers have crimson centres and come and go over many weeks. The delicate tracery of its dry stems makes pleasing winter silhouettes.

~ 9 ~

September

September is an easier month than August. The days may be getting a little shorter but there is a dampness and crispness in the air which pleases the plants and enriches the colours of the flowers.

One always associates michaelmas daisies with September, although really they don't get into their stride until more than halfway through the month. A few of the pygmy asters open early. 'Peter Harrison'* in a soft pink, about a foot tall, the paler more compact 'Rosebud'*, and the good white 'Snowsprite'* all start flowering early in September. The others come later in the month. 'Victor'*, the dwarfest of them all, is quite late, and the 'Countess of Dudley'*, a good pink with darker buds, is very late. In between there are various blues, in different heights and habits, but I think the most satisfactory is 'Blue Bouquet'*, with 'Lady-in-Blue'* a close second.

Among the taller ones pink 'Elisabeth Bright'*, which hasn't a trace of mauve in its tones, is always early, and so is an old one I still enjoy, a tight little pink, rather deep in colour, called 'Charles Wilson'*. I like it for the smallness of the flowers. They are a relief after the great shaggy heads of some of the new asters, some of which might almost be taken for annual asters. 'Peace'*, 'Plenty'* and 'Prosperity'* are among the early ones, and so is 'Royal Blue'* and 'Little Boy Blue'*. *Aster acris*, both tall and dwarf, are also in the first flush. The dwarf form of *Aster acris* is neat enough for the rock garden—if it is a fairly large one—and certainly for the front of the border. It makes a soft mound of blue which is a good subject to grow in front of a group of pink or red penstemons such as 'Pink Bedder'* or 'Castle Forbes'. I can't think why I bother to grow the tall form of *acris**. It is never very satisfactory and even when staked adequately looks untidy and skinny. But I never find it easy to cast out plants I have grown a long time. It seems ungrateful and unkind, but I know my garden would be better if I discarded some of the plants that are difficult to grow attractively.

I will never part with a little early red called 'Beechwood Rival'*, although there are newer and better reds now available. My sister gave me this aster when I first embarked on a garden, so I have had it over twenty years and still enjoy its dwarf stature and small crimson flowers. I must have given away hundreds of plants from my original piece; I divide it each year, which is easy as it is a neat little aster and has neat roots.

It is strange that there are still gardens where physostegia isn't grown. It is such an easy plant, with its straight bamboo-like stems and heads of orchid-pink flowers. I used to think it was called "the obedient plant" because it grew straight and gave no trouble, but of course, it is the flowers that are obedient. Push those neatly stacked flowers to one side or the other and they remain just where they are put. *P.* 'Vivid'* is the plant usually grown, and it is still the best in spite of new forms that arrive with glowing recommendations. *P.* 'Rose Bouquet'* and *P.* 'Summer Spire'* are both taller and the flowers are supposed to be pinker, although it is not very noticeable. *P.* 'Summer Spire'* gives colour in late autumn and winter because its tall and slender stems turn a dull crimson. The white-flowered physostegias are very pretty, but with me they don't grow straight and stiff like *P.* 'Vivid'* and fall about most untidily, just as the pale-flowered species *P. virginiana*, from which *P.* 'Vivid'* is developed, is quite incapable of holding up its weak back. I used to grow this because of the delicate colour of its flowers but could find no way of supporting its lanky stems. They increased well, but dealing with them was like handling wet hay.

*Acidanthera murielae** is a gambler's plant. One year it will flower like an angel, and the next it leaves it so late that frost spoils every bloom. It seems to need renewing each year. I haven't found that it mattered if the bulbs are planted later than it says on the packet. Sometimes I don't get mine in till June and still they flower. I try to plant in a little nest of sand and peat, enriched with bone-meal, and water them carefully if the weather is dry.

There is something rather provocative about these triangular white flowers, with their distinct black centres. The scent, when picked, is most seductive and they are nearly as exciting to watch opening as *Gladiolus grandis tristis**, with its rush-like stems which bend and swell in angular jerks.

I don't know why I have only lately been conscious of *Gaura lindheimeri*. A friend who has a lot in her garden says she has grown it for years. I know the garden quite well and can't think how I missed it. It is a late bloomer and perhaps I have never been there in September and October. Of course, after I admired it in this garden I kept running across it in other gardens, which is often the way things happen.

For a year or two I grew gaura and found the plant most entrancing, with its myriad fluttering creamy white flowers, flowers that are not quite like any others. The bud is tinged with pink and when the flowers open the bud sheath makes a background to the petals and gives a soft pink glow to the flowers. I don't know any other flower which has its petals arranged at the top, with a thick bunch of half-inch stamens making the lower part of the flower. The stamens are topped with brown and are clustered round a pale green stigma.

There are quite a number of flowers on each stalk and the buds keep opening as the lower flowers fade.

Gaura is rather a flimsy plant; the stalks are quite tall but they grow rather in a tangled mass, and I think need to be put among other tall plants, but plants of a more solid character so that the dancing white flowers of the gaura come foaming out from a dark background. I planted mine in the open, which was a mistake. I hadn't realised how tall the plant would be. Next I gave it as a companion *Epilobium rosmarinifolium**, which is about the same height and has somewhat the same untidy habit. When rearranging the bed my gauras were moved to a better position in the autumn and they didn't recover. The plant comes from Texas, likes a light, sandy soil and must not be moved till spring. It can be grown from seed and is worth a little trouble.

It is a pity that some really beautiful plants have irritating ways. When *Senecio tangutica** is in full splendour I can't help admiring its striking heraldic foliage and handsome golden heads. The flowers are golden filigree when they open and when the colour has gone the skeleton is shimmering silver. Unlike most plants that turn into silky down, this senecio will keep its shining beauty for a long time if it is cut for the house, but it must be cut at just the right moment. It is too late when the great pointed head has turned to silver; you must chop off your long stalks when the flower-heads are covered with rather bedraggled wisps that look as if they had been dipped in water. In the warmth of the house they soon transform themselves into little balls of down, with metallic bracts behind them. The bracts alone are quite handsome, and look attractive even after the fluff has blown away. That is the credit side. The debit side is not so good. Put *Senecio tangutica** at one end of your border and before you can turn round it will appear at the other end, and pop up in odd places on the way.

I have a very special little sheltered bed between the angle of the back of the cowhouse and the end of the malthouse. This small triangular bed is the haven for rather special plants that I want to keep under my eye. *Lobelia laxifolius** is one of the plants I grow there, and I have *Buddleia* 'Loch Inch' and *Ceanothus burkwoodii** on the wall. Foolishly I planted a small piece of *Senecio tangutica** in this bed, probably because I didn't quite know where else to put it. It very soon took complete possession of my precious sanctuary, and when I decided I must move it because I want to grow the less usual hellebores there, such as *H. torquatus, H. lividus* and *H. purpurascens*, it was quite determined it would not go elsewhere. Although I have got rid of it—so I thought—half a dozen times it continues to reappear. It reminds me of winter heliotrope (*Petasites fragrans*) which I was sold in my very ignorant days and which I planted in this same special corner. Somehow or other I managed to get rid of that determined interloper, so perhaps

I shall succeed with senecio in time. I don't intend to banish it altogether; I shall put one piece in a less valuable spot, because I wouldn't lose it completely. A dry summer helps. I notice that it doesn't at all approve of dry conditions, and I am cruelly planting it now in the driest place in the garden.

The refined form of this groundsel, *S. przewalskii**, is a much more graceful plant, with slender tapering spires of tiny yellow flowers and sharply cut leaves. It needs more moisture than the common plant and shows signs of real distress when it does not get it. It too dries well for the house. So far I have seen no signs that it is a runner but that may be because I put it at the top instead of the bottom of a bank and it is not really happy.

Another senecio that gets really busy in the autumn is the climbing *S. scandens*. It is a most easy and accommodating plant and I think will grow anywhere. I didn't realise this when I foolishly planted it on one of my precious south walls—at the back of the lower rock garden, near the barton gate. I don't know if it is the favoured position or its natural exuberance, but it has made itself into such an enormous smother of green and gold that it is at the mercy of every autumn gale. I am thinking of putting it in a less exposed and less valuable position because I think it would be happy anywhere.

Actually I do not need to move the parent plant as I get many seedlings and can find plenty to try in different parts of the garden. It does well on west and east walls, as well as the one facing south where it mingles with *Senecio leucostachys**, making a lovely symphony of silver, gold and soft green.

I was warned when I introduced the little pink *Convolvulus althaeoides* into the garden that I was letting myself in for trouble. I ought to have heeded the warning when I found how difficult it was to establish. So often plants that are stubborn in the beginning are even more difficult to banish. Certainly this is so in the case of the little pink-flowered convolvulus, with its innocent little flowers and fascinating trails of delicate silver foliage, which start life almost green. I put it— several times before it condescended to grow for me—in the bank at the top of the Lido, and now it has burrowed and wriggled its way over the whole bank. If I want to get rid of it the only thing to do is to dig out the whole bank and start afresh. The next time I shall sink a long drain pipe and cement it at the bottom, and then I suppose Mme Althaeoides will refuse to grow! Actually, there is nothing growing in the bank that is at all incommoded by the convolvulus; the agapanthus and nerines don't deign to notice it. Members of the ginger family that grow here—*Hedychium densiflorum* and *gardnerianum*—are far too tall to be affected and so are the cistuses, but it piles itself on top of *Geranium macrorrhizum* and the white version of *G. phaeum*. It likes to twine through *Cotoneaster horizontalis* and *Genista radiata*, and dodges about among the eryngiums and stachys that grow on the bank. My plant is, I think, *Convolvulus elegantissimus**, and the less beautiful green version is *C. althaeoides*.

Some of the convolvulus family are very well behaved. *C. mauritanicus** spreads slightly, but she does it in a ladylike way, just pushing out gently on all sides but never invading other people's domains. It is not always easy in the beginning and I have given bits to several people who complain that it won't grow for them. I don't think it likes being treated in a haphazard way but will respond if you take enough trouble with it. I like to pull bits off plants, with a few roots attached, and poke them in somewhere else, perhaps with a little sand and peat to help them take hold, and a sprinkle of water to refresh them after their journey. But *C. mauritanicus* won't be treated as casually as that. It pays to pot up the severed fragments in a good sandy potting mixture and when your pot is nicely full of roots, plant out the contents in its permanent position. Then it will make a solid mat, which gets bigger and bigger as the years go by, but remains a compact mass. I planted mine at the bottom of the rock garden near the gate and it now fills the whole pocket. Like our little pink friend it blooms late, and as we get into October and even November it works itself up into a frenzy of flowering and the dark green mat is spangled with charming blue flowers.

By sheer accident one of my September effects was created by ignorance. When I and my husband came to Somerset in 1938 someone in Lancashire asked what they could buy us for the garden and I asked for "autumn crocus"— colchicum. When the bulbs came in the summer I had just finished making rock gardens on the south side of the walls that separated us from the orchard, and of course my new "crocuses" had to go in the new rock garden. Now, of course, I should find a place for them in a special corner or under a hedge or wall. They can be planted at the edge of a shrub plantation, if one has one, or in a woodland garden that is not too shady, for bare earth is no background for these ethereal beauties. There is something very undressed about a glistening white colchicum rising from an earthy bed, and I do not wonder that they are called "naked ladies". You almost feel you must offer a cloak to shield them from the cold, so a nice green background must be conjured up somehow. The rarer colchicums are much too valuable to take their chance under a tangle of coarse ground cover, and the problem is to find something that will make a loose green background and will not develop into a dense mat. In their native home they grow in meadow grass, but very few of us can provide grass that will not be cut in the spring, when the "autumn crocus" produces its gigantic leaves. The great glossy leaves which are so beautiful in their prime are a depressing sight when they are on the way out, and that is why I try to find homes for the colchicums in places where the foliage can make its exit gracefully. When I planted a single bulb on the lowest part of the rock garden the small plant of *Convolvulus mauritanicus** was some way off, but it has grown over the years just as that single bulb has increased to twenty or more. And the colchicums, which happen to be a very deep and lively orchid-pink, appear in September in the middle of the 3-ft clumps of convolvulus. The colour combination is good, for the slaty blue of *C. mauritanicus** in no way competes with the colchicum. But perhaps the best part of this happy accident is the splendid material offered by the convolvulus for arranging over the dying yellow leaves of the colchicum.

I always think of *Phygelius capensis* as a September flower, although some years it starts its season much earlier. I think it likes a wet summer, then it blooms its head off from July till November, and those great heads of coral tubular flowers are very pleasant when there are many blues and greys among the michaelmas daisies. I grow only the ordinary form and am always meaning to get the brighter, redder *P. coccineus**. The more refined *P. aequalis*, in a softer, paler version, with a hint of green and pale bells deepening to orange, is unfortunately not so robust.

There are plenty of penstemons left to brighten the garden. 'Myddleton Gem' is particularly enchanting with its small, crimson, white-throated bells. I try to collect as many plants as possible that were grown by the late E. A. Bowles, and cherish his little penstemon.

The misty blue flowers of *P. heterophyllus* are more friendly because of their touches of pink. Too many blue flowers together tend to be cold, but introduce pink or lavender to the planting and it becomes less distant. The refined version of this penstemon, *P. h.* 'True Blue'*, is usually more esteemed than the type, but I would not want to grow more than two or three plants together, whereas the wide expanse covered by a good plant of *P. heterophyllus* is always cheerful. The reddish leaves probably help too. This is the only herbaceous penstemon I would call a ground-cover plant. Its horizontal habit of growth means that it is seldom more than 9 in above the ground but it can make a plant a yard across.

Sedums and September go together. We are all used to *S. spectabile*, with its flat heads of deep pink that go so well with *Perowskia atriplicifolia**, but not so often seen is the larger, paler edition which is *S. albo-roseum**.

I was once told by a reliable gardener that the variegated herbaceous sedum is a form of *S. albo-roseum**, but I notice that the nurseries who list this attractive plant call it *S. telephium variegatum**. It is as easy as any other sedum but one has to watch for the stems that go back to green and detach them at once. It should be grown in shade to get the best variegation.

The various new and brighter versions of *S. spectabile* are a great improvement on the old-fashioned plant, with its rather crude pink flowers. *S.*

s. 'Brilliant', 'Carmen' and 'Meteor' are new and better forms of *S. spectabile*, but the real break came when *S. s.* 'Autumn Joy'* was introduced. It is a much better plant in every way, taller, straighter and more luxuriant and its large heads of flowers are a much deeper, richer colour. And they keep that colour so well that I never think of cutting this sedum down till the spring, and then I put it off as long as possible.

Sedum telephium seems to have many variations. I have one which grows rather tall with very notched leaves and dark crimson flower-heads, which look like rich velvet. Then there is *S. telephium roseum**, in which the young foliage comes through in shades of pink, turning to normal green as it gets older. *S. telephium* 'Munstead Red' is a most sumptuous plant, with flat heads of dull red and little sprigs of flowers growing at each leaf joint for good measure. I regularly pass two gardens where this sedum is very well grown. In one there is a most impressive mound against a cottage wall, and in the other a whole bed high above the road is tightly packed with it and it looks—as one drives past—like an oriental carpet. One called *S. t.* 'Coral Cluster' has bright coral-coloured flowers.

That is not the end of the herbaceous sedums. For years I have been puzzled by a stranger that somehow got into my garden and to which I couldn't give a name. It is big and fleshy and rather indeterminate in colour, and the flower-heads are the same pale bronzy crimson as the leaves and stalk. Now I learn that it is *Sedum maximum**, the rather dowdy member of the family to which the magnificent *Sedum maximum atropurpureum** belongs. This magnificent plant is twice as tall as most of the sedums and needs a little staking if it is in an exposed position. I like to see it grown against a background of silver or very pale green. Some people consider bronze-foliaged plants are not quite the thing for the garden. They don't actually call them ugly but they certainly don't rave about them. But I think more of us are coming to realise that the use of different coloured foliage takes a garden out of the ordinary rut, and a group of this handsome sedum can be really exciting.

Sedums seem to mix themselves up, like other plants. You never know how a chance seedling will develop. I am always meeting new ones in other people's gardens. My latest find is a very tall and well-developed specimen, with large leaves which are tinged with red, but not all red like *S. m. atropurpureum**. The stalks are tinged as well and the immense flower-heads are green, at least they were on the plant I saw, but it is possible they might be going to turn red later on. These big sedums are good value in the way of colour, but they have not the neat habit of *Sedum spectabile*, which gives no trouble at any time in its life.

Most of the yellow sedums are dwarf and better suited to a rock garden or crazy paving, but *S. aizoon* is 18 in high and a good border plant. The flowers are bright yellow, but grown in a pleasant green setting they are toned down. There is another useful sedum with pale green flowers that looks well growing between stones at the front of the border. It is too big for the rock garden and does not grow straight and sturdily enough for an ordinary herbaceous bed but is delightful on the top of a wall. I haven't yet discovered its name.

One of the most attractive new plants I have met of recent years is *Scutellaria canescens**. I am not sure if it is really new, perhaps only to me, but when I first saw it I had to stop and gloat over it, and I returned again before I left the garden to have another look.

It is not very tall, perhaps 15 in high, and it makes a neat, bushy plant simply smothered with small slaty blue flowers. Perhaps slaty blue makes one think that the plant is drab, which it certainly isn't. The flowers are very delicate and the whole effect is soft and feathery. It is a lovely thing to grow with some of the more robust colours of early September, but I haven't yet found the right way to treat it. I have had it and lost it twice, just as I lose the delicious little lavender satureia which also blooms in September. Both are rather woody plants and there is something about my garden that they don't like. But I am determined to find out the right way to keep the two plants happy; both have that lovely hazy colouring that one needs for garden harmony.

I don't think I am alone in finding these two plants somewhat difficult. They used to appear in several nurserymen's lists but have been dropped. Strangely, the scutellaria got through the terrible winter of 1962–3 without trouble, so it may be damp rather than cold that it dislikes.

Satureia subspicata* is a tiny shrub with deep lavender-blue flowers. It looks rather like a glamorous winter savory, of which it is a relation. Perhaps not very striking, but one of those interesting little plants that give a cache to a garden.

There are some plants that appeal because of their rarity rather than their beauty. The individual flowers of the tiny *Nerine foliosa* are very delicate and spidery. The workmanship is exquisite but they don't make much show grown in the ordinary way; I think they are best if one has a bank or raised bed to give them. Then their delicate beauty can be seen and admired. There is another small nerine, *fimbriata*, and this too is fragile and lovely and needs to be planted at eye level.

All the nerines look their best in a narrow bed at the base of a south wall. I have seen them grown in ordinary flower beds in sheltered districts, but I like them best making a colourful fringe at the bottom of a wall. In most places they need that wall and the south aspect if they are to flower well, and it seems to suit their personality. For most people the ordinary *Nerine bowdenii* is rather a miracle. It looks so much more like a greenhouse plant than an ordinary hardy perennial, but its easy ways are being discovered and many people are adding it to their gardens. The form attributed to the late Mark Fenwick is undoubtedly a better plant but unless the two are grown side by side the average gardener is quite satisfied with *N. bowdenii*. There is a white nerine, but though I took the greatest care of it I did not succeed in growing it. For most people the attractiveness of nerines is their brilliant cerise at a time when that colour is scarce, so why a white one? White flowers have great charm and I'd like to have a white version of every flower in the garden.

Every year I hope to find new and interesting annuals. *Argemone mexicana* was growing in the Cambridge Botanic Gardens and I was enchanted by the delicacy of its colouring. It makes a symphony in soft grey-green and primrose, and I believe comes in other pastel shades as well. This poppy-like plant is a hardy annual and I am hoping will seed itself. The seed-pods are distinct and decorative, and probably are the reason for its common names of "Devil's fig" or "prickly poppy".

*Humea elegans** growing in a wall border at Hampton Court with plumbago and other not very hardy plants made me decide to try again with this most aromatic of all plants. It is quite beautiful when growing and nothing scents the house in winter so sweetly and mysteriously as its feathery brown plumes. It is most rightly called the incense plant.

The green form of *Amaranthus caudatus* has definite charm, but I think it is usually more effective when picked and carefully arranged than when growing. Those long and graceful racemes should be seen hanging in all their beauty, not brushing the earth with their weight, so the way to grow it is on a high bed, so that the full beauty of the plant is seen.

I was given seeds of the tassel flower, *Cacalia coccinea*, and I had no idea how very pretty and obliging it would be. I dislike orange flowers when they are that hard, crude colour that grates and clashes, but the orange of the tassel flower is dark and soft, and is well backgrounded by the bright green of the foliage. Once it starts the plant never stops flowering and its bright little flowers are still swaying in the cold winds of November.

The seed of the green-flowered *Nicotiana rustica* was given to me and raised for me by friends. I don't notice a very strong scent with the plant but its little frilled green flowers are delightful, and it makes a tall and solid plant and so far has come up every year since I have had it.

~ Part Two ~

There is no blue quite like the real sky-blue of *Salvia patens*. This plant used to be grown much more than it is today. It was treated as a dahlia but had to go with so many other nice things when labour, or the lack of it, decided what kind of gardens we must have. I believe that *Salvia paten*s will winter outside in some districts if it is planted very deep and given a nice warm cover. I have a friend who plants *Stachys lanata** on top and the salvia loves its grey blanket and comes up faithfully each year. Another way is to take cuttings as one does for penstemon. They root easily, as do all the salvias, and seem to flower more readily than the old plants do.

The yellow-flowered alpine strawberry, *Fragaria indica**, makes a lovely show in September, with its round red berries. They are so fat and luscious that one is tempted to eat them, but though edible they are tasteless and rather unpleasant and there is no temptation to despoil the plant. The birds seem to agree about this too, so their dark leaves and shining fruit make most beautiful, although rampant, autumn ground cover. I don't know what controls the flowers of the myrtle. In spite of being cut back quite badly in the winter it will sometimes produce a good crop of fuzzy cream flowers in September, particularly after a wet summer. I notice that when my myrtle flowers other people's do too, so I think the weather is responsible. Plenty of water in dry weather may be the answer. We can't stop it getting pinched and brown in the winter but we can try for a froth of bloom in the autumn, to be followed by shiny black berries.

Fuchsias are a great standby at this time of year. They seem to come into their stride now and one is grateful for those graceful little bushes simply dripping with crimson and purple, cerise and pink and white. I have half a dozen little fuchsias that survive my winters and cheer the autumn garden. Upright or spreading, single, double, pale and dark—alas, I have no names for them as I was given cuttings by friends and neighbours, who gave them no names. The ones I do know and can recommend are 'Mrs Popple', who grows bigger and more vigorous each year, and makes a splurge of strong colour until November. Fuchsia 'Tom Thumb' is at the other end of the scale, a perfect miniature and seemingly just as hardy. Then there is the big and graceful *F. magellanica*, with its delicate white and pink flowers, and the soft and spreading variegated form. My favourite fuchsia is 'Mme Cornelissen' with its flowers of crimson and white. Although listed as hardy I am not sure about her hardiness, having lost her more than once, and yet she survives in places far colder than where I am. Some people cover their fuchsias with bracken and evergreen boughs in the winter, which is probably a wise precaution but one I never take.

Chrysanthemums belong to the autumn and their scent conjures up bonfires and fallen leaves. So I do not take kindly to chrysanthemums in July; on the other hand I would be very pleased if I could persuade some of my favourites to bloom before the end of October—or even later. There are several that do, of course;

the old-fashioned 'Anastasia', an enthusiastic pom-pom in mauve-pink. She has a bronze counterpart and I used to have one of the same kind in pale pink. 'Dr Tom Parr'* flowers early and is altogether satisfactory. The colour is rose madder which fades to a pinkish bronze. A crimson dwarf called 'Brightness' is lovely but hasn't the stamina of the old varieties. I want chrysanthemums that are as reliable and trouble-free as other herbaceous plants, and those that have to be renewed every year are really a luxury. It is a luxury in which I indulge in the case of 'Tapestry Rose', a delightful single with soft coral-pink petals and green centres. It may be a Korean but if so it has a little more staying power than the other Koreans, which never stay long for me; but even 'Tapestry Rose' has usually to be renewed every year or two.

The cottage chrysanthemums are even later in their blooming. Sometimes they leave it so late that they have to compete with wind, rain and sodden leaves. A pleasant single pink called 'Innocence' is usually out by the end of September. It isn't as tall as some of the other cottage types, the yellows and bronzes, and that interesting old gentleman, the 'Emperor of China'. I have given up growing some of these in the orthodox way as it seems impossible to make them grow straight, even with the most careful staking. I planted the bronze variety under a tall bush of *Helichrysum gunii*. The first year it worked according to plan. The helichrysum produced its pink flowers in late spring, and in September, when all it had to show were brown tufts, the chrysanthemum thrust its long stems through the needled foliage and the bronze flowers were framed by dark green. Then came a disastrous winter and the poor helichrysum succumbed. I didn't cut it to the ground, as I did many things, but left about 2 ft of dead wood. The chrysanthemums did what they could with this support fountaining above the tree stump. Some of the longest stems couldn't manage to stay upright and where they sagged to the ground they rooted, which suggests possibilities of doing better things with the lanky chrysanthemums. The cottage yellow is tall but not so tall as the bronze, and it looks quite well if grown close to the tall *Anaphalis yedoensis** so that the soft yellow heads of the chrysanthemums intermingle with the fluffy white heads and silver leaves of the anaphalis.

The 'Emperor of China' is a pink chrysanthemum with darker buds and deeper shades in the flowers. The leaves carry on the same theme with many crimson leaves among the green. It is not quite so tall as the others. A dwarf pink called 'Gloria' is a pleasant little chrysanthemum for the front of the border, and a little later another old variety with tiny, gold-centred, crimson flowers comes into bloom. The only name I have for this is Tiny, and though it fits it I feel there must be another more responsible name. It isn't as easy as some of the others, and I am very careful when I try to increase it because I should hate to lose those eager little flowers which positively glow at me across the garden.

Perhaps my favourite of all the hardy chrysanthemums is the last to flower, the beautiful scented 'Wedding Day', with its large, single white flowers with their green centres. I have this one growing through a shrub too. I planted it below a good bush of *Phlomis fruticosa* and it has pushed its way up through the branches, as I intended it should, and the beauty of its flowers is enhanced by the soft grey-green leaves.

A useful orchid-coloured flower which is at its best in late September is *Chelone obliqua*. Its pouched flowers grow against the 2-in stems, which are straight and strong and do not need staking. The white version of this plant is easier to place, but quite accidentally I planted the type flower close to *Sedum telephium* 'Munstead Red', with good effect.

Also in orchid pink, but in a much deeper tone, *Senecio pulcher* flowers in autumn—that is, if it flowers at all. For some reason this groundsel is difficult to find and not at all easy when once it is found. It has long fleshy leaves, slightly jagged at the edges; the daisy flowers are fleshy too and grow on stems that should be 2 in high but are often more dwarf. A nurseryman, who called to see me when this flower was in bloom, looked at my plant and said, "I see you don't grow this very well either." I was, in fact, rather proud that I had managed to keep my *S. pulcher* for five or six years, and was grateful that it flowered at all. I grow it in a narrow bed beside a stone path and see that it gets plenty of water. I wonder if it would do better in a really wet place, but so far I haven't had the courage to lift or divide it. Another senecio that I grow, *S. smithii*, definitely prefers a damp place and does well in the wettest place in the ditch.

We are ungrateful in the way we chivvy certain plants when they are not adding to the garden scene but appreciate their beauty quite enthusiastically at their flowering—or fruiting—time. The thick, questing roots of the giant form of *Physalis franchetii** are always in my bad books. They appear in places where I have never planted this "Chinese lantern" and stray a long way from the spots where they are supposed to grow, choking more important plants. But one forgets all that in September when the "lanterns" start to turn. The colour they eventually attain is a clear mandarin-red and they reach it through green, yellow and shades of orange. The light green leaves add to the picture and for a finishing touch there are often some of the small cream flowers open at the top of the spike. This gorgeous colour is very welcome in the autumn and particularly when one comes on it suddenly under trees. Then there is never enough of the glowing plant for it looks so lovely amid all the green that it hurts to pick many of the spikes. And yet they are needed for drying and to satisfy all the requests that come from the people who don't bother to grow it and realise its potentialities only when they see its brilliant autumn display.

Strobilanthes atropurpurea doesn't get much attention at any time, which is a pity because its dark blue flowers are really very pleasing in a quiet way and go well with the dark, hairy leaves. It comes when strong, dark colours are needed to temper the richness of goldenrods and the many yellow daisies that bloom in August and September. A member of the acanthus family, this 2-in perennial is quite hardy but most of its relations are greenhouse plants. Its name means "cone-flower", from the buds, which are cone-shaped. I grow it with *Erigeron philadelphicus*, which flowers early and late.

Another September plant which really should be better appreciated is *Stokesia cyanea**, "Stoke's aster". The large-fringed lavender cornflowers grow on 9-in stems, so it is a good choice for the front of the border. Its rather narrow, long leaves are glossy and quite attractive in winter. It goes well with sedums.

Ceratostigma plumbaginoides is esteemed when it is in flower but for the rest of the year gets black looks because of its rather possessive ways. It soon outgrows a pocket in the rock garden and edges its way along crevices and under stones until it has covered a great deal of space that belongs to other flowers. Its wiry roots do not seem to have any beginning or any end and are quite tough. In September, of course, it starts its autumn display, its leaves turning crimson to show up the intense blue of the small flowers. It doesn't always flower well, and I understand the way to bring it to its senses is to plant it in very poor soil in such tight quarters as are afforded by the top of a wall or a narrow pocket between stones which has no way out. Bergenias make a good contrast.

The little pink and white daisies of *Erigeron mucronatus** come and go throughout the summer and seem to take a new interest in life in the autumn, when the plants are more thickly trimmed with flowers than at any other time. This little plant can be a nuisance with its seeding ways and the way to grow it is at the bottom of walls and in crevices as at the R. H. S. Gardens at Wisley. The very severe winter of 1962–3 showed us that it isn't quite as tough as we thought, and I think the plants that survived will get more respect in future.

We have always taken for granted the ravishing deep pink *Schizostylis* 'Mrs Hegarty'*. Admittedly, it didn't make such strong plants as the later, paler 'Viscountess Byng'*, whose flower spikes are taller and fleshier, but it grew quite well and every scrap of stem or root made a new plant, so everyone had a shock when the bad winter nearly wiped out all the stocks of this, the most popular Kaffir lily.

Though *Cyclamen neapolitanum** usually appears in small quantities in August, it is in September that it really flowers in earnest, and the corms are covered with myriads of fluttering little pink flowers which do not get their full background of leaves till October. *C. graecum*, with its lovely leaves, flowers in September and

October. The flowers can be white or pink, but often we have to be content with leaves only.

Liriope is such a modest little plant that one is inclined to forget all about it until the spikes of deep blue flowers appear among the dark, grassy leaves. It comes from China and is evergreen; the best plants I have ever seen were growing in shade but some people grow it in sun. There seem to be two species, *Liriope muscari* and *L. graminifolia**, but they look very much the same to me. I have recently been given a white liriope, and that should be even better for autumn, because the white flowers will look well in dark corners. I call the colour of my liriope dark blue; sometimes it is described as violet-purple, but whatever it is the plant has great character and a single specimen grown in a paved terrace or a large rock garden makes quite a sensation. It is not the type of plant to grow with other things of the same height. Alone with grey stones round it, it shows up very well.

A variegated plant which looks like liriope and often has white flowers is called *Opthiopogon spicatus**. It is not so tough or generous as the liriope, although it is a near relation. *Liriope hyacinthiflora** has spikes of pale pink, but I haven't grown it yet. All the various types have the same thickly encrusted spikes of flower, rather like crystallised lavender.

Although *Eryngium giganteum* flowers earlier in the summer, it is in September when it loses its colour substance and becomes a whitened ghost. The great gardeners of the beginning of the century appreciated this prickly subject, which has all the soft colour and good contour of an eryngium when it first comes out but becomes white and papery instead of fading. The famous Miss Willmott of Warley loved it so much that it is sometimes known as "Miss Willmott's Ghost" and the late Gertrude Jekyll loved it too. It is a biennial and sows itself generously, but with its long tap-roots it must be moved before it gets too big.

Most of micghaelmas daisies wait until October to come into thier full glory, but the *A. amellus* varieties are earlier, and such old friends as 'King George'* in rich blue, 'Brilliant'* in deep pink and the pale pink 'Sonia'* come out in September. One of the most refined of these single asters is 'Ultramarine'*, which has rather smaller flowers in very dark blue, on long stalks. But I have never found it as easy as the others, which are still with me, while 'Ultramarine'* is not. A newer one, and a very reliable variety, is 'Lac de Genève'* in medium blue.

Aster frikartii* is a hybrid between *A. amellus* and *thompsonii*. It is taller than either and rather more delicate in colouring and construction although very strong constitutionally. It needs to be planted rather far back in the border and its delicate form and colour show up against pink dahlias. People have different ideas of colour. I would call the large flowers of *A. frikartii** ('Glory of Staffa') lavender-blue, and the centres golden, yet I see it is described by one nursery as "peacock-blue with orange centre". Many of the ericoides and cordifolia asters bloom in October, but there is one which is at its best in September. *A. ercoides* 'Delight' is a most graceful plant, with branching, whippy stems covered with tiny white flowers. It lasts well in water and does for the flower arranger what *Aster tradescantii** does later on.

~ 10 ~

October

Against the reds and golds of the turning leaves the autumn gentians make a wonderful carpet of blue. To get a real effect I think these gentians should be grown as a drift and not dotted about in small clumps. I shall never forget a long bed of gentians in full flower in the garden of Sissinghurst Castle, or the carpets of blue on either side of a path that winds down through the trees to the lake in front of Forde Abbey.

Those of us with lime-ridden soil have to resort to all manner of expedients to keep our lime-hating gentians. In one garden I know they were planted in old buckets and washtubs, filled with peat and sunk in the soil, with adequate holeage, of course. I have tried all sorts of things. For some reason they don't get on too well in small troughs filled with peat, but in a wet year I have adequate success in a raised peat bed, made with outside walls of peat blocks and a filling of peat mould.

They are quite happy in old kitchen sinks, sunk below ground level and filled to the brim with peat mixed with a little sand. But again they need plenty of water. In a wet summer those hidden sinks are a sheet of blue, with *Gentiana macaulayi** and *G. newburyi** competing with *G. sino-ornata* in their lustiness.

I used to have a *G.* 'Kidbrook'* seedling but it disappeared one dry summer. *G.* 'Inverleith' still lingers on in a sink near the garden door. It doesn't increase, but on the other hand it hasn't died, so I leave it where I can enjoy to the full the intense blue of the flowers. I don't know whether it is particularly ungainly in its growth or whether I notice it more in the sink, but it does seem to have unusually long and unkempt straggling stems after it has finished flowering.

My latest adventure with *Gentiana sino-ornata* seems to be the most successful of all. When we bought this house we had to make our own electricity and a little stone shed had been built on to the back of the house. When we had mains service the little shed was used for apples, tools and odds and ends, and I can't think why I didn't realise it was an unnecessary excrescence years ago. Not only did it spoil an expanse of beautiful wall, but it took up space that could be used more usefully.

When at last I came to my senses and had the shed removed I realised I had space for a bed facing north, one of the most desirable places in the garden for all manner of plants.

I was offered some greensand, so I made the bed with that on a good layer of drainage stones. Large lumps of hamstone break up the bed, and when extra soil is needed I now use peat. Here I planted *Gentiana sino-ornata*, among other plants, and even in the driest summer they are completely happy and I can divide them several times a year if I want to.

It always interests me to see how Mother *sino-ornata* carries her young. Sometimes one lifts a clump and it practically falls to pieces, being made up of many little plants, with a tiny tuft of green on top and two white thrusting roots which straddle the big fleshy stem-root of the parent. If the gentian is really enjoying itself and making long arms in all directions they are soon pegged down to the soil with dozens of little plants again straddling the parent stem. On digging up such a stem it looks at first as if it were developing roots all along its length, but on inspection one discovers that they are tiny new plants and each can be lifted off the stem and planted elsewhere. This often happens in the autumn, so that there is no end to the number of plants that can be produced if one has time. It doesn't matter how often it is done because no breaking apart is required, the little plants are not attached in any way and are perfectly happy when replanted in damp soil. A good plant to grow near autumn gentians is the queer little *Fuchsia procumbens*, with green and red flowers, but it needs a very sheltered spot.

Many people wonder why we bother to grow the white flowered *Gentiana saxosa*. The whole point about gentians, they say, is the wonderful blue of their flowers. I agree; all the same I want to grow the white gentian. *G. saxosa* is a very charming little flower that is a joy to grow in any garden. One can forget about its being a gentian and grow it as a fascinating alpine plant, with white flowers and dark, shining leaves. Not everyone gets excited about white *Gentiana sino-ornata* any more than *G. saxosa*. And, again, if it was some other genus we should rave about its snow-white trumpets with a touch of green at the base.

To me *Schizostylis* 'Mrs Hegarty'* is the most beautiful of all the schizostylis, but not everyone agrees. The colour is a pure deep coral. For some reason there is often a muddle between *S.* 'Mrs Hegarty'* and *S.* 'Viscountess Byng'*, and Lady Byng, being the stronger, is always being sent instead of 'Mrs Hegarty'*. I have nothing against Her Ladyship, with her thick, fleshy stems and slender pale pink flowers as delicate as satin. I want them both, 'Mrs Hegarty'* to contrast with the cheerful scarlet *S. coccinea*, and *S.* 'Viscountess Byng'* to carry on when the others have finished.

There are two other red Kaffir lilies. The one found by Professor Tom Barnard* and named after him is more carmine than scarlet and the flower is more open and star-like. The other is the giant form of *coccinea*. The stems are often 2 in long and the flower big in proportion. But I must admit that a well-grown ordinary *S. coccinea*, if it has plenty of moisture, can sometimes grow nearly as big as a giant.

The schizostylis we are all looking for is a white-flowered one. I understand that an occasional albino occurs in their native South Africa, and I have asked friends to send me corms or seed, but so far there has been no white schizostylis.

The time schizostylis flower is also affected by the weather, I think. In a wet year they start in bloom quite early, *S. coccinea* sometimes in August, 'Mrs Hegarty'* soon after and 'Viscountess Byng'* in September. But the flowers in a dry year are very late, with Lady Byng only starting to flower at the beginning of November and carrying on till Christmas. I have picked a big bunch of these delicate pink flowers on Christmas Day in a year when we had no bad frosts until the New Year.

I am glad that we are paying more attention to kniphofias these days. When I was young we weren't so discriminating. There would be a clump of the ordinary orange kniphofias in nearly every garden but they didn't get much attention. Dead heads and dead leaves would be removed, bits would be taken off to be given away or thrown out when the clump got too big, but no one worried about different colours or different types of plant.

Not being fond of orange in the garden, I never paid much attention to kniphofias (or tritomas) until I was introduced to the lovely ivory 'Maid of Orleans'. Her delicate tone and generous habit have endeared her to me, and I enjoy too the green-tipped spikes of *Kniphofia* 'Bee's Lemon', and pale yellow of *K.* 'Brimstone'.

But orange and tawny kniphofias are still very popular. I was amused to hear some visitors to my garden discussing some of those that I grow: "I don't call them 'Red-hot Pokers' when they are yellow. I think they ought to be orange."

I am sure my visitors would approve of the free-flowering species, *snowdoni**, which is still sending up long and delicate spikes of bright coral at the end of October. This is the only kniphofia that runs, so far as I know, and that makes it very easy to increase. The dainty little orange *K. galpinii** also flowers late in the year, and so does *K.* 'Elf'*, not quite such a dwarf as its name would suggest. It is bigger than *K. galpinii**, rather more sturdy in build and with flowers of a brighter colour.

Only recently I was given a kniphofia of quite a different character. *K. comosum** has a mop head, with rather prominent stamens and flowers of a light, clear tangerine. The effect is rather shaggy, and distinctly showy, but the plant has the reputation of being slightly tender and needs planting in a hot, dry place.

When I was given *K. northii** I did not realise that I was introducing such a surprising plant into the garden. Instead of narrow, upright leaves, which become untidy and flop about over other plants, this plant has enormous stiff leaves which make gigantic rosettes. They are smooth, grey-green in colour and so exotic that it is difficult to believe they are members of the homely "Red-hot Poker" family. The solid flower spikes are in proportion, their greeny yellow flowers tipped with coral.

K. caulescens is a smaller edition of this exotic, more grey than green, with stems like elephant trunks which grow sideways and root in the ground. The flowers are solid too and their soft coral tones fade to pale greeny yellow.

I would not plant either of these kniphofias with ordinary civilised plants in a well-regulated herbaceous border. Both they and the other plants would feel a little embarrassed, but planted in an isolated position, in the same way as one would grow a yucca, they are a great success. They flower earlier than two other kniphofias which are outstanding in a more orthodox way.

I knew *K.* 'Prince Igor' was a large kniphofia, but I wasn't prepared for the 5-ft spikes that rose up among more lowly plants in my garden. And when those stout stems produced 18-in spikes of brilliant colour it looked as though flaming torches were being carried through the garden. They were so much higher than anything near them that it did not really matter what companions they had, but the variegated form of the single kerria which happened to be growing alongside made pleasant contrast, with its delicate, fluttering leaves.

Even later than the Prince, *K.* 'C.M. Prichard'* is also big, but not nearly so tall. The flower-heads are rather wide in proportion to their length, and are shaded from coral to lemon-yellow. It has as companions in the long border the cottage-garden daisy, *Chrysanthemum uliginosum*. This plant is also built on massive lines with roots in proportion. In an ordinary bed it soon races up to 4 or 5 ft, and I believe in a really damp place it will easily reach 7 or 8 ft. The white flowers, with their greenish centres, are not outsize but are firm and flat, and a contrast to the lavender-blue *Aster frikartii* which grows nearby and is still blooming in October.

I do not think there is any excuse for the October garden to be dull. Cimifugas flower extremely late, but it is worth waiting for them. They don't like dry conditions and should be given as damp a place in the garden as possible. Although *C. cordifolia** and 'White Pearl'* may sometimes start flowering in August they go on for some time, and *C. racemosa* and *C. ramosa** are at their best in September and October. *C. ramosa** is a particularly spectacular plant, tall with large and graceful foliage and great plumes of creamy white flowers.

Some people are worried by the peculiar scent of the ferny leaves of this plant, which is supposed to be abhorrent to bugs. It gives the plant its colloquial name of "bugbane" and its Latin name.

It is always encouraging when an old plant comes back into cultivation. Years ago *Bidens atropurpurea* was grown regularly. With its tuberous roots it was treated like a dahlia. Now it is known as *Cosmos atrosanguineus* and the few nurseries that do list it charge quite a high price. It is one of the richest-looking flowers I know, with typical cosmos flowers in smouldering mahogany. The colour of the flowers is intensified because the centre is exactly the same colour as the petals, and the few tiny yellow specks from the stamens don't lighten the flower at all. The scent of the flowers is rich too, for they smell just like hot chocolate, the richest chocolate one can imagine, and when I put my nose to this cosmos I am back in a little patisserie in Brussels.

There is a white form, but it is rather washed out against the deep colour of *C. atrosanguineus*.

The cordifolius asters flower later than some of the others. There are some beautiful plants in this category: 'Silver Spray', 'Blue Star' and *elegans**. The old variety called 'Photograph' is in the same group, and has soft blue flowers very slightly larger than the others.

Aster tradescantia* is another old one, and a member of the ericioides family. It is extremely graceful, with long arching stems and feathery foliage, with many small white daisy flowers. One of its particular attractions is the way the yellow centres of the flowers remain yellow. The centres of many of these asters discolour and become dingy after the flowers have been out a few days, but not *tradescantia*.

That complaint cannot be applied to another little aster that opens late in the season: *A. diffusus horizontalis* a real brunette, with dark reddish leaves and cherry-coloured centres to the small blue flowers. It seldom reaches 2 in and the flat, flower-studded stems put it in a class quite by itself.

'Empress' is a larger edition and, like *A. diffusus horizontalis**, it gains in beauty as it ages. When the flowers first come out they are rather washy and lacking in character and every year I am puzzled and wonder why I gave house room to such an insipid plant. But after it has been out for a week or ten days I find myself drifting back to admire its display of flowers, which thickly cover every stem. The flowers seem to increase in size as the days go by. The lavender petals get more shaggy and the ruby centres deeper in colour.

Gardeners are divided into two classes, those who grow michaelmas daisies and those who don't. I am in the first category and there are times when I wish I had the strength of mind to scrap all the hybrids and grow only the species, but I realise the garden would lose a lot of colour if I did, though I should not have the yearly worry of what to do with all the different asters I collect in the course of a year. In big gardens the problem is solved by having a michaelmas daisy border, and the wonderful horseshoe bed filled with them in the Savill Gardens in Windsor Great Park is a magnificent sight in the autumn. Grown in this way one can compare and decide which are the best and which can be scrapped without sacrificing a garden asset.

As a complete contrast to the gaiety and richness of asters and dahlias there are two subdued little autumn plants that I like very much. Both flower in October and both have character and charm, but they need to have the stage to themselves; one might feel their colour was rather indeterminate against more flashy plants. *Calamintha nepetioides** is a neat little bush under 12 in high, covered with small flowers in the softest, palest lavender. It is not difficult to please. I grow it in full sun, and I noticed it growing just as happily in a shady border in the garden of Hidcote. I saw *Scutellaria indica japonica** in a terrace bed at Hidcote too. It is a plant that needs moisture and then it makes quite a large sprawling mat of grey, velvety foliage. The flowers are deep lilac, they start quite early in the year and they are usually still blooming in October. It is by no means a spectacular plant but has charm and shows up brighter flowers.

The dwarf polygonums are cheerful October flowers. They flower on and off all through the year, but I think we notice them more in October, or it may be that they are really getting into their stride then and give their best display.

The tiny *Polygonum vaccinifolium** really needs to be grown in a wide sweep to be effective. I always admire the wonderful display it makes in the rock garden at Kew, covering large surfaces of their enormous rocks. It grows quite happily for me among stones at the side of the path, and now I am leaving it alone it is increasing quite nicely. I used to think it was an easy plant and when anyone asked me for a bit I tore off a lump and thought my plant wouldn't mind. But it did, and very soon I had hardly any left. I have seen it looking lovely with *Cyclamen neapolitanum**.

*Polygonum affine**, for all its leathery appearance, is a much easier plant. Some people say it does not flower well for them, but it has always behaved well for me. I grow it in several stony places in the garden, and I think it likes best to grow among the stones that edge the drive and then it can slip down from the stones and anchor itself in the path. It seems happier at the edge of a path than anywhere and I sometimes tear off pieces and put them along the edge of the path against the stones, where weeds delight to grow. I was amused one day when a visitor asked me for a bit and pointed to a lump I had carefully planted at the edge of the path, "I am sure you don't want that bit there." It was too difficult to explain that I like things growing where they shouldn't sometimes. Now I use it in the various scabby places at the edges of paths and round garage doors, at the base of water butts, and where the hard surface of the path has gone and something needs to be grown to keep down the weeds.

The new *P. affine* 'Darjeeling Red'* has flowers of real crimson, although they don't always come the right colour when they start. I put in this plant and was most disappointed when the first flowers were the same pale pink of the ordinary variety. Afterwards the flowers were deeper and more vivid, so I needn't have worried.

Several new forms of *Polygonum affine** have come to us from recent expeditions and they are grown extremely well in the rock garden at Kew. The most brilliant is the Loundes' variety*, with much finer flowers.

Although I admit its good qualities, I find *Corydalis luteus* rather too persistent in its seeding habits and spend much time tearing it from walls and flower beds. Now the pale-flowered form, *C. ochreleuca**, is another matter and my complaint with it is that it doesn't seed at all—at least not with me. With great care I put my newly acquired plant in a part of the garden where I have none of the common variety, and I hoped I should soon have a colony of seedlings, but so far there haven't been any. Most evergreen corydalis seed themselves well. The ferny leaved *Corydalis cheilanthifolia* sows itself and produces its yellow-green flowers for months on end. They look very pretty against the bronze leaves. Even more attractive is the soft rose madder *Corydalis rubra* which has foliage in the most delicate half-tones and flowers to match.

*Antirrhinum asarina** either likes you very much or not at all. In some gardens it seeds itself so much that it is a nuisance and in others it won't grow at all, let alone seed. I like its pale primrose flowers and grey-green leaves and its habit of trailing down over stones, and for years I tried it in different parts of the garden without success. It was not until it was planted in a large stone sink filled with greensand that it settled down at all, and once growing well it started seeding, and very soon there were trails down the front of the trough and seedlings in every corner, mingling with the bright blue flowers of *Parochetus communis*.

Eomecon chionantha has something of a halo, probably because it is not very well known. Perhaps that is just as well, because most of the people who grow it find it a nuisance. It has very nice leaves shaped rather like a large nasturtium and with a pleasant glaucous finish. It is sometimes called the "Cyclamen Poppy"; I don't know why because its leaves don't look much like cyclamen leaves. Its other name, "Poppy of the Dawn", doesn't raise any queries in one's mind. The flowers are pretty and they do look like small poppies with white petals and large yellow centres. They start in summer and will go on till October and November, but do not flower very much for me, and other people seem to have the same experience. The plant is a runner and I often wonder if it would flower better if we could find some means of controlling its wandering stems and make it give a little more thought to producing flowers. I agree its foliage is almost as beautiful as that of bocconia, but I feel I should like it more if it kept to one place instead of appearing some yards from the parent plant. It is a wily plant, for one treats its succulent stems with great respect, thinking they are as brittle as those of *Dicentra spectabilis*, whereas they have the iron will of such plants as *Corydalis luteus**, which looks brittle and fragile and yet finds a foothold in all sorts of places, from which it cannot be easily removed.

~ Part Two ~

It is a good thing that some of the less spectacular plants flower late in the year; it is so easy to overlook them at their ordinary flowering time if that comes when a great many plants are in bloom, most of which are more showy. I noticed a plant of marjoram blooming in a friend's garden in late October and learned it was the Bury Hill form of *Origanum vulgare*, with heliotrope and indigo flowers on slender dark stems. In a sunny spot it makes a good companion for *Oxalis floribunda**.

Origanum laevigatum is even more attractive, but it is a good thing that it flowers late in the year when there is not much competition. From a tight carpet of dark, glaucous leaves less than an inch high rise 12-in slender stems which have corymbs of small violet flowers. It grows rather slowly and so is not very easy to increase. I have it growing next to the blue flax *Linum perenne*, with the rich claret *Cosmos astrosanguineus*, very near, and the colours blend very happily.

*Serratula shawii** is another rather subdued little plant which has considerable charm if only one takes the trouble to find it. The flowers are of the cornflower type, rather small and in a subdued shade of mauve. They nestle in delicate bronze ferny foliage. The plant doesn't increase very fast but its roots run slightly and hang on, so that when once it has been grown in the garden small pieces will come up in the same place each year, even though the original plant has been moved elsewhere. It makes a good companion for the grey leaves of *Geranium rynardii*.

The other serratula I grow, *S. coronata*, flowers a little earlier and is as big as the other is tiny. The flowers are the same thistle shape and dark purple in colour and they come on 5-ft stems. The whole plant is very strong and massive and could well be used in a place where something as big and dense as a shrub is needed.

Blue flowers tone most beautifully with dwarf chrysanthemums, particularly the little blue daisies that flower so frenziedly in the autumn. Though *Aster pappei** and *Agathaea coelestis** do start flowering in late summer, it is not till late

September and October that they really get going, and then they seem to produce as many flowers as they can before frosts finish their season. They are not hardy and must be kept going with cuttings. If one has a greenhouse the flowering plants can be lifted, potted and transferred to the greenhouse where they will flower all through the winter. *Aster pappei** has very fine, dark green foliage and in *Agathaea coelestis** the leaves are wider, more the size and shape of box, but both have the small kingfisher-blue daisies that are so welcome in the autumn.

White flowers are needed to tone down the crude yellow of *Chrysanthemum* 'Janté Wells'. I don't know the history of this plant but I can never believe that it is an old one. The colour is too hard and uncompromising for cottage gardens. Nor is this chrysanthemum as tough as the others. I never lose the other pom-pom chrysanthemums in the winter, but I cannot keep 'Janté Wells', which is another reason why I think it is a recent acquisition. I don't want plants in the garden that have to be renewed each year, so I have ceased to bother with it and have no real regrets. I like a little yellow in the garden in every month of the year but prefer a paler, more muted shade than that of 'Janté Wells'.

While the old chrysanthemums can be relied on to give a good show and can therefore be planted in the middle of a wide border, the toad lilies, which also flower late in the year, are not spectacular and need an intimate place in a narrow bed. Tricyrtis are Japanese plants and have great originality and charm if studied at close quarters, but are lost if planted far from the path. The leaves are pointed ovals and they grow up the slender stems with the curiously shaped, spotted flowers at the top. Sometimes, as in *T. hirta*, the petals are pale pink with purple spots. The pure white form grows taller with me and misses something by the absence of soft colour and, of course, the spots. It is sometimes advised that the toad lilies need a moist, acid soil, but I have not found this and so far they have done very well in my heavy, limy soil. Some people deplore the fact that they flower so late, but I don't think they'd get as much attention if they bloomed earlier. It is partly because they have so little competition that they prove so fascinating. I do not grow the other varieties, *T. macrantha*, *T. formosana* and *T. macropoda*, but all are fascinating.

Though the dwarf *Anaphalis triplinervis* has been covered with fluffy white flowers for some weeks, it is not until late in October that one realises what a good plant it is. By this time the flowers, which have been semi-open from midsummer, have become fluffy white daisies with pale gold centres and remain like it for many more weeks. Some people cut them before they open, hang them up and then later use them in dried arrangements. This is probably a better way than cutting them when fully out —as some of us do. This anaphalis is a good plant at all times of the year. Its silver rosettes of foliage are good without the flowers, and from October to December—or even longer in good years—they make mounds of white and ivory against pointed white leaves and show up well in dark corners or make striking contrast to purple rhus. A softer, more mellow effect is gained by using the plant with domes of golden variegated box, golden sage or the soft grey-green leaves of *Alchemilla mollis* and *Othonnopsis cheirifolia** with its flat blue-grey leaves.

By October the medium-sized *Anaphalis margaritacea* has lost its beauty and its shrivelled stems are best cut down. This species does not make much ground-level foliage, its running stems ending in small silver shoots, and its main beauty comes in early summer when the 18-in stems are furnished with soft, silver-green leaves with typical anaphalis flower-heads.

I always enjoy the tall *Anaphalis yedoensis** in the autumn and winter, and I never cut it down until the spring. It is a plant that needs careful staking, because autumn winds can make a shambles of its 3-ft stems. But when well supported it is really a great addition to the late autumn garden and is still pleasant in early spring. The narrow 3-in leaves that grow all the way up the silver stems have three deep veins, and are green with silver linings. As they turn and twist they look more silver than green and, even when still, have a distinct silver edge. The usual anaphalis flowers come on branching tufts at the top of the stems. Behind it towers *Thalictrum glaucum*, all grey-green and soft yellow.

Although *Aster thompsonii* often begins to flower in July or August it is in late October that it gets its greatest share of admiration, for then its neat little clumps of orange-eyed, lavender-blue flowers stand out well. By then the rosy sedums have flowered but are not finished, for the rich, flat heads of *S.* 'Autumn Joy' and *S.* 'Munstead Red' keep their colour till the spring. The late Gertrude Jekyll always advised planting *Sedum spectabile* and its variations next to perowslia, with its graceful wands of small lavender flowers, and I find *Aster thompsonii* a pleasant addition to the group if grown in front of sedums. This little aster comes from the Himalayas and I grew it for years as plain *Aster thompsonii*. It was never more than 9 in or 10 in high and always neat and compact. Now I keep meeting a plant called *A. thomsonii nanus**, which is so similar to my plant that I think it must be the same, and so I wonder why the "*nanus*" when the original plant was about as dwarf as it could be.

Convolvulus mauritanicus* is another plant that is particularly flowery in late October although it starts flowering in the summer. The name convolvulus frightens some gardeners, but not all the family are dangerous; in fact some are rather tender and need a warm corner. *C. cneorum*, with leaves of silver satin and delicate pink flowers, is one, and *C. mauritanicus** is another. It can be killed by intense cold, in spite of the fact that it disappears below ground in the winter, and makes a network of underground stems which give it a great many chances of survival. All through the summer its long trails of ruffled green stems are starred with deep blue limpet flowers. It is never showy, with so much foliage, and is improved in summer by the pink-flowered *Phuopsis stylosa* which grows below and provides moss-like foliage in a different shade of green. Behind it the hardy *Fuchsia* 'Mrs Popple' is hung with its purple and magenta flowers.

There are not many shrubs flowering just at this time. Sometimes *Viburnum fragrans**, *V. candidissima** (with white flowers) and *V. bodnantense* (with pink) have begun their season, but it is too soon for *Prunus subhirtella autumnalis** and the winter-flowering honeysuckles. Laurustinus (*Viburnum tinus*) waits till November and so does *Mahonia japonica* as a rule.

It is not only the flowers that bring colour to the October garden. Berries and leaves make vivid patches of colour, colour that in the case of some of the berries, lasts well into winter. The glistening white fruits of *Sorbus hupehensis* take on a rosy sheen as they age, and in the case of *Sorbus vilmorinii* the process is reversed. The berries are red to begin with and fade to white with a pink blush. One is accustomed to take sorbus trees very much for granted, but we have discovered in recent dry summers that they do not like drought.

Great strides have been made with the snowberries. I am particularly charmed by *Symphoricarpus* 'Mother of Pearl'*. It is a low and spreading little tree with small clusters of soft pink berries, which last a very long time. *S.* 'White Hedge'* is even more spectacular because it is so heavily weighted with large and glistening white berries that I have had to give it support. It is an upright little bush and has slender, whippy stems like the wild snowberry but does not run so badly. These snowberries grow under the shade of apple trees near the orchard with another white one named after Constance Spry*. *S.* 'Magic Berry'* has deep carmine berries, but I don't think it is quite such a success as the others.

Shrubs that give both autumn tints and colourful berries are welcome indeed. Our common spindleberry, *Euonymus europaeus*, with its lovely old-rose fruits, has foliage that turns crimson in autumn. The leaves of *Euonymus alatus* are even more intense a crimson, and with me the fruits of *E. planipes* are particularly big and brilliant in colour.

The birds take most of the wonderful blue-black berries on the vaccineum (blueberry), which is grown in peat, but they do not deprive me of the leaves, which colour most gloriously at this time of year.

One of my favourite shrubs in the autumn and winter is *Stranvesia undulata**, which has many good points. First of all, it has rather sideways growth, which makes it good for filling a corner. It should produce bunches of matt-surfaced, scarlet fruit in October, and though my plant doesn't fill this part of its duty very well it does have magnificent autumn colour and the bush is brilliant with scarlet and gold all through the autumn. It adds to its good points by keeping those leaves for a long time. Other shrubs are not so accommodating. *Rhus potaninii* is a shapely little tree, with attractive bark in etched grey-green, and when its leaves are aflame it is a wonderful sight. But a high wind, early frost or even heavy rain will send them flying. I enjoy the Stag's Horn sumach, *Rhus typhina*, when its fingered leaves are red and orange, and crimson-plush fruits stand up like candles; but the display is soon over. *R. typhina laciniata** has more finely cut, fern-like leaves and is a plant of great delicacy.

Autumn colour is not always scarlet. Golden leaves can be very beautiful and no tree is more striking in its autumn finery than the *Ginkgo biloba*. When its two-lobed, fan-shaped leaves turn from glaucous green to pale gold, the maidenhair tree takes on a new character. Then the leaves make a thick carpet on the ground, leaving the outline of this unusual conifer to make an interesting silhouette against the winter sky. Ginkgos are becoming fashionable and are now often suggested as good trees for a small garden. Although eventually they reach substantial proportions they take some time to do it.

The scarlet oak, *Quercus coccinea* (especially the form *superbus*) is a wonderful sight in autumn, particularly if *Hydrangea paniculata* is grown under it. The great trusses of flower turn from white to flesh-pink as they age and keep their beauty for some time.

The large leaves of the vine, *Vitis coignetiae*, sometimes turn to all shades from gold to rich crimson. They don't do it for all gardeners; no doubt the soil has something to do with it. This vine needs plenty of room if it is to look its best. I shall always remember it growing up the wall of Buckland Abbey in Devonshire. It covered a wide area and each large leaf was backed by grey stone. It was in late autumn when I saw it and the enormous, rough-textured leaves were in every imaginable shade from soft green through yellow and orange to many shades of red.

The purple vine, *Vitis vinifera purpurea**, has rich claret-red foliage throughout the summer, and in autumn produces a bloom which gives mystery to its rich purple colour. The leaves of wine-purple and rich red contrast well with the soft blue of the late-flowering cordifolia asters and *Ceratostigma willmottiana**. I once saw this vine grown with the tender *Cobaea scandens*, and the pale green of the cobaea, with its flowers of pale green, lilac and purple was a lovely sight.

A berberis that is particularly brilliant in the autumn and is lovely growing with the cobaea is *B. thunbergii* 'Vermilion'. The leaves turn as bright a scarlet as the berries.

The various purple forms of rhus are lovely throughout the year but I always think the soft autumn tints of the Smoke Tree, *Rhus cotinus**, have a subtle beauty even more lovely than the purples. The bluish green leaves turn yellow and soft shades of pink. The taller *Rhus cotinoides** is more obviously brilliant, its pale leaves turning vivid orange-scarlet.

Against the brilliant crimsons and gold the soft green and silver of pampas grass (cortaderia) is particularly successful. For normal gardens the dwarf form, *Cortaderia argentea pumila**, is the best choice. It is never more than about 5 ft and its compact habit is easier in most gardens. It needs the scene to itself and shows up best with grass as a background. I have it at the top of a flight of steps with a grass walk behind.

~ 11 ~
November

By this time the less devoted gardeners have hung up their tools and retired indoors to continue gardening by the fire, studying catalogues and making plans.

But for the enthusiasts the gardening year is by no means finished, although its joys are not quite so obvious. The flowers that bloom very late in the year get more attention because there are fewer of them and they come as an extra dividend. But they get nothing from their setting. Wind and rain spoil the look of any border, the smaller plants can be buried in drifts of leaves and sodden lawns, and paths are not inviting.

But there is still plenty of colour from leaves and stems.

The stems of *Physostegia* 'Summer Spire'* become a fine shade of red. This "Obedient Plant" is rather taller than the others of the family and it should not have been planted in the lowest, rather narrow terrace bed, where I like to see the small special alliums, *Aster thompsonii* and the old double Sweet William, *Dianthus barbatus magnificus*. But a sprawling bush of *Senecio monroii** is near the physostegia and takes off the height, while its silver-lined leaves, with their fluted edges, make pleasant contrast to the knotted stems of the physostegia.

The coloured leaves of the paeonies, *P. mlokosewitschi* and *P. obovata alba**, have now become brown and shabby but the big leaves of the bergenias become brighter every day. For real bright crimson *Bergenia cordifolia* is the best value. Its heart-shaped leaves are leathery and not as shiny as some. But their green turns to brilliant shades of crimson, and the sight of the crimson leaves is very cheering. The oval leaves of *B. crassifolia* colour in a different way. These leaves turn back at their edges, they are very shiny and turn warm shades of amber and crimson. I do not find *B. schmidtii** and 'Bee's Pink' colour much, and it is too early for the narrower-leaved types, which turn to wondrous shades of crimson, to start their winter display.

Many of the geraniums give autumn colour, particularly all the forms of *G. macrorrhizum* if they are grown in the open in poor soil. *G. punctatum* seems to prefer to drain its leaves of colour before they start colouring. Not all the leaves do this and I have noticed it particularly in a planting under *Euonymus planipes*. It always surprises me that the flower arrangers haven't discovered this. Sometimes I think I am very mean to the good tempered "bloody" cranesbill, *G. sanguineum*. This is the easiest, most generous of creatures, flowering all through the year and putting up with any amount of snubbing. I don't mind the rather crude magenta-pink of its flowers but I resent its habit of infiltrating other people's territory. Where it finds a roothold it hangs on with the utmost determination, and if that happens to be between stones one might as well give up. But in autumn and winter it softens the blow with brilliant colour in its leaves, all the time keeping up its successions of perky crumpled flowers. The white-flowered form and the soft lavender *G. s.* 'Glen Luce'* are less invasive.

G. wallichanum 'Buxton's Blue' does not need to produce a touch of autumn colour to win our favour. Its beautifully shaped and marked leaves and the clear blue flowers, with their white centres, are among the joys of autumn, and when the leaves turn red as well the effect is most sumptuous. The pink-flowered form, *G. grevillianum**, though it would be highly esteemed if there were no question of comparison, never quite comes up to its blue-flowered relation.

Of course the herbaceous plumbago, *Ceratostigma plumbaginoides*, is at its best late in the year; I never know if the deep blue flowers would look so intense and such an unfathomable blue without their crimson leaves. In the autumn I forget the way the plant sends its wiry roots out on all sides, not very obviously, mind you, but just enough to crowd out small plants that were quietly minding their own business.

The tiny tangerine-coloured *Potentilla tonguei** seems to do much of its flowering in the autumn and those bright little flowers with their crimson centres come on the ends of long stems of dark leaves, many of which are almost as bright as the flowers.

At the bottom of my low walls where I plant the various forms of *Saxifraga umbrosa* there are crimson leaves on the form *S. u. geum**, and the golden variegated *S. umbrosa* has definite tinges of crimson, particularly where it is grown in the open.

Though much of the brilliant colour on the shrubs has blown away with the leaves, the dark, glistening foliage of *Viburnum utile* adds a cheerful note because of its splashes of gold and crimson. I am often asked about this viburnum: it isn't well known and its sole claim to fame seems to be that it is one of the parents of *V. burkwoodii**, *V. carlesii* being the other one. In my garden each of the proud parents does far better than the offspring and I often wonder why they bothered to make a match of it, but I may have been unlucky with the plants of *V. burkwoodii** I have.

There are always a few hellebores well before Christmas, and which they are varies with the season. I think the most usual one to open the season is *H. olympicus**. It is cream with a strong green tint, and I have seen it opening early in other people's gardens as well as my own. It usually flowers again in the spring, and I generally find that the second effort is best for producing seed. Some less greedy people don't bother to harvest from the first flowering, pinning all their faith on the second attempt, but I always take all I can get.

If I was pinned down to an average date for *H. corsicus** to start flowering I should say just after Christmas, but some years there are flowers in early November. They will still probably go on looking quite presentable till late spring. The golden stamens give a luminous look to the rounded green flowers and the handsome leaves, grey-green and toothed and netted with veins, make a wonderful background.

Perhaps we are earlier in Somerset—certainly, I do not think that other gardeners find *H. atrorubens** opening regularly before Christmas. It always does with me, sometimes early in November. By the time it opens it has usually lost its leaves so the purple bells on their 6-in stems are very obvious. Without the leaves it is easy to see the buds starting to open practically at ground level and then more buds appearing as the stems grow. I see some nurseries still call *H. atrorubens** the "pink Christmas Rose". I often find it hard to convince some gardeners that this is not a variety of the true Christmas rose, *H. niger*, which is always white.

There should be Christmas roses in November but it is not always easy to find them. I am always being asked which variety will definitely flower before Christmas and I have to admit I do not know. I know several gardens where there are lovely, pink-flushed forms flowering away very early, sometimes even in September and October, but the owners can never give me a name—because they don't know. There are some good named forms which have exceptionally fine flowers, such as *H. n. macranthus**, *n. altifolius**, 'St Bridget', 'St Margaret' and *n. maximus**, but I don't think any one of them can be definitely said to flower very early. The late B. Ladhams had a particularly good form* with pink-flushed flowers. The best form I have is called 'Eva' and it came from Harrogate. It is finer than *H.* 'Potter's Wheel' but it doesn't flower very early.

The first flowers of the stinking hellebore, *H. foetidus*, may open soon. They are usually only tiny green buds this month, but those hanging green buds are a promise of the winter display we shall have for weeks on end, pale green flowers and bracts above dense dark foliage, beautifully cut and shining. The leaves of so many of the hellebores get tattered and brown in the bad weather, but in *H. foetidus* they stay beautiful for most of the winter.

Usually it is the plants that are common that flower best and the rarer things are more shy. *Iris unguicularis* does not flower for everyone, however kindly treated, but a recently introduced very pale blue form seems actually eager to flower. This is named 'Walter Butt' after the well-known gardener. It is not only the first to flower but its large, rather flat flowers follow on without hesitation while other kinds are thinking about it. It always flowers in November while the ordinary form seldom does, although I sometimes find an early flower on the small *I. angustifolia*.

I don't pretend my next November flower is quite so reliable. For years I have been trying to grow *Lobelia tupa* but it has never come to maturity. After one of the coldest winters in memory it grew to manhood and produced a flower. I am glad I have seen it flower once for the plant has an "air" about it. I know its soft grey-green pointed leaves because they have made fleeting visits to my garden. But I wasn't prepared for the handsome head of blood-red flowers about 8 in high on 4-in stems. I understand the plant will grow to 8 in when "properly cultivated". But there is no hint what proper cultivation should be. This lobelia comes from Chile and as a rule Chilean plants do best in shade, having been used to life in the jungle. I admired my head of *tupa* from a distance and wished there were half a dozen of them, but didn't look at it very closely. After a heavy gale I found one morning that the stem had snapped just above the supporting cane. I had hoped to get a photograph but instead I was able to study its splendours by the fire. And it proved a most exciting flower when examined under a magnifying glass. The typically labiate flowers consist of a large lower petal with a deeply indented lip, and above there is a very bright red tube which encases the style and stamens. The top of the tube is enlarged and black, not unlike the head of a safety match, but slightly bent to one side so that it resembles the head of a bird or a snake. To foster the illusion still more the red stigma protrudes, with silky white anthers on each side almost like the tusks of a walrus. I notice that according to the books, *L. tupa* should bloom in September, not November.

The lobelia is planted in a warm corner made by a low hedge and the south end of the malthouse. Near it are a few of the shrubby salvias that also flower late in the year. And early, for *Salvia neurepia** starts flowering in July and August and is still at it in November. I like this salvia the best of the red ones; it is a real cherry-red without a hint of blue. The leaves are rather a light yellow-green and the flowers show up well with them. There are several other salvias sometimes sold as *S. neurepia**, but if they have slightly magenta-ish flowers they are not the true neurepia. I wish that *S. neurepia** was reliably hardy. It succumbs to a really hard winter because its rather brittle stems are all above ground and so it is vulnerable. The deep blue *Salvia ambigens** comes through severe winters much better because it goes to ground and reappears in time for its late flowering.

The sub-shrub *S. bethelli** doesn't pretend to be quite hardy, and provident gardeners always have cuttings in the frame. It blooms all through the summer and is still producing its magenta-pink flowers, which look so well against the purplish foliage in November, and so is the exotic looking *S. leucothae**, with violet flowers from woolly buds.

The crimson-flowered *S. grahamii** is the toughest of the shrubby salvias but the flowers are rather small, and so are the dark leaves, and the bush is rather thin and straggly. I have mine growing near the barton gate and it benefits by associating with a bergenia growing in front of it, with comfortable, solid leaves. *Salvia candelabra** grew there once too, with a good background of large woolly leaves for its long arms and soft lavender-blue flowers. *Verbena venosa** (*rigida*) plays about among the stones at its feet and is always still blooming in November.

That dainty little carpeter, *Pratia treadwellii**, is still covering one part of itself with small white flowers, while the other half is studded with purple berries. The flowers look rather like small lobelias. I noticed it growing and flowering in the grass in Mr Walpole's garden at Mt Usher, near Dublin, so it would appear that it likes to escape the unyielding embrace of stones and play hide-and-seek in a lawn.

Every year I am worried because my sternbergias are so late in flowering. While everyone else has great patches of golden flowers all I can find are thin green buds among the strap-like leaves. The usual sternbergia is *S. lutea* and the narrow-leaved form, *S. angustifolia**, is said to flower better. It has been suggested that mine may be *S. sicula*, which opens later and has rather smaller flowers.

~ Part Two ~

By the end of November *Senecio scandens* is still flowering well and its small starry flowers look well against the pale green foliage. It is planted next to another senecio, *leucostachys**, which really needs the south wall to bring it through the winter safely. The two plants grow together in delightful abandon, the silver leaves of one making a wonderful contrast for the golden flowers of the other. The soft ivory flowers of *S. leucostachys** are an added beauty.

The climbing senecio is also acting as shield for another tender shrub, *Convolvulus cneorum*, so I hope it will not be cut too drastically. The senecio really has no business at all to be in such a favoured position, but with all its obligations I think I shall have to leave it now. Before, I had *Coronilla glauca** there and enjoyed its wealth of yellow bloom in the winter, and I think I had a woolly idea that *Senecio scandens* would take its place. I have started two new coronillas against the same wall, the ordinary glaucus one and the lovely variegated form. At the moment they are well barricaded against draughts by shrubs in front and I hope will not succumb this time. I was even foolhardy enough to put a plumbago in the same bed. There were several trusses of lovely blue blossom in the summer, and since then a tangle of creepers has all but obscured it, but I hope will give it enough protection to bring it through. *Convolvulus cneorum* does best in poor soil, I have discovered. Rich living produces a lush plant and it often gets killed.

Gentiana sino-ornata is still flowering very happily when the sun shines. It is not quite so happy on cold, wet days, but there are many blossoms still, and they make a wonderful show, all wide-eyed and smiling in the sunshine. I wonder if I have mastered the gentian problem at last by growing it in sunken sinks filled with peat, but I have known many gardens where they seemed perfectly content and went on for years and years, and then suddenly petered out (gardens with lime-free soil where they had nothing to grumble about), so I keep my fingers crossed when I see my gentians flowering and happy.

Some people treat *Saxifraga fortunei* with very great respect, but I find it likes to be treated casually. So long as it has shade, moisture and humus I think you can do anything with it. I have heard it said that it won't put up with disturbance, but I divide and replant mine whenever I feel the need of more plants. This always takes place in the winter, of course, when everything is damp, and it settles down without a whimper. I think it must be that because it is thought to be difficult this plant is not very widely grown. The only time when I have seen any signs of distress is in a long, dry summer, and then it shrivels up and will depart this life without ado unless it gets water. So far it has never seeded for me, but I have seen little plants playing round their parents in the gardens of my friends.

Seed from the late flowerers is always a problem. Nerines are pretty good and one gets a harvest most years, but belladonna lilies are not so reliable. The last and tallest of the green eryngiums, *E. pandanifolium*, always gives cause for anxiety. It is a plant everyone wants, so big and spiny and congested that it would be a herculean task to divide it; seed is the answer, but when it is in full flower in the middle of November there is always worry if the seed will ripen. Also, strong winds can easily snap off the tall heads of flower. They come on stems that are often 14 in high and more, and are most impressive when the myriads of tiny round mushroom-coloured flowers are silhouetted against the sky.

Another plant that delays its flowering until late in the year and always seems to me at its most luxuriant in November is the "Mexican Incense Bush", *Eupatorium micranthum**. The meaning of its name is "bearing minute flowers" and they last so well in water that they are sometimes used as an autumn substitute for gypsophila. It makes a good rounded bush usually about 4 ft high, but taller in some districts. The pinky white flowers come on long stalks and are sweetly scented. In Somerset it goes through normal winters but is badly hit by very hard weather.

*Viburnum fragrans** usually starts its long season in late October and early November and it comes and goes all through the winter months. A sunny day brings forth a crop of pink-flushed scented flowers and in very cold weather the supply of flowers stops. *Prunus subhirtella autumnalis** behaves in the same way. It can be white or pink and on sunny winter days the snowy blossom looks lovely silhouetted against a blue sky. Very bad weather discourages all effort, but the relays of flowers come and go till late spring, and towards the end of the season the tiny green leaves appearing among the flowers makes it even more entrancing.

We have to call the shrubby veronicas hebes now, although some nurseries still stick to veronica. My favourite remains the dwarf hybrid, 'Morning Glory'*, which I think is *V.* Primley Gem*. There are always a few blossoms and in November it settles down to a winter's hard flowering. The bush is covered with short sprays of lavender flowers and will remain so for months to come.

I used to be rather rude about the big-leaved veronicas. They reminded me too much of public gardens, and usually they get rather big and there are not many flowers, and those are rather small. I didn't think they were worth bothering about, but I have come to the conclusion that treated in the right way they can be an asset.

The right way, I think, is to keep the plants small, taking cuttings every year and starting afresh when the plants get too big. In this way you have little bushes about a foot high and the flowers look almost too big in proportion. Most of them are supposed not to be too hardy in inland districts, but for several years I have managed to keep my small plants without winter damage. Several have almost-red foliage and they flower till January. Even the white and green variegated forms of *Hebe andersoni** and *H. speciosus** have come through, and I have had welcome spikes of purple, crimson and lavender all through the winter. I never know why 'Midsummer Beauty' is so named, because it certainly does not confine its flowering to the summer. Its long lavender spikes are lovely in November and it is scented, which seems strange for a veronica. It looks almost like a buddleia. The veronicas have neat and glossy foliage and make a good background for other plants.

Clerodendron bungei (foetidum) is always an uncertainty. It gets cut to the ground every winter and the new growths that make a leisurely appearance are only just about ready to flower when the first frosts of the winter are imminent. So it is a race, and if the clerodendrons win we get flat heads of rich pink flowers nestling in their purple-flushed leaves. It is called a "sub-shrub" in the textbooks, but I think "super-herbaceous plant" would be a better description.

I can't remember how I first got it, nor where I planted it in the beginning.

It must have been somewhere at the top of the terrace garden, for now it amuses itself by coming up in the bed, in the middle of the little nitida hedge, in the bed under the hedge and in the paved path beside it. I dig up and give away a dozen or so every year, which prevents it becoming a forest, but it doesn't seriously check it. It is quite colourful, with large reddish leaves and big flat heads of very bright pink. I believe it can become almost a tree, but it never achieves more than 2–3 in with me. Starting from ground level in midsummer it just about achieves its 3 in when it is cut down, at the height of its beauty. Though the flowers are supposed to be scented, I have never been able to detect it, but perhaps that is because the plant's unpleasant smell is stronger. I do not wonder it is called *foetidum*. The small tree, *Clerodendron trichotomum*, manages better. Its leaves smell most unpleasantly but the flowers have a lovely scent, which is so strong that it drowns the unpleasant smell. The bright blue berries would make this tree worth growing, whatever its smell.

When I planted my front garden with a border of hydrangeas, it was suggested to me that I was being rather unenterprising to put in only the hortensis type of hydrangea, in different shades of white and pinks. What a pity, while I was at it, that I didn't have some of the species as well. Later I did put in *Hydrangea villosa**, and at the height of its beauty it is really very lovely and a pleasant change from endless pink. But its after-appearance is not so good. All through the late autumn and nearly till Christmas the bread-and-butter hydrangeas are extremely beautiful and add much richness to the garden. The leaves turn pleasantly and the flower-heads turn the most wonderful shades of crimson, copper and green. The large bush of lace-cap *Hydrangea mariesii** at the north-east corner is a most sumptuous spectacle, with glorious foliage spreading far and wide, and tier after tier of great colourful flowers, even more intensely coloured than those on the hortensis types.

After enjoying all this richness there is no pleasure in looking at *H. villosa**, shivering in his corner. What remains of the flowers is a grey and dreary wispiness, and the leaves that were so large and handsome are twisted and colourless. You can see all his angular bones, with little flesh adhering, and you dwell on him as little as possible. Other species hydrangeas which I have in other parts of the garden are no more attractive. *H. petiolaris** is a lovely thing when in full bloom but looks miserable when it has finished flowering. I don't know anything more adorable than a little bush of *Hydrangea involucrata hortensis**, covered with its little double pink flowers, and because of its loveliness it gets a prominent position in the garden. There is nothing attractive about it when its flowering is done, and I would like to arrange my planting so that something would grow up in front of it for the latter half of the year. It is not easy to pick on just the right subject. *H.* 'Grayswood'* is more pleasant in its latter stages. The leaves turn rich tones of crimson and the flowers keep a little of their colour, which is blue and vivid pink.

I leave the heads on my ordinary hydrangeas until spring. For many months they have good colour and are an asset, then they become skeletons and, I think, still attractive enough to keep. I was glad when I read that it is better for the plant if the flower-heads are left on in the winter. In the first place they protect the buds that are forming on the stalk below and, second, there is magnesium secreted in the flower-heads that finds its way back into the plant. I am always very glad, all the same, when spring comes and I can trim off the heads, which by that time are definitely the worse for wear. By then the leaves are beginning to show.

There are some roses that always flower late, not just in a freak year. I always enjoy November roses, whether it is 'Madame Abel Chatenay', that wreathes the dining-room window, or 'Zephrine Drouhin', who pops up from behind the barton wall at a time when I thought all good roses had gone to sleep. But the one I think pleases me most is 'Dr Van Fleet'*, who is growing on the north wall opposite the front of the house. Why I planted him there I cannot imagine. There are some roses, such as 'Mermaid', that quite like a north wall, but I don't think this is one of them. True, I have 'Guinée' growing over the north wall in front of the dining room, but here the wall is lower, and the stems are trained down the south side so that most of the flowers come on the top of the wall or down the front. But 'Dr Van Fleet'* was planted under quite a high wall, and very near a *Garrya elliptica*, which was not a piece of intelligent planting on my part, but I enjoy the results. In November I am enchanted by the shell-pink flowers opening against the wall, with the heavy limbs of the garrya making a canopy above them. I am never tempted to pick my late roses because I love to see them growing in the autumn mists, and to smell them in the early morning, when the garden is sparkling with heavy dew, or in the dusk when the smell of late roses mingles with wet leaves.

Another rose that is particularly irresistible in its second blooming is that green rose, *Rosa chinensis viridiflora**. And the flowers that open in November remain beautiful till January.

Other roses that are lovely this month are the hybrid musks, 'Felicity'* and 'Penelope'. I can't raise much enthusiasm for 'Masquerade' when it is a mixture of crimson and yellow, but at this time of year the crimson tints tend to disappear and it becomes a pleasing soft yellow.

With hydrangeas and roses my small front garden can be very gay in

November. Nerines flower till December, and there are often winter irises in bloom with them. *Abutilon megapotamicum* trained against the south front of the house is always in bloom, and those small hanging crimson flowers, with their little yellow petticoats below, receive even more admiration late in the year when flowers are scarce.

When I was given the variegated form of *Iris japonica* I was warned that it was not as hardy as the ordinary form, so I planted it in the front garden, and so far it is quite happy and increasing very well. The delicate white and green leaves are almost as good as pale flowers, as they sway gently in a sheltered corner. And of course there are its orchid-like flowers in the summer.

I always have several plants of the Corsican hellebore at the west end of the front garden, and they open before others in less favoured sites in the garden.

It is interesting to note that the actual flower Francis Bacon mentions to cheer the heart in late November, December and January is the periwinkle. In his famous essay *Of Gardens* he lists flowers, shrubs and fruits to make the garden attractive through each month in the year, and after re-reading the essay and meeting the modest little periwinkle among the "holly, ivy, bays, juniper, cypress, yews, pines, fir trees, rosemary, lavender, periwinkle, the white, the purple and the blue", I felt I should go out and apologise to my great mound of shining green foliage, from which the pure blue flowers look out so trustingly on a cold day. Evergreen, luxuriant, and indomitable, I contend that *Vinca major* is one of our best winter plants. I am ashamed that sometimes I curse it for the very qualities I admire.

One has pleasant surprises sometimes in November. After giving me nothing but leaves all through the year—beautiful leaves I admire, shapely and colourful—*Eomecon chionantha* sometimes chooses this month to produce one of its lovely white flowers, a cross between a poppy and an anemone, with deep yellow centre. This plant is sometimes called the cyclamen poppy and there is a likeness in the leaves.

Late cyclamen start their winter season now. *C. cilicicum* flowers well in November and buds on the others are forming. There are still a few blooms among the *C. neapolitanum**, and it is now that *C. pseudibericum* produces its leaves to show that it is still with us.

Many people regard ivy as an enemy. I suppose it is in the wrong place. It can destroy walls and get under the eaves of houses, but I believe it is not as disastrous for trees as some of us have been taught. Be that as it may, one of the wayside plants I enjoy in November is the common ivy, *Hedera helix*. I love the way it covers up the unsightly holes in crumbling walls, wreathes tree stumps and brings soft green coverage to many an eyesore. When it ceases to climb and grows horizontally it will flower and at this time of year it is covered with its little tight clusters of green flowers, with tiny yellow anthers.

In spite of my love for green flowers I would not dare allow ivy of this kind to ramble at will up my walls. Beautiful as it is, I am firm in removing it from my walls, although I enjoy it on other people's. But I enjoy the great glossy leaves of fatshedera falling down the ditch bank, and its flowers, which are just like those of the roadside ivy, open in November. A cross between Irish ivy and the Japanese aralia (*Fatsia japonica*), it is a remarkable evergreen plant, and has a loose, graceful habit which makes it useful for an informal setting. I like almost better the variegated form, and hope to induce it to trail down the broken wall behind my top rock garden. So far I have small plants only and cannot expect flowers on them for a year or two.

Atriplex is regarded as a seaside plant but it does just as well inland. A well-grown plant of atriplex grown where it can be seen from all sides is a pleasant sight on a late autumn day. The foliage is like grey satin and the plant can be kept to reasonable limits if it is firmly pruned in the spring. We don't grow atriplex for its flowers but for its foliage, so let's plant it somewhere to improve the winter scene. Like all plants that do well by the sea it is tough; wintry winds and rain do not spoil the leaves, although they look so fragile, and the shrub itself bends with the wind but doesn't break.

~ 12 ~

December

Not all the flowers we enjoy in December should be legitimately included in this book. In some years there are still many roses blooming; China roses in particular often bloom in December, the ordinary monthly rose, *R. chinensis*, producing its pink flowers almost every month in the year.

There are usually odd flowers of penstemon left. The tall *P.* 'Mrs Hindley'* often blooms late and so does the bright cerise rose 'Independence'. When the two grow near each other and both have a burst of flower the effect is striking. The rose turns a dull purplish tint as it ages and is lovely with the penstemon. Early primroses, stray violets, occasional anemones, late-flowering liriopes and perhaps a spray or two of the chaenomeles (which is the unwieldy name we now have to use for our tough old friend that we knew first as japonica and then as cydonia, and occasionally as Japanese quince) all add colour.

And all the time we are cherishing the last flowers of the year the real December flowers are opening. One of the best plants Robert Fortune introduced to this country from China is the winter jasmine, *Jasminum nudiflorum*. At no time is it unattractive because the evergreen stems and leaves are a fresh, bright green and in the summer it is a valuable foliage plant. The usual way to grow it is up a wall and it is accommodating enough to grow in any aspect, so inevitably it gets a north wall more often than not. From the orange-tinted buds the golden flowers open on bare stems and keep on opening for many weeks. It isn't necessary, of course, to grow it on a wall. It makes a good bush if kept trimmed, or it can be grown behind a tree stump or a low wall and allowed to fountain over the top, displaying its flowers even better than when growing on a wall.

That this jasmine is a quick grower can be seen by the way the cottagers use it to make living porches. It makes a solid thicket of green but the constant clipping does mean that some of the flowers are snipped off in the process of trimming.

I also grow the variegated form of this plant but have to admit it is more for its botanical interest than its beauty. The variegation is in yellow and a very rich yellow at that; in fact, looking at the plant from a distance you could almost think it was flowering. There is a variegated form of the summer-flowering *J. officinalis* with rich golden variegated leaves, and it too looks rather piebald and has none of the beauty of the silver-variegated *J. officinalis*, which has delicate tones of silver, pale green and pink. Alas, it increases slowly compared with the exuberance of the golden variety.

The winter-flowering jasmine is undaunted by bad weather and goes on producing its golden flowers when the rest of the garden is sparkling with frost.

Viburnum fragrans* starts to flower in November too and it also comes and goes all through the winter. It is never quite so spectacular as *Prunus subhirtella autumnalis** because when grown in the open it doesn't grow so tall as the prunus, nor does it make such a large, open tree. As a rule it makes a closer, lower bush with bigger clusters of flowers. Against a wall it will grow taller and this seems a good way to grow it. The flowers are white, opening from pink buds and deliciously scented, and they may be spoilt by very heavy frost, but the next to open will be perfect. The young foliage is often pink.

There are several varieties of this shrub. A dwarf edition, *V. f. compactum**, is useful for smaller gardens and gives colour in flower beds in the winter and welcome foliage afterwards. *V. f. candidissima** is all white, as its name suggests, and the white buds and pure white flowers are shown up by dark brown stems. It looks best grown as a specimen, and will grow to about 12 in in time.

When I admired *V. grandiflorum* in a famous garden in Porlock I was given cuttings and was excited at the thought of growing this tall shrub, with bigger, deeper pink flowers, which turn to blush-pink as they fade. Knowledgeable friends assured me I wouldn't be able to grow it, and they were right. It is not completely hardy, for one thing, and perhaps it didn't like the lime in my soil. Luckily, its offspring from its alliance with *V. fragrans** has no foibles and grows as strongly as the type. This shrub usually goes under the name of *V. bodnantense* 'Dawn'. It has deep pink flowers, not as large as those of *V. grandiflorum* but a very good colour. *V. foetens** is also similar to *V. fragrans**. It was first introduced to me as a good shrub for growing under taller trees, for it must have shade. It has white flowers in rather looser clusters and its leaves are smoother than normal. It seems to be more tolerant of other people's gardens than *V. grandiflorum*.

While we are discussing members of the viburnum family, I think *V. tinus*, our old friend laurustinus, should come into the picture. If this was in any way a difficult plant we should pay far more attention to it. As it is so easy it often gets the worst positions in the garden. I was quite shocked recently when I visited some friends whose big garden had been neglected and was being brought back to its original beauty. As can't be helped in newly-planted gardens, the effect was thin and spotty in places, and I was very pleased when I saw two plants of laurus tinus growing against a low wall and filling in the space at each side of stone steps. The dark green leaves of the shrub and its happy way of crouching into a corner with its voluminous growth spread gracefully round made a lovely picture, and I felt here was a little permanent planting at last. But the owners of the garden felt the ordinary plant was far too common for such a conspicuous place and had ideas for seconding it and putting in its place something more unusual.

Laurustinus can be used in many different ways. As a specimen shrub it will be attractive the year through, and from late autumn till March there will be flat heads of lacy white flowers opening from pink buds. It makes a wonderful "natural" hedge, for the flowers are followed by blue berries that later turn black. And as the shrub thrives in shade it has infinite possibilities. (To make a change the variegated form can be grown.)

There are improved forms of this invaluable plant, of which *V. t. lucidum** is the best known and undoubtedly finest. It gets its name from its shining leaves, which are larger than the ordinary plant. The flowers are larger too, and whiter, and the plant grows quicker. This is the "French lauristinis" which one sometimes meets in the gardens of connoisseurs.

Another variety which also has larger glossy leaves and larger flowers is *V. t.* 'Clyne Castle', and *V. t. hirsutum** is described as having bristly stems and leaves. In his *English Flower Garden* William Robinson mentions other forms of lauristinus which do not seem to be in general cultivation. *V. t. rotundifolia** has rounded leaves and also has a variegated form. *V. t. variabile** and *froebeli** are also suggested as worth growing.

Although *Mahonia japonica* often starts to flower in November, it is in December that its real season begins with relays of scented flowers in long racemes. There is much confusion about the names of these flowering mahonias. The one we all want, with long sprays of flower, is *M. japonica* and used to be known as *M. bealei** or *Berberis bealei**. Then it was decided that *M. bealei** is the form with short, upstanding and rather congested spikes of flower and holly-like leaves. Even now the situation is not at all clear. Sometimes the names are reversed and in some lists the name is given as *M.* (or *B.*) *japonica bealei*, for good measure. Is it any wonder the layman is confused? Whatever its true name, it is a most delightful shrub, with glossy leaves good all through the year, and richly tinted in autumn. It is advised to plant it in shade in cool, peaty soil, but it will succeed in the open in limy clay if it has good drainage and adequate water.

I have two planted in the open and I have been told that they can't be completely happy because they turn red in autumn, which is said to be a sign that they are not doing as well as they should. If that is so it is a very pleasant sign, for those crimson leaves are one of my autumn delights. The flowers are just starting too, and the long sprays of primrose peeping from under the turning leaves is very pretty. I pick the individual sprays of flowers, but I never cut off a whole flowering shoot until all the flowers are over. Then I remove every single head that has flowered, and these heads can be used for cuttings if one is clever at rooting such things. About 6 in down the stem is swollen and roughened, and it is here that I cut. My bushes look simply dreadful after I have done with them, and I have had nurserymen shake their heads at my destructive ways. But they change their tune when they come back a few weeks later. For two shoots appear from every stem that has been cut, and very soon the bush is even more heavily leafed than before. It also means that the bushes are kept low and spreading, and pleasantly compact, which is what I need in my small garden. I have seen very angular, untidy bushes of *Mahonia bealei**, which are not pretty grown in the open. There is far too much trunk visible and only sparse tufts of leaves. Such an elongated shrub can be quite attractive grown against a wall, and one I like very much has the whole top of the bush growing over the wall, and spilling the fragrance of its flowers on the other side.

The more aristocratic *M. lomariifolia* flowers in October and November and its flower sprays are as long as those of *M. japonica* and have the upright habit of *M. bealei**. They emerge from a toby-frill of leaves, which are smaller and neater than those of the other two forms. I find something rather stiff and forbidding about this plant and cannot love it as I do the commoner, and it is not only because the flowers have no scent. Major Lawrence Johnstone brought the seeds back from China in 1931 and it is not completely hardy, even in Somerset. But even if it loses its leaves and the stems seem to be bereft of life it usually grows again from the bottom. Visitors to the Savill Gardens in Windsor Great Park will have seen the beautiful hybrid between this plant and *M. japonica*, which is called *M.* 'Charity'*. It has the distinction of *M. lomariifolia* and the toughness of *M. japonica*.

Great care should be taken when planting *Chimonanthus praecox (fragrans)* that it will have plenty of room to develop. We always want it as near the house as possible and sometimes forget how big it will grow eventually. When the long, leafy branches begin to screen windows they have to be cut back and many of next winter's flowers with them. This is what happened to me and now most of those precious, fragrant flowers come on the top branches too high to shade the windows and too high for me to pick from the ground. Soon, of course, I shall be able to reach them from a bedroom window; meanwhile I have to be content with a sprig or two to scent the house. Even one tiny flower will bring enough spicy scent to fill a small room. It annoys me when people call the flowers drab and dull. Probably we shouldn't look at them twice in June, but in December their transparent, claw-like petals get close scrutiny and it is difficult to decide if the colour is straw or beeswax. The inner petals are a dull crimson and seen with the light behind them glow with brilliance. The two other varieties are more showy but the scent is not so strong. *C. p. grandiflorus* has larger, yellower flowers with inner petals of crimson, and *C. p. luteus* has large, open flowers in pale yellow and no crimson at all. To see a well-grown specimen after rain, when every flower sparkles with raindrops and the wintry sun makes the flowers glisten, is something to remember. All varieties take a few years to start flowering and seem to do best in poor soil.

A shrub that is often at its best in December—in my garden, at any rate—is the slightly tender *Cestrum parqui*. It is a Chilean plant, which should flower in the summer, but in my garden the second blooming in December is better—or has one more time to enjoy it? The yellow-green flowers certainly show up better when there are fewer other flowers in bloom but one misses the scent. The flowers are fragrant only at night and these have to be enjoyed in the summer. I grow it beside *Eucalyptus gunnii* against a south wall.

It is lucky for those of us who garden on lime that the many forms of *Erica carnea* bloom in the winter. There is no excuse to have bare ground under shrubs. As in many things the unnamed variety grows most willingly and it is a good plant for rough places and large areas where something quick and easy is needed. I planted this attractive soft, mauve-pink heather when I first came here and it has made wide plants, in spite of pieces I take off from time to time. Since then I have tried to introduce some of the brighter colours but the small plants that I have bought have been very slow to increase, and haven't shown the willingness of the ordinary mountain heather.

I still think *E. c. vivelli** is the best of the deep reds, and it has coppery foliage that adds depth. *E. c.* 'Eileen Porter' is a new variety with very bright carmine flowers, but it is slower to increase even than *E. c. vivelli**. *E. c.* 'Ruby Glow' is another rich-coloured variety, and *E. c. praecox rubra** is a very deep pink; *E. c.* 'James Backhouse', 'King George' and 'Pink Pearl' are other good pinks. The white form of *E. carnea*, *E. c. alba**, is a neat little plant, and there is also 'Snow Queen', another good white.

All these varieties are useful for places where compact cushions are wanted, but for banks and wilder places the Springwoods are the best varieties to choose. They have a horizontal, sprawling habit and show up best on a slope. 'Springwood White' is more vigorous than 'Springwood Pink' and its flowers are long and urn-shaped with protruding brown stamens. But both make most excellent ground cover, smothering weeds and covering wide areas.

Another good winter heather for ground cover is *E. darleyensis**, a deep pink and a strong grower. Others of the same cross of *E. carnea* with *E. mediterranea* are 'A.T. Johnson'* and 'George Rendall'* in pink and 'Silberschmelze'* (Molten Silver), a lovely white with upright spikes and foliage that has a tinge of bronze.

Heathers make a good winter effect growing under shrubs. The deeper pinks and mauve shades are lovely under grey-green conifers, the pale pinks show up well under glaucous shrubs and whites as an underplanting for golden shrubs are very pretty. There are two evergreen golden hebes; *H. armstrongii* is a small spreading bush with old-gold foliage, *H. hectori** is a bright golden green and *Cassinia fulvida**, sometimes known as "golden heather", is an upright bush of burnished gold. It can be kept compact by quite drastic cutting in spring.

~ Part Two ~

Mid-December is the time of year when I rejoice to see my big euphorbias bending over the tips of their long stems; I never get tired of watching this wonderful trick of nature. One day the stems are quite straight with a nice little rosette at the top of each. Then they stiffen up, and I spend my odd moments gently feeling them to see if the stiffening process has started. When it has I know that very soon they will slowly bend over to take the shape of a crozier. I always imagine this is to protect the forming flower buds from the rigours of winter, for when the flowers eventually open the whole head is miraculously up right again. I notice that in most of the nursery lists spring is the time given when these euphorbias are in bloom. They are still a magnificent sight in spring but they often start flowering soon after Christmas. In my garden *E. wulfenii** is a little before *E. charasias*, but there isn't much in it.

I had a great friend who made herself a little winter garden at the bottom of her garden. It is small and formal, with box-edged beds round a garden vase, and larger beds outside, with narrow brick paths between. Though all the plants growing there are lovely—sternbergias and crocuses in late autumn, winter cyclamen and hellebores in every shade—it is the euphorbias standing sentinel at the corner of every bed that give character to the garden. The one she used is the compact *E. charasias* with black "eyes", Mr Bowles' "Frog's Spawn Bush".

The average date when *Iris stylosa** starts to flower is about December 14th. In some years, particularly if we have had a cold, wet summer, it will be even later, and after a very hot, dry summer it can even be a month earlier. I think the behaviour of winter-flowering irises depends very much on the place where they are growing. Mine planted against the front wall of the house are always the first to flower. I have many others under south walls, but they are later. Probably there is a certain amount of warmth from the house, and that brings them on quickly. It is a pity that the various white forms of *Iris stylosa** are so much slower to get going. I have the ordinary white, and a white form of *I. stylosa speciosa*, but they are very slow to increase and exceedingly shy when it comes to flowering. There are other forms of *I. stylosa** with much finer foliage and smaller flowers. *I. angustifolia* has narrow leaves and in *I. creticum** they are even narrower.

Although the ordinary blue and pink pulmonaria, *P. officinalis*, does not flower till late February and early March, the green-leaved, red-flowered form we call *rubra* starts cocking an eye at me in December. I am very fond of this pulmonaria, with its clean, light red flowers. They are very bright and are well back grounded by the rather fresh green leaves, which have not a spot on them. I have another pulmonaria with flowers of the same colour but this has spotted leaves, although the markings are not as pronounced as on some of the blue-flowered forms. This red-flowered pulmonaria is attributed to Mr Bowles and I can think of nothing more cheerful to meet on a cold winter's day. It is sometimes called the "Christmas Cowslip".

I grow many pulmonarias for the beauty of their leaves. There are some that are much more distinctly marked and which are probably forms of *P. saccharata*. The leaves are long and narrow in contrast to the almost heart-shaped leaves of the common lungwort. I always plant these well-marked pulmonarias in a special place, and I hope in time I shall have nothing but handsomely spotted forms. That is what I say, but the common pulmonaria thinks differently. While I am busy selecting my good forms it is very busy planting its young in all the good places where I want to grow my "fancy" pulmonarias. I really haven't the heart to pull out and destroy all these little intruders, so I continue to have some good and many ordinary pulmonarias in the garden. One with leaves that are completely silver with no markings at all I have called *P. argentea** and I am trying to increase it, so it gets divided whenever there is anything to divide.

From the middle of November the fascinating leaves of *Arum italicum pictum** have been poking their noses through the ground. I always feel most grateful for this plant for producing such beautiful and fascinating leaves at this time of the year. The background of the leaves is very dark green and they have most distinct white markings, which makes them a great source of interest in winter. They flower in the ordinary way at the ordinary time but they do seem to have even brighter seed-heads, which last quite a long time. I always think the ordinary "Lords and Ladies" is one of the loveliest flowers we have in the garden, and it makes me feel a brute when I uproot them without ceremony. The soft green flowers are lovely, and the bright orange berries which follow bring a welcome note of gaiety into the garden. But I grow so many other arums which are all botanically interesting, that I should be in a hopeless mess if I allowed all the wild ones to survive. As it is, most of my interesting arums have the same orange seeds on the same upright stem, so there is really no need to be sentimental about the ordinary woodland arum. I have never seen seed-heads after the stinking *Arum dracunculus vulgaris** has flowered. I don't get those wicked-looking, ox-blood flowers every year, but I often find seedlings so they must set seed.

We can't expect to get all our enjoyment from the garden in winter out of flowers. The flowers we do have are very precious; in fact one flower in winter is worth a hundred at any other time of the year, but there are other ways of making the garden attractive in winter. I get great enjoyment from a shrub, *Leycesteria formosa*, which has most beautiful stems all through the year. They are smooth and vivid sea-green in colour, and not unlike a very elegant bamboo. In the summer there are graceful, hanging cream flowers, with claret-coloured bracts. The bracts are still there in December, but beneath them are red berries instead of cream flowers.

Bergenias with crimson-lined leaves stand out well. *B. delavayi* is very rich in colour; *B. purpurascens* is nearly as good. *B.* 'Ballawley'* colours later and is a wonderful sight when the wide leaves are crimson-purple. The form of *Tellima grandiflora* called *T. g. purpurea** is not very different from the type throughout most of the year, but it stands out strikingly in the winter when its leaves turn bright red and look from the distance like a patch of crimson flowers.

The red stems of some of the dogwoods stand out too. The gold and yellow-green foliage of *Cornus alba spaethii** is lovely throughout the year and in the winter the dark crimson stems give glowing colour. Its silver-variegated counterpart, *C. alba elegantissima**, which looks lovely with the crimsons and blues of the summer border, also has crimson stems and so do two other elegant members of the cornus family with variegated leaves, *C. alternifolia variegata** and *C. controversa variegata**, which has heavy white and green foliage. Both have a flat, spreading habit of growth and are good shrubs for use in herbaceous borders. There is also a willow that has red stems in winter, *Salix britzensis**. Golden stems also add colour. *C. flaviramea**, with green leaves, has stems that are ochre-yellow in winter, and the weeping willow with gold bark, *Salix vitellina pendula**, glows warmly in the winter.

Even brighter, the green-leaved *C. alba* 'Westonbirt'* has stems that are bright sealing-wax red. It can be cut down drastically in the spring, to ground level if necessary, and this undoubtedly is a factor in getting good colour in the winter stems.

There are, of course, shrubs with golden leaves that bring warmth to the winter scene. I like to use the golden form of *Lonicera nitida* 'Baggeson's Gold' as a specimen plant. So far it seems to be quite slow-growing, and the plant I bought three years ago is still only about 2 in high, and has made an irregular, sprawling bush that looks right among dwarf herbaceous plants, and gives wonderful colour in December. Also good for growing near the front of the border with lower plants round it, *Cassinia fulvida** is more bronze than golden, and its small leaves make it look rather like a golden heather. Left to itself it gets rather leggy and can be cut drastically in the spring. I have also read that it can be pegged down and kept neat by being clipped, but I have never done this.

Its flowers are small and grow in flat heads, the colour of old ivory and fluffy like those of helichrysum. I leave them on for winter effect. This shrub does best in a hot, dry position in a light soil, but it puts a good face on my heavy clay. Although the dwarf golden bamboo, *Arundinaria auricoma**, is not evergreen, it keeps its leaves for a long time and they are still fluttering on their 30-ft stems in late December. These leaves are 6 to 8 ft long, with fine green lines on the gold. I tried growing it in shade but there the leaves take on a greenish tinge, so now I grow it in the open and plant *Anaphalis triplinervis* in front of it, for its silver leaves are beautiful all through the year and in December the "everlasting flowers" are often still presentable. They look bedraggled in very wet weather but even late in the year will fluff out again to tiny balls of silver when the sun shines.

A similar permanent effect can be made with *Hebe armstrongii* and one of the glaucous acaenas. The hebe is a spreading dwarf shrub, with foliage rather like that of a cypress in deep old gold. There are three acaenas with very blue glaucous foliage and they can be selected according to the position. Where there is plenty of room the biggest one, *A. ascendens**, makes a swirling mass of ferny foliage, which will fall over stones or blur a straight edge. Much neater in growth, another is known as Mr Bowles' form, with black stems and smaller leaves. So far I haven't been able to get its botanical name. The smallest of all is *A. buchanani*, a carpeting plant more sea-green than the others and keeping closer to the ground. *Othonnopsis cheirifolia** can be used with the hebe instead of an acaena. It seldom grows higher than 9–12 in and its bunches of close-packed, rounded leaves cover the ground thickly. I have never discovered when this plant is supposed to flower. It seems to produce odd flowers in every month in the year, and I often find several fleshy, yellow daisies in December.

*Hebe hectori** is also golden bronze with upright, shiny whip-cord branches. The prostrate and glaucous *Euphorbia myrsinites* can be grown in front of it to loll over a flat stone and bask in the sun when there is any.

In a normal December the blue-grey foliage of *Hebe cupressoides* is lovely and the scent of incense always seems stronger on a frosty day. Its soft colouring goes well with the velvety leaves of the purple sage, *Salvia officinalis purpurascens**.

Winter-flowering honeysuckle is sometimes rather disappointing because the few flowers are hidden by luxuriant leaves. I have always had *Lonicera fragrantissima* in the garden and periodically I decide to scrap it, but the threat is never carried out. It doesn't warrant an important place and seems to do best in the shade, where its leaves are not so luxuriant. A far better plant is *L. purpusii**, a hybrid between *L. fragrantisssma* and *L. standishii*, which is semi-deciduous. Instead of competing with a forest of leaves, in this plant the scented cream flowers are borne on naked stems and are far more effective.

Perhaps it is not fair to call the daphnes December shrubs, although I often get a few flowers this month. The white form of *Daphne merzereum* is often in bloom in December, although it does not reach its full beauty till January and February. *Daphne odora* has flowers in the winter and their strong scent is one of December's delights. I don't believe *Daphne blagayana* is supposed to flower quite so early, but it does with me, very often.

There is one rhododendron that flowers in December, *R. mucronuatum*, which is deciduous and has small magenta-pink flowers. It has mahogany stems, making it an attractive plant for all times of the year.

Some shrubs are valuable for their fruits and *Cotoneaster exburyensis** in full fruit early in December is a sight not soon forgotten. The yellow berries are carried in a loose and graceful way and a well-grown tree well covered with fruit is lovely on a winter's day. I think it should be grown as a thing apart; its silhouette is so beautiful that nothing should be allowed to spoil it. *C. frigida** has bright red berries and makes a big tree eventually.

The rather tough, wavy leaves of *Garrya elliptica* look as though they could withstand any amount of cold but, in fact, they are vulnerable to frost, and once they are blackened and blotched the beauty of the tree is spoiled for the whole season. I don't think this shrub is as completely hardy as we think and needs a sheltered position. I grow it against a north wall and it did very well when it was low enough to have the protection of the wall, but now it has grown high above the wall it is often spoilt by frost and bitter winds. If I trim it down to the level of the wall I lose all my flowering shoots, and there will be no 12-in catkins of palest green to cheer me at Christmas time.

The cream and green striped leaves of *Iris foetidissima variegata** are at their best in winter. Some of the variegated irises almost disappear, but from November onwards this iris becomes sleeker and its leaves stand out with striking brilliance. I like to grow it against a dark background or standing by itself about a planting of low green plants such as *Geranium macrorrhizum*, or even that useful little carpeter for shady places, *Symphytum grandiflorum**, which starts producing its orange-tipped cream flowers in November above dark, hairy leaves. The iris will grow in sun or shade, it increases well and I find does particularly well wedged between stones.

Almost as striking, the variegated form of *Vinca major* adds greatly to the winter scene. The best form is *V. m. elegantissima**, with large leaves which look as though they have been heavily splashed with cream paint. It can be grown in two ways. Between shrubs it brings brilliant relief, and can be trained as a neat bushy plant if all the runners are kept cut. Or it can be planted at the edge of a wall so that it hangs over. Another way to grow the periwinkle would be at the edge of a bed containing *Physalis franchetii**, which keeps some of its orange lanterns until Christmas.

Variegated ivies also show up well; the larger-leaved *Hedera colchica dentata variegata*, with golden variegation, and *H. canariensis variegata* 'Gloire de Marengo'* on shady walls or covering the ground under shrubs, and the smaller *H. helix* 'Harold'*, *H. h. tricolor** or *H. h. marmorata** tumbling down a shady bank.

The warm tones of *Magnolia grandiflora* 'Exmouth' add beauty to a winter's day. This form can be grown in the open and in this position the glossy green leaves with their cigar-brown linings are seen to good advantage. It is also said to flower sooner after planting than the ordinary *M. grandiflora*, but the plant bought about six years ago has not yet shown any inclination to flower. The stems of the willows which hold up the banks of the ditch are red-brown in the winter; such a shrub as *Neillia longiracemosa** has warm winter stems, and *Aruncus sylvester** and *Lysimachia clethroides* have bright brown stems in the winter.

The white stems of *Rubus giraldianus** have a powdery bloom, and the leaves are lined with white. It will grow to 10 in in time, but the dwarf *R. thibetanus*, with its graceful arching stems, seldom reaches more than 5 ft. It too has powdered white stems and "frosted" leaves. I never cut down my *Perowskia atriplicifolia** until the spring because the long white stems look nice all through the winter with all the other skeletons! It is a good thing that we are not cutting down our gardens as drastically as we used to. Lack of labour may be the cause almost as much as the aesthetic reason. Probably it began when we hadn't managed to cut down every herbaceous plant before winter overtook us and then discovered how beautiful the garden looked in its shagginess. Those stalks of michaelmas daisies are different altogether when rimed with frost, and instead of bare, flat beds there are delightful shapes, colours and skeletons outlined against the sky.

Somehow the wild teasel, *Dipsacus fullonum*, found its way into the garden and though it is inclined to overseed itself, there are many times when I am glad of its company. The delicate mauve flowers are beautiful and have a strange habit of opening first in a band round the centre of the core. But it is in the winter that they are most spectacular with their whitened stems and fascinating prickly heads. They seem indestructible, for after the winter they remain in one piece, and if one waited for them to disintegrate one would wait for years.

I always prefer the twisted trees when they have lost their leaves. With their curling and twisting branches making a graceful pattern against the winter sky they give endless pleasure.

I find the "corkscrew" hazel rather a deformed looking tree when fully clothed in the summer, as it has not the tall grace of the twisted willow, *Salix matsudana tortuosa**. But in the winter its twisting brown stems have a strange fascination, particularly when hung with catkins.

The bleached leaves of some of the grasses stand out well; even the untidy old "Gardener's Garters", *Phalaris arundinacea variegata**, becomes a warm ivory and adds to the beauty of the garden. It doesn't matter which of the various forms of miscanthus we grow—green, variegated or striped like a zebra—they all turn papery white in winter and their tall and graceful silhouettes show up well. Some flower in late autumn and the slender tufts of flower stand up above the leaves.

December may not be the best month in the garden, but there are flowers and shrubs to make it exciting if we look for them. Little hardy cyclamen are opening every day, there are violets and primroses, and lovely leaves and tree trunks. I enjoy my silver birches best in the winter and for those who grow it the satin bark of *Prunus serrula* (*P. serrula tibetica**) looks like polished mahogany. In a quiet way the trunk of *Rhus potaninii* is lovely too. It is grey-green and delicately fingered and adds to the charm of this shapely little tree. For those with eyes there are many good things to enjoy in the December garden.

Plant-name Changes

In her writings Margery Fish naturally used the plant names that were familiar to her and were considered acceptable at the time. But times have changed, and while many of the names she used are still current, and many that are not are nevertheless recognisable, some have changed completely.

In order to help contemporary gardeners understand exactly which plants Mrs Fish is discussing, we have asterisked within the text all the names that have changed and listed these with the current accepted name below.

In some cases Mrs Fish gives two different names for the same plant, yet modern thinking may apply these two names to two different entities. She may also give two different names for what she asserts are two different plants yet modern thinking assures us that the two plants are the same. In some cases she indicates that one name has been superceded by another while it may now be clear that the first name, or another name altogether, is actually correct.

So while acknowledging that a full and accurate explanation of these nomenclatural niceties would be impossibly cumbersome, we hope that our simple listing will prove helpful. In identifying the correct names we sought advice and clarification from *The PlantFinder*, a range of modern encyclopedias and monographs together with expert individuals. However, because Mrs Fish grew such an extraordinary range of plants, some obscure even by today's standards and some now completely lost, a few minor problems remain unresolved.

In general we have changed Mrs Fish's original text as little as possible but the accepted manner in which names are styled in type has also changed over the years. So in some cases we have simply modified the expression of an otherwise correct name in order to avoid unnecessary additions.

The science of plant nomenclature perhaps should be, but is certainly not, a precise one; however we feel sure that by making these additions we add to an appreciation of Mrs Fish's writing and of the plants she grew.

Plant name in the text	Correct current name
Acaena ascendens	*Acaena saccaticupula*
Achillea 'Cerise Queen'	*Achillea millefolium* 'Cerise Queen'
Achillea 'Gold Plate'	*Achillea filipendulina* 'Gold Plate'
Achillea serrata 'W.B. Child'	*Achillea ageratum* 'W.B. Child'
Acidanthera murielae	*Gladiolus callianthus* 'Murieliae'
Aconitum volubile latisectum	*Aconitum hemsleyanum*
Actaea alba	*Actaea pachypoda*
Actaea spicata rubra	*Actaea rubra*
Adonis dahurica	*Adonis amurensis*
Agathaea coelestis	*Felicia amelloides*
Alcea cannabina	*Althaea cannabina*
Allium afflatuense	*Allium hollandicum*
Allium babbingtonii	*Allium ampeloprasum* var. *babbingtonii*
Allium siculum	*Nectaroscordium siculum*
Alyssum citrinum	*Aurinia saxatilis* 'Citrina'
Alyssum saxatile compactum	*Aurinia saxatilis* 'Compacta'

Alyssum saxatile compactum
    'Dudley Neville'
	Aurinia saxatilis
	        'Dudley Neville'

Amsonia salicifolia	*Amsonia tabernaemontana* var. *salicifolia*
Anaphalis yedoensis	*Anaphalis margaritacea* var. *yedoensis*
Anchusa caespitosa	*Anchusa leptophylla* subsp. *incana*
Anchusa 'Loddon Royalist'	*Anchusa azurea* 'Loddon Royalist'
Anchusa myosotidiflora	*Brunnera macrophylla*
Anemone alleni	*Anemone nemorosa* 'Allenii'
Anemone blanda atrocoerulea	*Anemone blanda* 'Atrocaerulea'
Anemone blanda rosea	*Anemone blanda* var. *rosea*
Anemone blanda scythinica	*Anemone blanda* 'Scythinica'
Anemone japonica	*Anemone* x *hybrida*
Anemone nemorosa alba plena	*Anemone nemorosa* 'Alba Plena'
Anemone nemorosa robinsoniana	*Anemone nemorosa* 'Robinsoniana'
Anemone pulsatilla 'Red Clock'	*Anemone vulgaris* 'Rode Klokke'
Anthericum algerense	*Anthericum liliago* var. *major*
Anthericum graminifolium	*Anthericum ramosum*
Anthericum liliastrum	*Paradisea liliastrum*
Antirrhinum asarina	*Asarina procumbens*
Aquilegia coccinea	*Aquilegia canadensis* var. *coccinea*
Aquilegia viridis	*Aquilegia viridiflora*

Arisaema candidissima	*Arisaema candidissimum*
Arnebia echioides (*macrotomia*)	*Arnebia pulchra*
Artemisia 'Lambrook Silver'	*Artemisia absinthum* 'Lambrook Silver'
Artemisia tridentata	*Seriphidium tridentatum*
Arum dracunculus vulgaris	*Dracunculus vulgaris*
Arum italicum pictum	*Arum italicum* subsp. *italicum* 'Marmoratum'
Aruncus sylvester	*Aruncus dioicus*
Arundinaria auricoma	*Pleioblastus auricomis*
Aster acris	*Aster sedifolius*
Aster 'Beechwood Rival'	*Aster novi-belgae* 'Beechwood Rival'
Aster 'Blue Bouquet'	*Aster novi-belgae* 'Blue Bouquet'
Aster 'Brilliant'	*Aster amellus* 'Brilliant'
Aster 'Charles Wilson'	*Aster novi-belgae* 'Charles Wilson'
Aster cordifolius elegans	*Aster cordifolius* 'Elegans'
Aster 'Countess of Dudley'	*Aster novi-belgae* 'Countess of Dudley'
Aster diffusus horizontalis	*Aster lateriflorus* 'Horizontalis'
Aster 'Elisabeth Bright'	*Aster novi-belgae* 'Elisabeth Bright'
Aster frikartii	*Aster* x *frikartii*
Aster 'King George'	*Aster amellus* 'King George'
Aster 'Lac de Genèvé'	*Aster amellus* 'Lac de Genève'
Aster 'Lady-in-Blue'	*Aster novi-belgae* 'Lady in Blue'
Aster 'Little Boy Blue'	*Aster novi-belgae* 'Little Boy Blue'
Aster macrophylla	*Aster macrophyllus*
Aster pappei	*Felicia amoena*
Aster 'Peace'	*Aster novi-belgae* 'Peace'
Aster 'Peter Harrison'	*Aster novi-belgae* 'Peter Harrison'
Aster 'Plenty'	*Aster novi-belgae* 'Plenty'
Aster 'Prosperity'	*Aster novi-belgae* 'Prosperity'
Aster 'Rosebud'	*Aster novi-belgae* 'Rosebud'
Aster 'Royal Blue'	*Aster novi-belgae* 'Royal Blue'
Aster 'Snowsprite'	*Aster novi-belgae* 'Snowsprite'
Aster 'Sonia'	*Aster amellus* 'Sonia'
Aster thomsonii nanus	*Aster thomsonii* 'Nanus'
Aster tradescantii	*Aster pilosus* var. *demotus*
Aster 'Ultramarine'	*Aster amellus* 'Ultramarine'
Aster 'Victor'	*Aster novi-belgae* 'Victor'
Astilbe chinensis pumila	*Astilbe chinensis* var. *pumila*
Astilbe simplicifolia atrorosea	*Astilbe simplicifolia* 'Atrorosea'

Astilbe simplicifolia atrorosea 'Bronze Elegance'	*Astilbe* 'Bronze Elegans'
Astilbe simplicifolia atrorosea praecox alba	*Astilbe simplicifolia* 'Praecox Alba'
Astrantia biebersteinii	*Astrantia major*
Astrantia carniolica rubra	*Astrantia major* 'Rubra'
Astrantia gracilipes	*Astrantia minor*
Astrantia helleborifolia	*Astrantia maxima*
Atriplex hortensis	*Atriplex hortensis* var. *rubra*
Bellis aucubaefolia	*Bellis perennis* 'Aucubifolia'
Bellis 'Alice'	*Bellis perennis* 'Alice'
Bellis 'Bon Accord'	*Bellis perennis* 'Bon Accord'
Bellis 'Dresden China'	*Bellis perennis* 'Dresdon China'
Bellis prolifera	*Bellis perennis* 'Prolifera'
Bellis 'Rob Roy'	*Bellis perennis* 'Rob Roy'
Bellis 'The Pearl'	*Bellis perennis* 'The Pearl'
Berberis bealei	*Mahonia japonica Bealei* Group
Bergenia 'Ballawley'	*Bergenia* 'Ballawley'
Bergenia delavayi	*Bergenia purpurascens* var. *delavayi*
Bergenia milesii	*Bergenia stracheyi*
Bergenia schmidtii	*Bergenia* x *schmidtii*
Brodiaea laxa	*Triteleia laxa*
Buddleia fallowiana	*Buddleja fallowiana*
Buddleia 'Royal Red'	*Buddleja davidii* 'Royal Red'
Caltha palustris flora plena	*Calthus palustris* 'Flore Pleno'
Calamintha nepetioides	*Calamintha nepeta*
Campanula burghltii	*Campanula* 'Burghaltii'
Campanula 'Cantab'	*Campanula persicifolia* 'Cantab'
Campanula muralis	*Campanula portenschlagiana*
Campanula 'Telham Beauty'	*Campanula persicifolia* 'Telham Beauty'
Cassinia fulvida	*Cassinia leptophylla* subsp. *fulvida*
Cautleya robusta	*Cautleya spicata* 'Robusta'
Ceanothus burkwoodii	*Ceanothus* 'Burkwoodii'
Ceanothus veitchianus (floribundus)	*Ceanothus* x *veitchianus*
Centaurea candidissima	*Centaurea cineraria*
Centaurea gymnocarpa	*Centaurea cineraria*
Ceratostigma willmottiana	*Ceratostigma willmottianum*
Cheiranthus 'Miss Hopton'	*Erysimum* 'Miss Hopton'
Cheiranthus 'Moonlight'	*Erysimum* 'Moonlight'
Cheiranthus mutabilis	*Erysimum mutabile*

Chelone barbatus	Penstemon barbatus
Chimonanthus fragrans	Chimonanthus praecox
Chimonanthus grandiflorus	Chimonanthus praecox 'Grandiflorus'
Chimonanthus luteus	Chimonanthus praecox var. luteus
Chrysabactron hookeri	Bulbinella hookeri
Chrysanthemum balsamita	Tanacetum balsamita
Chrysanthemum balsamita balsamitoides	Tanacetum balsamita subsp. balsamitoides
Chrysanthemum 'Dr Tom Parr'	Chrysanthemum 'Doctor Tom Parr'
Chrysanthemum uliginosum	Leucanthemella serotina
Cimifuga cordifolia	Cimicifuga americana
Cimifuga ramosa	Cimicifuga simplex 'Prichard's Giant'
Cimifuga 'White Pearl'	Cimicifuga simplex 'White Pearl'
Clematis albo-luxurians	Clematis 'Alba Luxurians'
Clematis balearica (calycina)	Clematis cirrhosa var. balearica
Clematis florida bicolor	Clematis florida 'Bicolor'
Clematis henryi	Clematis 'Henry'
Clematis jackmanii	Clematis 'Jackmanii'
Clematis jouiniana praecox	Clematis x jouiniana 'Praecox'
Clematis macropetala alpina	Clematis alpina
Clematis markhami	Clematis 'Markhami'
Cobaea scandens alba	Cobaea scandens f. alba
Convolvulus elegantissimus	Convolvulus althaeoides subsp. tenuissimus
Convolvulus mauritanicus	Convolvulus sabatius
Cornus alba elegantissima	Cornus alba 'Elegantissima'
Cornus alba spaethii	Cornus alba 'Spaethii'
Cornus alba 'Westonbirt'	Cornus alba 'Sibirica'
Cornus alternifolia variegata	Cornus alternifolia 'Argentea'
Cornus controversa variegata	Cornus controversa 'Variegata'
Cornus flaviramea	Cornus stolonifera 'Flaviramea'
Coronilla glauca	Coronilla valentina subsp. glauca
Cortaderia argentea pumila	Cordaderia selloana 'Pumila'
Corydalis cashmiriana	Corydalis cashmeriana
Corydalis densiflora	Corydalis solida subsp. incisa
Corydalis luteus	Corydalis lutea
Corydalis ochreleuca	Corydalis ochroleuca
Corylus contorta	Corylus avellana 'Contorta'
Cotoneaster exburyensis	Cotoneaster salicifolius 'Exburyensis'

Cotoneaster frigida	Cotoneaster frigidus
Cyclamen atkinsii	Cyclamen coum subsp. caucasicum
Cyclamen europaeum	Cyclamen purpurascens
Cyclamen hiemale	Cyclamen coum
Cyclamen ibericum	Cyclamen coum subsp. caucasicum
Cyclamen neapolitanum	Cyclamen hederifolium
Cyclamen orbiculatum	Cyclamen coum
Cyclamen orbiculatum coum	Cyclamen coum
Cyclamen vernum	Cyclamen coum subsp. caucasicum
Cystisus kewensis	Cystisus x kewensis
Daphne cneorum eximea	Daphne cneorum 'Eximea'
Daphne grandiflorum album	Daphne mezereum var. autumnalis 'Alba'
Daphne mezereum album	Daphne mezereum f. alba
Delphinium 'Pacific'	Delphinium 'Galahad'
Delphinium 'Tibetan'	Delphinium grandiflorum
Dentaria pinnata	Cardamine heptophylla
Dianthus barbatus magnificus	Dianthus barbatus 'Magnificus'
Dianthus caesius	Dianthus gratianopolitanus
Dianthus 'Mme du Barri'	Dianthus 'Dubarry'
Dianthus 'Musgrave'	Dianthus 'Musgrave's Pink'
Dianthus 'Pheasant's Ear' (laced pink)	Dianthus 'Pheasant's Eye'
Dianthus 'Sops and Wine'	Dianthus 'Sops in Wine'
Dicentra eximea	Dicentra formosa
Dondia epipactis (Hacquetia epipactis)	Hacquetia epipactis
Dorycnium hirsutum	Lotus hirsutus
Dracocephalum prattii	Nepeta prattii
Elaeagnus pungens aurea	Elaeagnus pungens 'Aurea'
Epilobium rosmarinifolium	Epilobium dodonaei
Epimedium niveum	Epimedium x youngianum 'Niveum'
Epimedium pinnatum colchicum	Epimedium pinnatum subsp. colchicum
Epimedium 'Rose Queen'	Epimedium grandiflorum 'Rose Queen'
Epimedium rubrum	Epimedium x rubrum
Epimedium sulphureum	Epimedium x versicolor 'Sulphureum'
Epimedium versicolor sulphureum	Epimedium x versicolor 'Sulphureum'
Eranthis cilicica	Eranthis hyemalis Cilicia Group
Eranthis tubergenii	Eranthis hyemalis Tubergennii Group
Eranthis tubergenii 'Guinea Gold'	Eranthis hyemalis 'Guinea Gold'
Erica 'A. T. Johnson'	Erica x darleyensis 'Arthur Johnson'

Erica carnea alba	Erica carnea 'Alba'
Erica carnea praecox rubra	Erica carnea 'Praecox Rubra'
Erica carnea vivelli	Erica carnea 'Vivellii'
Erica darleyensis	Erica x darleyensis
Erica 'George Rendall'	Erica x darleyensis 'George Rendall'
Erica 'H. E. Beale'	Calluna vulgaris 'H. E. Beale'
Erica 'Mrs D. F. Maxwell'	Erica vagans 'Mrs D. F. Maxwell'
Erica 'Silberschmelze' (Molten Silver)	Erica x darleyensis 'Silberschmelze'
Erigeron mucronatus	Erigeron karvinskianus
Eryngium bromeliifolium	Eryngium agavifolium
Erysimum capitata	Erysimum capitatum
Erythronium 'Cream Beauty'	Erythronium revolutum 'Cream Beauty'
Erythronium 'Rose Queen'	Erythronium dens-canis 'Rose Queen'
Escallonia 'Gwendoline Anley'	Escallonia 'Gwendolyn Anley'
Eucomis punctata	Eucomis comosa
Euonymus radicans variegatus	Euonymus fortunei 'Variegatus'
Eupatorium micranthum	Eupatorium ligustrinum
Euphorbia androsacinifolia	Euphorbia esula
Euphorbia biglandulosa	Euphorbia rigida
Euphorbia epithymoides	Euphorbia polychroma
Euphorbia hibernica	Euphorbia hyberna
Euphorbia pilosa major	Euphorbia polychroma 'Major'
Euphorbia robbiae	Euphorbia amygdaloides var. robbiae
Euphorbia sibthorpii	Euphorbia characias subsp. wulfenii
Euphorbia valdevilloscarpa	Euphorbia villosa subsp. valdevilloscarpa
Euphorbia wulfenii	Euphorbia characias subsp. wulfenii
Exochorda giraldii wilsonii	Exochorda giraldii var. wilsonii
Fatshedera lizei	x Fatshedera lizei
Forsythia intermedia spectabilis	Forsythia x intermedia 'Spectabilis'
Forsythia viridissima bronxensis	Forsythia viridissima 'Bronxensis'
Fragaria indica	Duchesnea indica
Fritillaria citrina	Fritillaria bithynica
Galanthus atkinsii	Galanthus 'Atkinsii'
Galanthus graecus	Galanthus gracilis
Galanthus 'John Grey'	Galanthus 'John Gray'
Galanthus lutescens	Galanthus nivalis 'Lady Elphinstone'
Galanthus nivalis 'Green Tip'	Galanthus nivalis 'Pusey Green Tip'
Galanthus nivalis scharloki	Galanthus nivalis 'Scharloki'
Galanthus nivalis viridapicis	Galanthus nivalis 'Viridapicis'

Galanthus 'Poe'	*Galanthus* 'Hill Poe'
Galanthus 'Samuel Arnott'	*Galanthus* 'S. Arnott'
Galanthus virescens	*Galanthus nivalis* 'Virescens'
Gentiana 'Kidbrook'	*Gentiana* x *macaulayi* 'Kidbrooke Seedling'
Gentiana macaulayi	*Gentiana* x *macaulayi*
Gentiana newburyi	*Gentiana newberryi*
Geranium 'A. T. Johnson'	*Geranium* x *oxonianum* 'A. T. Johnson'
Geranium atlanticum	*Geranium malviflorum*
Geranium endressii 'Wargrave'	*Geranium* x *oxonianum* 'Wargrave Pink'
Geranium grevillianum	*Geranium lambertii*
Geranium 'Russell Prichard'	*Geranium* x *riversleaianum* 'Russell Prichard'
Geranium sanguineum 'Glen Luce'	*Geranium sanguineum* 'Glenluce'
Gladiolus byzantinus	*Gladiolus communis* subsp. *byzantinus*
Gladiolus grandis tristis	*Gladiolus tristis*
Hamamelis 'Adonis'	*Hamamelis* x *intermedia* 'Ruby Glow'
Hamamelis brevipetala	*Hamamelis* 'Brevipetala'
Hamamelis 'Hiltingbury Red'	*Hamamelis* x *intermedia* 'Hiltingbury'
Hamamelis 'Jelena'	*Hamamelis* x *intermedia* 'Jelena'
Hamamelis mollis pallida	*Hamamelis mollis* 'Pallida'
Hamamelis 'Orange Beauty'	*Hamamelis* x *intermedia* 'Orange Beauty'
Hamamelis 'Ruby Glow'	*Hamamelis* x *intermedia* 'Ruby Glow'
Hebe andersoni	*Hebe* x *andersonii*
Hebe hectori	*Hebe hectorii*
Hebe speciosus	*Hebe speciosa*
Hedera canariensis variegata 'Gloire de Marengo'	*Hedera canariensis* 'Gloire de Marengo'
Hedera helix 'Harold'	*Hedera helix* 'Harald'
Hedera helix 'Jubilee Gold Heart'	*Hedera helix* 'Ori di Bogliasco'
Hedera helix marmorata	*Hedera helix* 'Luzii'
Hedera helix tricolor	*Hedera helix* 'Tricolor'
Helichrysum angulosum	*Helichrysum italicum* subsp. *serotinum*
Helichrysum siculum	*Helichrysum stoechas* subsp. *barrelieri*
Helichrysum trilineatum	*Helichrysum spendidum*
Helleborus abchasicus	*Helleborus orientalis* subsp. *abchasicus*
Helleborus atrorubens	*Helleborus orientalis* subsp. *abchasicus* 'Early Purple'

Helleborus Bauer's hybrid	*Helleborus* x *sternii* 'Bauer's Hybrid'
Helleborus corsicus	*Helleborus argutifolius*
Helleborus kochii	*Helleborus orientalis*
Helleborus niger altifolius	*Helleborus niger* var. *altissimus*
Helleborus niger Ladham's var.	*Helleborus niger* 'Ladham's variety'
Helleborus niger macranthus	*Helleborus niger* subsp. *macranthus*
Helleborus niger maximus	*Helleborus niger* 'Maximus'
Helleborus olympicus	*Helleborus orientalis*
Helleborus orientalis 'Greenland'	*Helleborus* 'Greenland'
Helleborus sternii	*Helleborus* x *sternii*
Holcus mollis variegatus	*Holcus mollis* 'Albo variegatus'
Hosta albo-picta	*Hosta fortunei* var. *albopicta*
Humea elegans	*Calomeria amaranthoides*
Hydrangea 'Grayswood'	*Hydrangea serrata* 'Grayswood'
Hydrangea involucrata hortensis	*Hydrangea involucrata* 'Hortensis'
Hydrangea mariesii	*Hydrangea macrophylla* 'Mariesii'
Hydrangea petiolaris	*Hydrangea anomala* subsp. *petiolaris*
Hydrangea villosa	*Hydrangea aspera* 'Villosa'
Hyssopus aristatus	*Hyssopus officinalis* subsp. *aristatus*
Iris alata	*Iris planifolia*
Iris chamaeiris	*Iris lutescens*
Iris chrysofar	*Iris* Chrysofar Group
Iris creticum	*Iris unguicularis* subsp. *cretensis*
Iris foetidissima variegata	*Iris foetidissima* 'Variegata'
Iris histrioides major	*Iris histrioides* 'Major'
Iris kaempferi	*Iris ensata*
Iris kerneri	*Iris kerneriana*
Iris laevigata 'Rose Queen'	*Iris ensata* 'Rose Queen'
Iris mellita	*Iris suaveolens*
Iris sibirica 'Snow Queen'	*Iris sanguinea* 'Snow Queen'
Iris stylosa	Iris unguicularis
Iris stylosa angustifolia	Iris unguicularis subsp. *carica.* var. *augustifolia*
Iris stylosa ellisii	*Iris unguicularis* 'Ellis's Variety'
Iris stylosa speciosa lindsayae	*Iris unguicularis* 'Speciosa'
Iris tuberosa	*Hermodactylus tuberosus*
Kniphofia 'C. M. Prichard'	*Kniphofia rooperi*
Kniphofia comosum	*Kniphofia pumila*
Kniphofia 'Elf'	*Kniphofia* 'Little Elf'

Kniphofia galpinii	Kniphofia triangularis subsp. *triangularis*
Kniphofia northii	*Kniphofia northiae*
Kniphofia snowdoni	*Kniphofia thomsonii* var. *snowdenii*
Laburnum vulgare	*Laburnum anagroides*
Laburnum vulgare aureum	*Laburnum anagroides* 'Aureum'
Laburnum vulgare autumnale	*Laburnum anagroides* 'Autumnale'
Laburnum vulgare quercifolium	*Laburnum anagroides* 'Quercifolium'
Lamium galeobdolon variegatum	*Lamium galeobdolon* 'Florentinum'
Lathyrus (Orobus) vernus praecox	*Lathyrus vernus*
Leucojum vernum carpathicum	*Leucojum vernum* var. *carpathicum*
Leucojum vernum wagneri	*Leucojum vernum* var. *wagneri*
Lilium longifolium	*Lilium longiflorum*
Lilium 'Martagon'	*Lilium martagon*
Lilium szovitsianum	*Lilium monodelphum*
Lily-of-the-valley 'Fortin's Giant'	*Convallaria majalis* 'Fortin's Giant'
Lily-of-the-valley 'Mount Everest'	*Convallaria majalis* 'Mount Everest'
Liriope graminifolia	*Liriope muscari*
Liriope hyacinthiflora	*Reineckia carnea*
Lobelia laxifolius	*Lobelia laxiflora*
Lobelia vedrariensis	*Lobelia* x *gerardii* 'Vedrariensis'
Lonicera japonica aureo-reticulata	*Lonicera japonica* 'Aureoreticulata'
Lonicera purpusii	*Lonicera* x *purpusii*
Lychnis coronaria 'Abbotswood Rose'	*Lychnis* x *walkeri* 'Abbotswood Rose'
Lychnis dioica fl. pl.	*Silene dioica* 'Flore Pleno'
Lychnis viscaria fl. pl.	*Lychnis viscaria* 'Plena'
Lysichitum americanum	*Lysichiton americanus*
Lysichitum camschatense	*Lysichiton camtschatcensis*
Lysimachia leschnaulti	*Lysimachia leschenaultii*
Lysimachia verticillata	*Lysimachia verticillaris*
˘ôMahonia bealei	*Mahonia japonica* Bealei Group
Mahonia 'Charity'	*Mahonia* x *media* 'Charity'
Malva 'Primley Blue'	*Malva sylvestris* 'Primley Blue'
Mentha rotundifolia variegata	*Mentha suaveolens* 'Variegata'
Mertensia virginica	*Mertensia virginioides*
Muscari azureum album	*Muscari azureum* 'Album'
Muscari comosum plumosum	*Muscari comosum* 'Plumosum'
Muscari moschatum flavum	*Muscari macrocarpum*
Narcissus plenus odoratus	*Narcissus* x *odorus* 'Double Campernelle'

Narcissus pseudo-narcissus moschatus	Narcissus moschatus
Narcissus pseudo-narcissus obvallaris	Narcissus obvallaris
Narcissus recurvis	Narcissus poeticus var. recurvus
Neillia longiracemosa	Neillia thibetica
Nepeta 'Six Hills' var.	Nepeta 'Six Hills Giant'
Nepeta 'Souvenir d'André Chaudron'	Nepeta sibirica 'Souvenir d'André Chaudron'
Olearia gunniana	Olearia phlogopappa
Olearia mollis	Olearia ilicifolia
Olearia oleifolia	Olearia 'Waikariensis'
Opthiopogon spicatus	Ophiopogon intermedius
Orchis elata	Dactylorhiza elata
Orchis maculata	Dactylorhiza maculata
Orobus vernus albo-roseum	Lathyrus vernus 'Alboroseus'
Orobus vernus cyaneus	Lathyrus cyaneus
Othonnopsis cheirifolia	Othonna cheirifolia
Oxalis floribunda	Oxalis articulata
Paeonia corollina	Paeonia mascula
Paeonia lobata	Paeonia peregrina
Paeonia obovata alba	Paeonia obovata var. alba
Paeonia potaninii	Paeonia delavayi Potaninii Group
Papaver 'Perry's White'	Papaver orientale 'Perry's White'
Papaver 'Watermelon'	Papaver orientale 'Watermelon'
Penstemon 'Garnet'	Penstemon 'Andenken an Friederich Hahn'
Penstemon 'Geo. Home'	Penstemon 'George Home'
Penstemon heterophyllus 'True Blue'	Penstemon heterophyllus
Penstemon 'Hewell's Pink Bedder'	Penstemon 'Hewell Pink Bedder'
Penstemon 'Mrs Hindley'	Penstemon 'Alice Hindley'
Penstemon schönholzeri	Penstemon 'Schoenholzeri'
Perowskia atriplicifolia	Perovskia atriplicifolia
Phalaris arundinacea variegata	Phalaris arundinacea 'Picta'
Phlox ahrendsii	Phlox x arendsii
Phlox 'Border Gem'	Phlox paniculata 'Border Gem'
Phlox 'Brigadier'	Phlox paniculata 'Brigadier'
Phlox 'Mother o' Pearl'	Phlox paniculata 'Mother of Pearl'
Phygelius coccineus	Phygelius capansis
Physalis franchetii	Physalis alkekengii var. franchetii
Physostegia 'Rose Bouquet'	Physostegia virginiana 'Bouquet Rose'
Physostegia 'Summer Spire'	Physostegia virginiana 'Summer Spire'

Physostegia 'Vivid'	Physostegia virginiana 'Vivid'
Pimpinella major rosea	Pimpinella major 'Rosea'
Pinelia tubifera	Pinellia ternata
Plantago major rosalensis (Rose Plantain)	Plantago major 'Rosularis'
Pleione pricei	Pleione formosana Pricei Group
Polemonium 'Blue Pearl'	Polemoniumreptans 'Blue Pearl'
Polemonium flavum	Polemonium foliosissimum var. flavum
Polemonium humile	Polemonium 'Northern Lights'
Polemonium 'Lambrook Pink'	Polemonium 'Pink Pearl'
Polemonium pulchellum	Polemonium reptans
Polemonium richardsonii	Polemonium boreale
Polyanthus 'Barrowby Gem'	Primula 'Barrowby Gem'
Polyanthus 'Bartimeus'	Primula 'Bartimeus'
Polygonatum fl. pl. (Solomon's Seal, double)	Polygonatus odoratum 'Flore Pleno'
Polygonatum multiflorum major	Polygonatum biflorum
Polygonum affine	Persicaria affinis
Polygonum affine 'Darjeeling Red'	Persicaria affinis 'Darjeeling Red'
Polygonum affine Loundes var.	Persicaria affinis 'Donald Lowndes'
Polygonum vaccinifolium	Persicaria vaccinifolia
Potentilla tonguei	Potentilla x tonguei
Pratia treadwellii	Pratia angulata 'treadwellii'
Primula altaica grandiflora	Primula elatior subsp. meyeri
Primula bhutanica	Primula whitei 'Sherriff's variety'
Primula 'Blue Ribbon'	Primula 'Blue Ribband'
Prunus mume 'Beni-shi-don'	Prunus mume 'Beni-chidori'
Prunus serrula tibetica	Prunus serrula
Prunus spinosa rosea	Prunus cerasifera 'Rosea'
Prunus subhirtella autumnalis	Prunus x subhirtella 'Autumnalis'
Prunus subhirtella autumnalis rosea	Prunus x subhirtella 'Autumnalis Rosea'
Pulmonaria argentea	Pulmonaria saccharata 'Argentea'
Ranunculus aconitifolius fl. pl.	Ranunculus aconitifolius 'Flore Pleno'
Ranunculus acris fl. pl.	Ranunculus acris 'Flore Pleno'
Ranunculus bulbosum fl. pl.	Ranunculus constantinopolitanus 'Plenus'
Ranunculus repens fl. pl.	Ranunculus repens var. pleniflorus
Ranunculus speciosus fl. pl.	Ranunculus constantinopolitanus 'Pleunus'
Rhazia orientalis	Amsonia orientalis
Rhododendron arborea	Rhododendron arboreum

Rhododendron parvifolium	Rhododendron ponticum
Rhododendron repens	Rhododendron repens Forrestii Group
Rhus cotinoides	Cotinus obovatus
Rhus cotinus	Cotinus coggygria
Rhus typhina laciniata	Rhus typhina 'Dissecta'
Rosa chinensis viridiflora	Rosa x odorata 'Viridiflora'
Rosa 'Dr Van Fleet'	Rosa 'Doctor W. Van Fleet'
Rosa 'Felicity'	Rosa 'Felicia'
Rosa mutabilis	Rosa x odorata 'Mutabilis'
Rosa 'Paul's Scarlet'	Rosa 'Paul's Scarlet Climber'
Rosa rugosa 'Frau Dagmar Hartop'	Rosa 'Fru Dagmar Hastrup'
Rose plantain	Plantago major 'Rosularis'
Rubus giraldianus	Rubus cockburnianus
Rue, Jackman's Blue	Ruta graveolens 'Jackman's Blue'
Salix britzensis	Salix alba 'Britzensis'
Salix matsudana tortuosa	Salix babylonica 'Tortuosa'
Salix vitellina pendula	Salix alba 'Tristis'
Salvia ambigens	Salvia guaranitica 'Blue Enigma'
Salvia bethelli	Salvia involucrata 'Bethellii'
Salvia candelabra	Salvia candelabrum
Salvia grahamii	Salvia microphylla subsp. microphylla
Salvia leucothae	Salvia leucantha
Salvia neurepia	Salvia microphylla subsp. microphylla
Salvia officinalis purpurascens	Salvia officinalis 'Purpurascens'
Santolina incana	Santolina chamaecyparissus
Santolina 'Lemon Queen'	Santolina chamaecyparissus 'Lemon Queen'
Santolina neapolitana	Santolina pinnata subsp. neapolitana
Santolina sulphurea	Santolina pinnata subsp. neapolitana 'Sulphurea'
Santolina viridis	Santolina rosmarinifolia
Sarcococca hookeriana digyna	Sarcococca hookeriana var. digyna
Sarcococca humilis	Sarcococca hookeriana var. humilis
Satureia subspicata	Satureja montana subsp. illyrica
Saxifraga umbrosa geum	Saxifraga x geum
Schizostylis 'Mrs Hegarty'	Schizostylis coccinea 'Mrs Hegarty'
Schizostylis 'Professor Tom Barnard'	Schizostylis coccinea 'Professor Barnard'
Schizostylis 'Viscountess Byng'	Schizostylis coccinea 'Viscountess Byng'
Scilla azureus	Muscari azureum

Scilla tubergeniana — Scilla mischtschenkoana
Scrophularia aquatica variegata — Scropularia auriculata 'Variegata'
Scutellaria canescens — Scutellaria incana
Scutellaria indica japonica — Scutellaria indica var. parvifolia
Sedum albo-roseum — Sedum alborseum
Sedum maximum — Sedum telephium subsp. *maximum*
Sedum maximum atropurpureum — Sedum telephium subsp. *maximum* 'Atropureum'

Sedum spectabile 'Autumn Joy' — Sedum 'Herbstfreude'
Sedum telephium roseum — Sedum telephium 'Roseum'
Sedum telephium variegatum — Sedum telephium 'Variegatum'
Selinum carvifolium — Selinum carvifolia
Senecio greyii — Brachyglottis 'Sunshine'
Senecio laxifolius — Brachyglottis 'Sunshine'
Senecio leucostachys — Senecia viravira
Senecio monroii — Brachyglottis monroi
Senecio przewalski — Ligularia przewalskii
Senecio tangutica — Sinacalia tangutica
Senecio 'White Diamond' — Senecio cineraria 'White Diamond'
Serratula shawii — Serratula seoanei
Solidago 'Lemore' — x Solidaster luteus 'Lemore'
Solidaster luteus — x Solidaster luteus
'Solomon's Seal' — Polygonatus odoratum 'Flore Pleno'
Spiraea palmata — Filipendula palmata
Spiraea palmata rubra — Filipendula palmata 'Rubra'
Stachys lanata — Stachys byzantina
Stokesia cyanea — Stokesia laevis
Sternbergia angustifolia — Sternbergia luea 'Angustifolia'
Stranvesia undulata — Photinia davidiana var. undulata
Symphytum grandiflorum — Symphytum ibericum
Symphoricarpus 'Constance Spry' — Symphoricarpus albus 'Constance Spry'
Symphoricarpus 'Magic berry' — Symphoricarpus x doorembosii 'Magic Berry'

Symphoricarpus 'Mother of Pearl' — Symphoricarpus x doorembosii 'Mother of Pearl'

Symphoricarpus 'Variegated' — Symphoricarpus orbiculatus 'Foliis Variegatus'

Symphoricarpus 'White Hedge' — Symphoricarpus x doorembosii 'White Hedge'

Tellima grandiflora purpurea	*Tellima grandiflora* 'Purpurea'
Thalictrum aquilegifolium	*Thalictrum aquilegiifolium*
Thalictrum dipterocarpum	*Thalictrum delavayi*
Trillium stylosum	*Trillium catesbyi*
Verbena venosa	*Verbena rigida*
Veronica colensoi	*Hebe colensoi*
Veronica 'Morning Glory'	*Hebe* 'Primley Gem'
Veronica virginiana	*Veronicastrum virginianum*
Viburnum bodnantense 'Dawn'	*Viburnum* x *bodnantense* 'Dawn'
Viburnum burkwoodii	*Viburnum* x *burkwoodii*
Viburnum foetens	*Viburnum grandiflorum* f. *foetens*
Viburnum fragrans	*Viburnum farreri*
Viburnum fragrans candidissima	*Viburnum farreri* 'Candidissimum'
Viburnum fragrans compactum	*Viburnum farreri* 'Nanum'
Viburnum opulus compactum	*Viburnum opulus* 'Compactum'
Viburnum tinus froebeli	*Viburnum tinus* 'Froebeli'
Viburnum tinus hirsutum	*Viburnum tinus* f. *hirsutum*
Viburnum tinus lucidum	*Viburnum tinus* 'Lucidum'
Viburnum tinus rotundifolia	*Viburnum tinus* 'Rotundifolia'
Viburnum tinus variabile	*Viburnum* 'Variabile'
Vinca acutiloba	*Vinca difformis*
Vinca major elegantissima	*Vinca major* 'Variegata'
Vinca minor alba	*Vinca minor* f. *alba*
Vinca minor flore plena	*Vinca minor* 'Azurea Flore Pleno'
Vinca minor multiplex	*Vinca minor* 'Multiplex'
Vinca minor rubra	*Vinca minor* 'Atropurpurea'
Violet 'Conte de Brazza'	*Viola* 'Comte de Brazza'
Violet 'Maria Louise'	*Viola* 'Marie-Louise'
Vitis vinifera purpurea	*Vitis vinifera* 'Purpurea'
Watsonia beatricei	*Watsonia pillansii*

Index